Enjoy German

Heiner Schenke and Paul Coggle

First published in Great Britain in 2015 by John Murray Learning. An Hachette UK company.

British Library Cataloguing in Publication Data: a catalogue record for this title is available from the British Library.

Library of Congress Catalog Card Number: on file.

ISBN 9781473602977

10 9 8 7 6 5 4 3 2

Cover image © Carlos Malvar/Getty Images

Typeset by Integra Software Services Pvt. Ltd, Pondicherry, India.

Printed and bound in Great Britain by CPI Group (UK) Ltd., Croydon, CRO 4YY

John Murray Learning policy is to use papers that are natural, renewable and recyclable products and made from wood grown in sustainable forests. The logging and manufacturing processes are expected to conform to the environmental regulations of the country of origin.

John Murray Learning

338 Euston Road

London NW1 3BH

www.hodder.co.uk

Also available in ebook and audio

Contents

Meet the authors

Heiner Schenke is Principal Lecturer in German and Director of the institution-wide language programme at the University of Westminster. He has taught German at all levels and is the co-author of several German language and grammar books, including the *Teach Yourself German* series and *Willkommen*.

Paul Coggle was Senior Lecturer at the University of Kent, where he taught German at all levels. He has co-authored a number of German courses, including the *Teach Yourself German series* and *Willkommen*. He was Course Consultant for the BBC course *Deutsch Plus 2* and assisted the Language Centre, University of Cambridge in the development of multi-media German language materials.

Acknowledgements

The authors would like to thank their editor Bruno Paul for his support and guidance. They would also like to thank Anna Miell for all her invaluable comments and suggestions.

Introduction

WELCOME TO *ENJOY GERMAN*!

This course has been written specifically for the learner who:

▶ has already completed a beginner's course

▶ wishes to resume studying German after some interruption

▶ has intermediate proficiency and wants to attain an advanced standard in German

▶ prefers a self-study course or learns one-on-one with a tutor

▶ seeks to supplement classroom instruction with more guided practice

▶ needs to revise in view of sitting an advanced level examination.

If one or more of these descriptions applies to you, you will find *Enjoy German* consistent with your objectives. The course is designed to help you take your German to a higher level. The first few units are aimed at consolidating and building on your previous knowledge. The course then moves on to more complex language and issues in the later units. It is here that you will also be introduced to the more advanced points of German grammar, such as the forms and various uses of the subjunctive. Much of the audio is based on real-life interviews with native speakers of German. The course covers the four basic language skills – listening and speaking, reading and writing – and contemporary cultural aspects about life in Germany. It will lead you to develop your vocabulary and give you opportunities to express your opinion on a number of topics, as well as react to other people's opinions.

DEVELOP YOUR SKILLS

The language introduced in this course is based on realistic situations ranging from talking about your daily routines, interests and hobbies, to expressing your opinions about how to cope with job-related stress, discussing national stereotypes, debating environmental issues or contrasting education systems.

The first units are designed to consolidate and build on your prior knowledge, focusing on some of the essential language functions and grammatical points. You will then progress to dealing with more complex language and issues in the subsequent units.

If you are studying on your own, the audio recordings will be all the more important, as they will provide you with the essential opportunity to listen to German and to speak it within a controlled framework. Do try to balance your study sessions so you work evenly on your listening, speaking, reading and writing skills.

And most importantly, **Viel Spaß beim Lernen!** *Have fun while you learn!*

About this course

Enjoy German consists of a course book and audio pack, organized into ten thematic units, each with a self-assessment test at the end, and a reference section at the back of the book.

THE UNITS

The units are your language building blocks and are organized as follows:

Statement of aims

Tells you what you can expect to learn, in terms of what you will be able to do in German by the end of the unit, and the language points that will be introduced.

Conversations

In each unit, there are two conversations with a preview of vocabulary which have been recorded and are reproduced in the body of the units. The language spoken in these conversations covers all the basic structures and verb tenses, including more advanced forms such as the subjunctive. Each conversation is followed by comprehension exercises focusing on the content of the dialogue.

Listen and understand

This listening passage, typically a dialogue or a monologue, is supported by transcriptions at the back of the book. Here the main learning point is to develop strategies for understanding German spoken at native speed. It is recommended that you follow the teaching instructions closely, as listening is the area in which learners often require more guidance – as well as where they stand to make the most progress.

Language discovery

In the Language discovery sections you learn about the form of the language, reviewing structures you may already know as well as learning new ones. A series of questions precede the grammar explanations and ask you to notice the language in action, often as you have heard it in the conversations. This helps you confirm your prior knowledge as well as develop your ability to induce the rules of German. The explanations are written to encourage you to think about the language and how native speakers use it. The emphasis is as much on form as on usage.

Practice

In the Practice sections you will have ample opportunity to use the language that has been presented and to work specifically on your speaking, reading and writing skills. This section also includes more open-ended exercises which give you a framework for longer speaking or writing tasks. These activities will lead you gradually toward expressing your own opinion about topics and issues. Where possible, model answers for these tasks are included in the Key to the exercises at the back of the book.

Tips

At different stages throughout a unit, you will find tip boxes with further information related to the German language and culture. There are also useful tips for dealing with new language.

Go further with grammar

This section complements the quick 'language bites' you will have previously encountered in Language discovery with more complete language explanations and further examples.

Learning the forms of the language will enable you to construct your own sentences and paragraphs correctly.

Test yourself

There is a self-test at the end of each unit. Answers to these activities are provided in the Key to the exercises. The test and its accompanying checklist enable you to monitor your progress and achievement. Use it to determine if you are ready to move on to the next unit, or if you should spend a bit more time going over the unit once more.

Reference

You may wish to consult these reference sections at the end of the book as you work through the units:

▶ Key to the activities and exercises

▶ Transcripts of the **Listen and understand** recordings

▶ List of German irregular verbs

▶ Glossary of grammatical terms

▶ German–English glossary

▶ English–German glossary

▶ Grammar index.

How to study with *Enjoy German*

Make sure at the beginning of each unit that you are clear about what you can expect to learn.

First preview the **key vocabulary** and then listen to the **conversations** on the audio. There are usually a few questions to focus your listening on a broad aspect of the dialogue. Try to listen for that information and listen for the gist of what is being said before you look at the printed text. Listen to the audio several times until you are familiar with it. Don't forget that even when you *recognize* what you hear and read, you may still be some distance away from being able to *produce* the language correctly and fluently.

Make the most of the audio material by listening to the audio at every opportunity — sitting on the train, during work breaks or while you're getting ready in the morning, using what would otherwise be 'down' time. After you have listened to a conversation, go through the comprehension questions and check that you understood what was said. The answers to these are in the **Key to the exercises**.

You can then study the explanations in the **Language discovery** section in a systematic way. We have tried to make these explanations as user-friendly as possible and to present them in small chunks. In the end, it is up to you just how much time you spend on studying and sorting out the grammar points. Some people find that they can do better by getting an ear for what sounds right. Others need to know in detail how the language is put together.

You will then be ready to move on to the **Practice** section and work through the activities alone, with a study partner or in a group. Some of the activities are communicative in nature, focusing on the aims outlined at the start of the unit. You are the main actor here, so carry out the instructions given for each exercise, which may involve understanding and responding to what a German speaker has said, playing a role, writing a letter, taking a position, debating an issue, sharing a personal story and so on.

As you work your way through the activities, check your answers carefully in the **Key to the exercises**. It is easy to overlook your own mistakes. If you have a study buddy, it's a good idea to check each other's work. Most of the exercises have fixed answers. The temptation may be to immediately consult the **Key to the exercises**, but try not to do this. The whole point of these exercises is to improve your ability to use German in sustained conversations and to contribute your own ideas and personal views.

Before you move on to a new unit, go through the **Test yourself** section, which will allow you to assess what you have learnt in the unit. You can check your answers in the **Key to the exercises** section. If you did well in the test move on to the next unit, but if your performance was not satisfactory, study the relevant information in the **Language discovery** and the **Go further with grammar** sections again, and attempt a few of the activities until you feel confident that you have learnt the language points.

SYMBOLS

Throughout *Enjoy German*, you will find a system of icons to identify the purpose of a section or activity. They are:

Play the audio track

Figure something out for yourself

Learn key words and expressions

Exercises coming up!

Write and make notes

Read for gist and detail

Speak German out loud (even if you're alone)

Check your German ability (no cheating!)

Learn to learn

The Discovery method

There are lots of philosophies and approaches to language learning, some practical, some quite unconventional, and far too many to list here. Perhaps you know of a few, or even have some techniques of your own. In this book we have incorporated the **Discovery method** of learning, a sort of DIY approach to language learning. What this means is that you will be encouraged throughout the course to engage your mind and figure out the language for yourself, through identifying patterns, understanding grammar concepts, noticing words that are similar to English, and more. This method promotes language awareness, a critical skill in acquiring a new language. As a result of your own efforts, you will be able to better retain what you have learnt, use it with confidence and, even better, apply those same skills to continuing to learn the language (or, indeed, another one) on your own after you've finished this course.

Everyone can succeed in learning a language – the key is to know how to learn it. Learning is more than just reading or memorizing grammar and vocabulary. It's about being an active learner, learning in real contexts and, most importantly, using what you've learnt in different situations. Simply put, if you **figure something out for yourself**, you're more likely to understand it. And when you use what you've learnt, you're more likely to remember it.

And because many of the essential but (let's admit it!) challenging details, such as grammar rules, are introduced through the **Discovery method**, you'll have more fun while learning. Soon, the language will start to make sense and you'll be relying on your own intuition to construct original sentences independently, not just listening and repeating.

Enjoy yourself!

Become a successful language learner

1 Make a habit out of learning

Study a little every day, between 20 and 30 minutes is ideal. Give yourself **short-term goals**, e.g. work out how long you'll spend on a particular unit and work within this time limit; **create a study habit**. Try to **create an environment conducive to learning** which is calm and quiet and free from distractions. As you study, do not worry about your mistakes or the things you can't remember or understand. Languages settle gradually in the brain. Just **give yourself enough time** and you will succeed.

2 Maximize your exposure to the language

As well as using this course, you can listen to podcasts, watch television or read online articles and blogs. Do you have a personal passion or hobby? Does a news story interest you? Try to access German information about them. It's entertaining and you'll become used to a range of writing and speaking styles.

There are a wealth of websites you can access. You will find it's best to concentrate on short items to begin with. For instance, you may try *Heute 100 sec*, the daily news summary on www.zdf.de.

3 Vocabulary

Group new words under **generic categories**, e.g. professions, education, business; and the **situations** in which they occur, e.g. under professions you can write **Arzt** *doctor* and **Tierarzt** *vet*, **Krankenschwester** *nurse* but **Krankenpfleger** *male nurse*, etc.; and **functions**, e.g. describe a sequence of events, make plans for the future, express a personal opinion, etc.

▶ It's a good idea to make your own list of new words and phrases for each unit; joining nouns with their gender and plural will help you remember them, e.g. **das Bundesland (-ˮer)** *federal state*.

▶ Keep lists of words on your smartphone or tablet, but remember to switch the keyboard language so you can include all accents and special characters.

▶ Listen to the audio several times and say the words out loud as you hear or read them.

▶ Cover up the English side of the vocabulary list and see if you can remember the meaning of words. Do the same for the German. Work your way up to phrases and whole sentences.

▶ Create mind maps.

▶ Flip the language settings of your browser to German and navigate as is your custom. Try searching content using www.google.de or https://de.yahoo.com.

▶ Experiment with words. Look for patterns in words, e.g. try to learn words in families, e.g. **der Flug** *flight*, **das Flugzeug** *airplane*, **der Flughafen** *airport*, **Hin-** und **Rückflug** *return flight*; **normal** *normal*, **normalerweise** *normally*; **der See** *lake*, but **die See** *sea*, etc.

4 Grammar

Experiment with grammar rules. Sit back and reflect on how the rules of German compare with your own language or other languages you may already speak.

▶ Use known vocabulary to practise new grammar structures.

▶ When you learn a new verb form, write the conjugation of several different verbs you know that follow the same form.

5 Pronunciation

▶ Study individual sounds, then full words. Make a list of those words that give you trouble and practise them.

▶ Repeat the conversations line by line and try to mimic what you hear. Record yourself if you can.

6 Listening and reading

The conversations in this course include questions to help guide you in your understanding. But you can do more:

▶ **Imagine the situation.** Think about where a scene is taking place and make educated guesses, e.g. a conversation in a snack bar is likely to be about food.

▶ **Guess the meaning of key words before you look them up.** When there are key words you don't understand, try to guess what they mean from the context. If you're listening to a German speaker and cannot get the gist of a whole passage because of one word or phrase, try to repeat that word with a questioning tone; the speaker will probably paraphrase it.

7 Speaking

Practice makes perfect. The most successful language learners know how to overcome their inhibitions and keep going.

▶ When you conduct simple transactions in your daily life, pretend that you have to do it in German, e.g. telling someone what you would like to do next Saturday, explaining who you are, telling your employer why you deserve a pay rise and so on.

▶ Rehearse the dialogues out loud, then try to replace sentences with ones that are true for you.

8 Learn from your errors

▶ Making errors is part of any learning process, so don't be so worried about making mistakes that you won't say anything unless you are sure it is correct. This leads to a vicious circle: the less you say, the less practice you get and the more mistakes you make.

▶ Note the seriousness of errors. Many errors are not serious as they do not affect the meaning.

9 Learn to cope with uncertainty

▶ Don't give up if you don't understand everything. Keep following the conversation a while. The speaker might repeat or paraphrase what you didn't understand and the conversation can carry on.

▶ Keep talking. The best way to improve your fluency in German is to seize every opportunity to speak. If you get stuck for a particular word, don't let the conversation stop; paraphrase or use the words you do know, even if you have to simplify what you want to say.

▶ Don't over-use your dictionary.

▶ Resist the temptation to look up every word you don't know. Read the same passage several times, concentrating on trying to get the gist of it. If, after the third time, some words still prevent you from making sense of the passage, look them up in the dictionary.

1 Leute, Leute

In this unit you will learn how to:
- ▶ *share personal details about yourself.*
- ▶ *ask other people about themselves and what they do.*
- ▶ *ask different types of questions.*
- ▶ *identify gender and form the plural of nouns.*
- ▶ *use prepositions correctly when giving personal information.*
- ▶ *understand and write a personal blog.*

CEFR: *Can use a series of sentences and phrases to describe people's background and their jobs; can establish social contact (B1); Can understand texts that consist of high-frequency or job-related language (B2); Can write clear detailed text on a variety of subjects, e.g. a bio sketch (B2).*

Conversation 1

EIN INTERVIEW MIT FRAU PETERS

Sehen Sie sich zuerst die Vokabeln an und hören Sie dann, was Frau Peters über sich erzählt.

 1 01.01 **First look at the vocabulary, then listen to what Frau Peters says about herself. How is her hobby linked to her job?**

auf/wachsen	*to grow up*
berufstätig sein	*to be working, to work*
halbtags	*part-time (lit. half days)*
die Fremdsprache (-n)	*foreign language*
die Versicherungsfirma (-firmen)	*insurance company*
die Arbeit macht mir Spaß	*I enjoy my work*
fließend	*fluent(ly)*
fast	*almost*
selbstständig	*self-employed*
ich interessiere mich für ...	*I am interested in ...*
für Fortgeschrittene	*for advanced learners*
der Anfängerkurs (-e)	*beginners' course*

Reporter	Frau Peters, können Sie ein bisschen über sich erzählen?
Frau Peters	Ja, natürlich. Mein Name ist Ulrike Peters. Ich bin 1962 in Berlin geboren, bin dort auch aufgewachsen und lebe jetzt seit 12 Jahren hier in Köln.
Reporter	Und sind Sie berufstätig?
Frau Peters	Ja, ich arbeite halbtags als Fremdsprachensekretärin bei einer Versicherungsfirma. Normalerweise arbeite ich am Vormittag, von halb neun bis ein Uhr, und die Arbeit macht mir sehr viel Spaß.
Reporter	Und welche Sprachen sprechen Sie?
Frau Peters	Ich spreche fließend Französisch und Englisch. Ich habe vier Jahre in Bristol gelebt und dort an der Universität studiert. Außerdem kann ich ein bisschen Spanisch und Italienisch.
Reporter	Sind Sie denn verheiratet?
Frau Peters	Ja, ich bin seit fast 10 Jahren mit meinem Mann verheiratet und wir haben zwei Kinder.
Reporter	Was macht denn Ihr Mann?
Frau Peters	Mein Mann ist selbstständig. Er ist Architekt und hat ein kleines Architektenbüro hier in Köln.
Reporter	Und haben Sie ein Hobby?
Frau Peters	Im Moment habe ich leider nicht viel Zeit. Ich interessiere mich aber sehr für Sprachen und gehe einmal in der Woche zu einem Englischkurs für Fortgeschrittene. Die Klasse macht mir sehr viel Spaß.

2 Beantworten Sie die folgenden Fragen.

Answer the following questions. As with all exercises, you can check your answers in the Key to the exercises at the back of the book.

    a Where does Ulrike live?

    b What is her profession?

    c What languages does she speak and how well?

    d What does she say about her family situation?

    e What does she do once a week?

3 Richtig oder falsch? Korrigieren Sie die falschen Aussagen.

Decide whether the following statements are Richtig *true* **or Falsch** *false* **and correct the ones that are false.**

Beispiele: Frau Peters ist in Köln geboren. → *Falsch. Sie ist in Berlin geboren.*

Sie arbeitet halbtags bei einer Versicherungsfirma. → *Richtig.*

a Die Arbeit gefällt ihr nicht.
b Sie hat vier Jahre in England studiert.
c Sie ist seit über 10 Jahren verheiratet.
d Ihr Mann ist Angestellter in einem Architektenbüro.
e Sie geht zu einem Anfängerkurs in Englisch.

4 Welches Wort fehlt?

Complete the sentences with the appropriate word from the box.

| fließend | Spaß | verheiratet | halbtags | interessiert | selbstständig | ~~berufstätig~~ |

Beispiel: Frau Peters arbeitet. → Sie ist *berufstätig.*

a Sie arbeitet Teilzeit. → Sie arbeitet _____.
b Ihre Arbeit gefällt ihr. → Ihre Arbeit macht ihr _____.
c Frau Peters hat einen Ehemann. → Sie ist _____.
d Ihr Mann hat eine eigene Firma. → Er ist _____.
e Sie spricht sehr gut Französisch. → Sie spricht _____ Französisch.
f Ein Hobby von ihr sind Sprachen. → Sie _____ sich für Sprachen.

Language discovery 1

 You have already seen this language in action. Can you work out the rules?

1 **Look at the following questions from the Conversation. Which require a yes/no answer and which ones are open-ended? Can you see how their structure differs?**
   a Können Sie ein bisschen über sich erzählen?
   b Welche Sprachen sprechen Sie?
   c Sind sie denn verheiratet?
   d Was macht Ihr Mann beruflich?

2 **To talk about personal details, for instance to say where you work or study, etc. you need certain prepositions. Look at Conversation 1 again and find the missing words.**
   a Ich bin _____ Berlin geboren.
   b Ich arbeite _____ einer Versicherungsfirma.
   c Ich habe in Bristol _____ der Universität studiert.
   d Ich bin _____ fast 10 Jahren _____ meinem Mann verheiratet.
   e Ich gehe _____ einem Englischkurs.

1 VERSCHIEDENE FRAGEN *DIFFERENT TYPES OF QUESTIONS*

In German there are two main types of question. The first starts with a question word, such as **woher?**, **was?**, **wie?**, **wo?**, etc.:

Woher kommen Sie? **Was** macht Ihr Mann beruflich?

Here the question word is usually in the first position and followed by a verb.

The second type of question is often called a *yes/no* question, because it requires an answer in the affirmative or the negative. Here the verb appears in the first position:

Sind Sie verheiratet? **Ist** Ihr Mann berufstätig?

If there are two verbs, the auxiliary verb (**sein/haben**) or a modal verb like **können** goes into first position while the main verb goes to the end:

Bist du schon einmal nach Deutschland **gefahren**?

Können Sie ein bisschen über sich **erzählen**?

Note that in spoken German the question word or verb is often preceded by **und** or **aber**:

Und welche Sprachen sprechen Sie? **Aber** kommen Sie nicht aus Berlin?

Sometimes an expression of time or a preposition can also go before the question word:

Seit wann wohnt er in München? **Bei** welcher Firma arbeitest du?

2 PRÄPOSITIONEN *PREPOSITIONS*

To say where you're from, where you work or study, etc. you need to use the appropriate prepositions which sometimes don't correspond to the English usage. Here are a few important prepositions for this purpose:

Ich komme **aus** Berlin.	*to come **from***
Er arbeitet **als** Architekt.	*to work **as***
Ich arbeite **bei** einer Versicherungsfirma.	*to work **for/at** a company*
Sie arbeitet **in** einem Büro.	*to work **in** an office*
Er studiert **an** einer Universität.	*to study **at** a university*
Sie wohnt **seit** 12 Jahren in Köln.	***for** twelve years*

There are more examples in the **Go further with grammar** section at the end of this unit.

 Practice 1

1 Wie heißen die Präpositionen?

Darren wrote a short biographical note about himself in German but wasn't sure about which prepositions to use. Can you help him?

Ich bin am 3. Dezember 1996 **(a)** _____ Manchester geboren. Meine Mutter kommt auch **(b)** _____ Manchester, aber mein Vater kommt **(c)** _____ Dublin. Im Moment studiere ich **(d)** _____ der Universität hier. Nebenbei jobbe ich **(e)** _____ Kellner **(f)** _____ einem Hotel im Stadtzentrum. Ich bin nicht verheiratet, aber ich habe **(g)** _____ vier Jahren eine Freundin, Tracy. Sie kommt **(h)** _____ Bath und ist Physiotherapeutin **(i)** _____ einem Krankenhaus. Später möchte ich gern **(j)** _____ Informatiker **(k)** _____ einer großen internationalen Firma arbeiten.

2 Welches Fragewort fehlt?

Find the missing question word.

a _____ heißt du?

b _____ kommst du?

c _____ alt bist du?

d _____ bist du aufgewachsen?

e _____ Sprachen sprichst du und wie gut?

f Seit _____ lernst du Deutsch?

g Und _____ machst du beruflich?

h _____ sind deine Hobbys?

3 Was passt zusammen?

Here is a scrambled up interview with Mark Taylor. Match the right answer with each question (a–h).

a Wie heißen Sie, bitte?

b Kommen Sie denn aus Kanada?

c Und wo sind Sie geboren?

d Sind Sie verheiratet?

e Haben Sie Kinder?

f Und sind Sie berufstätig?

g Wie lange lernen Sie Deutsch?

h Haben Sie ein Hobby?

1 Ja, seit 14 Jahren.

2 Ja, ich arbeite bei einer Filmfirma.

3 Ich lerne es seit fünf Jahren.

4 Mein Name ist Mark Taylor.

5 In der Nähe von Detroit, Michigan.

6 Ja, ich interessiere mich für alte Bücher.

7 Ja, eine Tochter und zwei Söhne.

8 Nein, aus den USA.

 ## 4 Und Sie? Was antworten Sie?

Now answer the questions from Exercise 3 for yourself.

> **LANGUAGE TIP**
>
> Here is some useful vocabulary when talking about personal relationships:
>
> | | |
> |---|---|
> | **verheiratet** | *married* |
> | **single/ledig** | *single* |
> | **geschieden** | *divorced* |
> | **verwitwet** | *widowed* |
> | **Ich habe einen Freund.** | *I've got a boyfriend.* |
> | **Ich habe eine Freundin.** | *I've got a girlfriend.* |

Listen and understand

DREI KANDIDATEN STELLEN SICH VOR

In einer Fernsehshow stellen sich drei Personen vor. Hören Sie sich die Aufnahme an und finden Sie die fehlenden Informationen.

 1 01.02 **Three candidates introduce themselves on a German TV show. Look over the vocabulary, then listen and complete the grid with the information you hear.**

> **LEARNING TIP**
> The main purpose of **Listen and understand** is to practise your listening skills and help you to understand more authentic German. For that reason, the conversations do not appear in the units, but in a **Listen and understand transcripts** section at the back of the book. Listen to the audio several times and try to get as much information as possible before checking the script.

V vor/stellen — *to introduce*
die Ausgabe (-n) — *(here) edition*
in der Nähe von — *close to, near*
das Bockbierfest (-e) — *bock beer festival*
der Krankenpfleger (-) — *male nurse*
ein zeitraubender Job — *a time-consuming job*
die Hotelfachfrau (-en) — *hotel manageress*
die Pension (-en) — *guesthouse*
tuhren — *(here) to run*
die Runde (-n) — *round*

	Alter	Familienstand	Wohnort	Beruf	Hobbys
Martin			Apolda, in Thüringen		
Petra				Hotelfachfrau	
Max					

You can check your answers in the **Listen and understand transcript** or in the **Key to the exercises**.

2 Welche Antwort stimmt?

Decide which of the two answers is true.

  a Apolda
  1 ist eine Stadtteil von Weimar.   **2** liegt in Thüringen.
  b Das Bockbierfest ist
  1 sehr bekannt.   **2** nicht so bekannt.
  c Petra und ihr Mann führen
  1 eine große Pension.   **2** eine kleine Pension.
  d Sie haben
  1 nicht viel Freizeit.   **2** das ganze Jahr Freizeit.
  e Max surft
  1 am Wochenende.   **2** in den Ferien.

Different regional public broadcasting organisations in Germany.

 3 01.03 **Sagen Sie's auf Deutsch!**

Can you supply the German equivalents for the following phrases, which you heard in the last conversation? Listen to confirm your answers and practise imitating the native speaker's intonation.

   a Can you please introduce yourself briefly.

   b What do you do for a living?

   c What do you do in your spare time?

   d What sort of hobbies do you have?

   e I like going to the cinema.

   f In the holidays I go surfing.

Conversation 2

IM INTER-CITY-EXPRESS NACH BERLIN

Susanne und Marcus lernen sich auf der Zugfahrt nach Berlin kennen.

 1 01.04 **Susanne and Marcus get to know each other while travelling on a train to Berlin. Listen to the dialogue. Why is Susanne visiting Berlin and what is Marcus complaining about?**

auf Dauer	*in the long term*
die Fahrerei	*travelling (with negative connotations)*
kostspielig	*expensive*
der Studienplatz (-¨e)	*university place*
darauf freue ich mich	*I am looking forward to that*
offen	*open, open-minded*
lebendig	*lively*

Marcus	Fährst du das erste Mal nach Berlin?
Susanne	Ja. Ich wollte Berlin schon seit langem besuchen, aber hatte nie genug Zeit. Und du? Warst du schon mal in Berlin?
Marcus	Ja, schon öfters. Meine Freundin wohnt dort und darum fahre ich fast jedes zweite Wochenende dorthin.
Susanne	Und woher kommst du?
Marcus	Ich wohne in Hannover.
Susanne	Na, das ist ja nicht so weit.
Marcus	Nicht so weit? Tja, aber auf Dauer ist diese Fahrerei ganz schön kostspielig.
Susanne	Und was macht deine Freundin in Berlin?
Marcus	Sie studiert Film an der HdK, der Hochschule der Künste. Sie ist natürlich sehr glücklich, dass sie dort einen Studienplatz bekommen hat.
Marcus	Und was willst du in Berlin machen?
Susanne	Ich besuche eine alte Schulfreundin von mir, die seit einem Jahr in Berlin wohnt und in einer Kneipe arbeitet. Sie will mich ihren Freunden vorstellen und mir natürlich das Berliner Nachtleben zeigen. Darauf freue ich mich schon.
Marcus	Mir gefällt Berlin sehr gut. Ich finde, dass die meisten Leute sehr offen sind. Überhaupt kann man hier Menschen aus der ganzen Welt treffen. Das macht die Stadt sehr lebendig. Dir wird es bestimmt sehr gut gefallen.

2 Beantworten Sie die Fragen auf Deutsch.

Listen again, if necessary, then answer these questions in German.

    a Fährt Susanne das erste Mal nach Berlin?

    b Warum fährt Marcus nach Berlin?

    c Was macht die Freundin von Marcus in Berlin?

    d Was möchte eine Schulfreundin Susanne in Berlin zeigen?

    e Wie findet Marcus die meisten Leute in Berlin?

> **LANGUAGE TIP – ICH FREUE MICH AUF …**
>
> Haben Sie gemerkt, was Susanne sagte, als sie über das Nachtleben in Berlin sprach: **Darauf freue ich mich schon.** *I'm looking forward to that (already).*
>
> Den Ausdruck **ich freue mich auf** benutzt man sehr oft im Deutschen. Man kann zum Beispiel sagen:
>
> **Ich freue mich auf** das Wochenende.   *I am looking forward to the weekend.*
>
> **Ich freue mich auf** die Ferien.   *I am looking forward to the holidays.*

 3 Ergänzen Sie.

Study the dialogue once more and complete these phrases with the missing information.

    a Susanne wollte Berlin …

    b Marcus kommt …

    c Die Fahrerei ist auf Dauer …

    d Seine Freundin ist glücklich, dass …

    e Susanne möchte gern …

    f Marcus sagt, in Berlin kann man …

    g Das macht die Stadt …

Language discovery 2

 You have already seen this language in action. How good is your language intuition?

1 The following nouns have been grouped according to their gender. Can you say which ones are masculine, feminine or neuter? Which part of the word can help you determine the gender of nouns?

    a _____ Universität, Realität, Tasche, Freiheit, Krankheit, Pension, Option

    b _____ Motor, Faktor, Egoismus, Optimismus, Honig, König

    c _____ Büro, Auto, Experiment, Dokument, Doping, Meeting

2 Can you supply the plural forms of the following nouns? What are typical plural endings for each group?

masculine: der Sohn – die _____   der Gast – die _____   der Kurs – die _____

feminine: die Sprache – die _____   die Person – die _____   die Information – die _____

neuter: das Konzert – die _____   das Fest – die _____   das Kind – die _____

1 GESCHLECHT *GENDER*

Some endings can help you to work out the gender of certain nouns. Here are a few guidelines:

Masculine nouns   -ant, -ig, -ismus, -ist, -ling, -or
Feminine nouns   -e, -ei, -enz, -heit, -ie, -ik, -ion, -keit, -schaft, -tät, -ung, -ur
Neuter nouns   -chen, -ing, -lein, -ment, -o, -um

Note that there are some exceptions to these general guidelines such as **der Moment** or **das Abitur**.

The vast majority of nouns ending in **-e** are feminine (**die Frage**, **die Kneipe**, etc.), but watch out for a few exceptions such as **der Name** or **das Wochenende**.

2 PLURALFORMEN DER NOMEN *PLURAL OF NOUNS*

Like knowing the genders, forming the plural is often seen as quite difficult in German. Here is an overview of the most common forms which might make it easier for you:

1 Many masculine nouns add an **-e** in the plural and very often an umlaut:
    der Tisch → die Tisch**e**   der Ball → die B**ä**ll**e**

But there are important exceptions, where no umlaut is added, e.g.: der Tag → die Tag**e**; der Schuh → die Schuh**e**

2 Most feminine nouns add **-n** or **-en**:
    die Tasche → die Tasch**en**   die Frau → die Frau**en**

There are also a number of common feminine nouns which add an **-e** + umlaut:
    die Hand → die H**ä**nd**e**   die Stadt → die St**ä**dt**e**

3 Neuter nouns often add **-e**, but no umlaut:
    das Bier → die Bier**e**   das Haar → die Haar**e**

Another commonly found ending is **-er** + an umlaut where possible:
    das Kind → die Kind**er**   das Buch → die B**ü**ch**er**

Note: Most important nouns from English and French simply add -s in the plural:
    der Chef → die Chef**s**   das Team → die Team**s**   das Hobby → die Hobby**s**

Practice 2

1 Wie heißen die Artikel? Ergänzen Sie.

> **a** *die Bundesrepublik* **b** ____ Nation **c** ____ Fahrerei **d** ____ Instrument
> **e** ____ Kapitalismus **f** ____ Impressionismus **g** ____ Museum **h** ____ Zentrum
> **i** ____ Klasse **j** ____ Kultur **k** ____ Hoffnung **l** ____ Reaktor **m** ____ Wochenende

2 Give the plural form of these nouns:
    a der Beruf → die *Berufe*
    b der Kurs → die _____
    c der Gast → die _____
    d der Zug → die _____
    e die Kneipe → die _____

f die Zeitung → die _____

g die Stadt → die _____

h das Haus → die _____

i das Restaurant → die _____

j das Büro → die _____

Reading

1 Lesen Sie, was Nico in seinem Blog über sich geschrieben hat.

Read what Nico wrote about himself in his blog. Without looking at the vocabulary list which follows, can you figure out what Nico's hobbies are, what he is so happy about and where he wants to go on his holiday?

Nicos Blog

Ich über mich

Ich bin 18 Jahre alt, besitze seit zwei Monaten einen Führerschein (Klasse A, B und C) und gehe in die 12. Klasse des Heinrich-Heine-Gymnasiums in München, das heißt, ich mache dieses Jahr Abitur.

Meine Hobbys sind Computerspiele, Internetsurfen, Chatten und Modellbau und seit neuestem Autofahren. Seit einer Woche bin ich stolzer Besitzer eines Mazda 3, 1.4, nur 10 Jahre alt, das ist sehr aufregend. Ich bin sehr glücklich, dass ich ein eigenes Auto habe, aber leider frisst diese Kiste sehr viel Benzin.

Immerhin habe ich schon ein paar Touren zum Starnberger See und nach Nürnberg gemacht. In den Ferien möchte ich gern mit dem Mazda bis nach Italien fahren.

Was ich nach dem Studium machen will, weiß ich noch nicht genau. Ich denke, dass ich in München bleiben werde. Später würde ich gern mal als Programmierer arbeiten, vielleicht bei Siemens. Aber erst mal muss ich das Abitur machen.

V der Führerschein (-e)	*driving licence*
das Abitur	*German school-leaving exam taken at age 18+*
der Modellbau	*model building*
der Besitzer (-)/die Besitzerin (-nen)	*owner*
aufregend	*exciting*
die Kiste (-n)	*(here) old banger (car)*
das Benzin	*petrol*
fressen	*(usually) to eat (of animals); (here) to guzzle*
der Starnberger See	*a large lake about 25 km from Munich*

2 Lesen Sie den Text noch einmal und beantworten Sie die Fragen.

Now read the text once more and answer the questions.

   a Was macht Nico dieses Jahr?

   b Seit wann hat er seinen Führerschein?

   c Sitzt er in seiner Freizeit gern am Computer?

   d Seit wann hat er ein eigenes Auto?

   e Was ist das Problem mit seinem Auto?

   f Als was möchte er später arbeiten?

3 Mein Blog.

Write a bio sketch for your personal blog, using the vocabulary and structures covered in this unit. State where you were born and brought up, if you're in a relationship, what you do for work, what your hobbies are, the language skills you have and what you think about the town/city where you live. Mention what you want to do in your holiday.

Go further with grammar

1 PRÄPOSITIONEN *PREPOSITIONS*

As you saw in **Language discovery 1** earlier, the prepositions used in German are often different from those which English speakers might expect. Here are a few guidelines to help you decide which preposition to use in a given context. The list is not comprehensive, but it does give you the most commonly found usages.

a Origins/Details

*to live **in***	Claudia wohnt **in** Dresden.
*to come **from***	Ich komme **aus** Berlin.
*to be married **to***	Sie ist **mit** Michael verheiratet.
*to be separated **from***	Er hat sich **von** Silvia getrennt.

b Work

*to work **in** an office*	Sie arbeitet **in** einem Büro.
*to work **as***	Er arbeitet **als** Architekt.
*to work **for** a company*	Ich arbeite **bei** einer Versicherungsfirma.

c Time

*20 years **ago***	**Vor** 20 Jahren ...
***For** 20 years*	**Seit** 20 Jahren ...

d Study/Leisure time

*to go **to** school/to attend school*	Die Kinder gehen **in** die Schule/ Die Kinder gehen **zur** Schule.
*to study **at***	Er studiert **an** der Humboldt-Universität.
*to go **to** a course/to attend a course*	Sie geht **zu** einem Englischkurs.

Don't forget that a preposition + definite article is frequently combined to form one word:

an + dem	Er ist **am** 3. Dezember geboren.
in + das	Jörg geht **ins** Büro.
zu + dem	Frau Heinze muss **zum** Arzt.
zu + der	Er geht **zur** Arbeit.

For more information on **Präpositionen**, see **Unit 5** and **Unit 7**.

2 GESCHLECHT *GENDER*

In **Language discovery 2** you saw that there are guidelines to help you work out and remember the gender of nouns in German. Here are a few more pointers that you may find helpful.

Männlich *Masculine*

Days of the week, months and the four seasons: **der Dienstag, der April, der Sommer.**

Makes of car: **der BMW, der Toyota, der Mercedes.**

Alcoholic drinks: **der Wein, der Schnaps, der Gin** (exception: **das Bier**).

Weiblich *Feminine*

Names of motorbikes and ships: **die Honda, die Titanic.**

Names of many flowers: **die Rose, die Butterblume.**

Sächlich *Neuter*

Most metals: **das Eisen, das Gold, das Silber.**

Names of hotels, restaurants and cinemas: **das Ritz, das Odeon.**

Infinitives used as nouns: **das Tanzen, das Bungeespringen.**

3 PLURALFORMEN DER NOMEN *PLURAL OF NOUNS*

In addition to the guidelines given in the unit earlier on, please note that nouns ending in **-el, -en, -er, -chen** usually do not add a plural ending, and in most cases add an umlaut to form the plural:

der Spiegel → **die Spiegel**	**die Mutter** → **die Mütter**
der Magen → **die Mägen**	**das Mädchen** → **die Mädchen.**

 Test yourself

When you have completed the following exercises, check your answers in the Key to the exercises. In the case of Und jetzt Sie! **(here Exercise 4), also compare your answers with those given on the audio.**

We recommend that you continue to work on this unit until you can answer over three quarters of the questions correctly.

1 Wie heißen die Wörter?

Complete the words with the missing letters.

    a ein anderes Wort für Teilzeit: h _ l _ _ _ _ _

    b man hat eine eigene Firma: _ _ _ _ st _ _ _ _ _ _ g

    c wenn man arbeitet: b _ _ _ _ _ t _ _ _ _

    d nicht single: _ _ _ _ e i _ _ _ _ _

    e man ist nicht mehr mit seinem Partner zusammen: g e t r _ _ _ _

    f ein Kurs, wenn man nicht viel weiß: ein _ _ f _ _ g _ _ _ _ _ _

    g eine andere Sprache: _ _ _ _ d s p _ _ _ _ _

    h braucht man zum Autofahren: F _ _ _ _ _ s c h _ _ _

    i ein Schulexamen: A _ _ t _ r

    j ein anderes Wort für teuer: k _ s t _ _ _ _ _ _ _

    k die Leute sind tolerant: die Leute sind _ f f _ _

2 Stellen Sie Fragen.

Philipp Häfner was interviewed for a magazine in Berlin. Here are his answers. Can you work out what the questions were?

Beispiel: Mein Name ist Philipp Häfner. → *Wie ist Ihr Name, bitte?/Wie heißen Sie?*

    a Nein, ich komme nicht aus Berlin, aber ich wohne jetzt in Berlin.

    b Aufgewachsen bin ich in Salzburg.

    c Ich spreche fließend Englisch, Französisch und Italienisch.

    d Ich bin Koch und arbeite in einem Restaurant.

    e Nein, ich bin single.

    f Nein, ich habe keine Kinder.

    g Ich gehe gern in Konzerte und fotografiere gern.

3 Der, die oder das?

Using your prior knowledge and what you've learned in this unit, group the nouns in the appropriate column of the box.

~~Woche~~	Temperatur	Ferrari
~~Mittwoch~~	Sommer	Audi
Sonntag	Winter	Gymnasium
Natur	Dezember	Mädchen
Landschaft	Sprache	Märchen
Region	Pension	Tanzen
Passion	Fußballmannschaft	Schwimmen
Rose	Freundschaft	Nationalität
Silber	Schnaps	Identität
Gold	Wein	Intelligenz

der	die	das
Mittwoch	Woche	

4 01.05 Und jetzt Sie!

Herr Brandt is a guest on a TV show. Take on his role, using the English prompts to guide you.

LEARNING TIP

Rehearse your answers before role-playing the conversation along with the audio.

Moderator	Herr Brandt, können Sie ein bisschen über sich erzählen?
Sie	*Say yes, of course. Say that your name is Matthias Brandt and that you were born in Hanover, but that for 20 years you have lived in Berlin.*
Moderator	Und sind Sie berufstätig?
Sie	*Say yes, you are self-employed. Say that you are an architect.*
Moderator	Und sind Sie verheiratet?
Sie	*Say yes and that you have one daughter, Steffi. Explain that your daughter is a student and studies at the University of Heidelberg.*
Moderator	Und haben Sie ein Hobby?
Sie	*Say that you like going to the cinema and that you like reading. Say that you are also interested in languages.*
Moderator	Leben Sie gern in Berlin?
Sie	*Say yes. Say that the people in Berlin are friendly and Berlin is really interesting.*

SELF CHECK

	I CAN...
○	... share personal details about myself.
○	... ask other people about themselves and what they do.
○	... ask different types of questions (*yes/no* and *wh-*) correctly.
○	... identify typical gender and plural endings of nouns.
○	... use prepositions correctly when giving personal details.
○	... understand and write a personal blog.

2 Mein Tagesablauf

In this unit you will learn how to:

▶ *talk about daily routines including work and home life.*
▶ *describe a sequence of events and their frequency.*
▶ *understand an article about commuting to work.*
▶ *apply the principles of German word order.*
▶ *use separable and inseparable verbs.*

CEFR: *Can understand standard spoken language on familiar topics of everyday social and professional life, e.g. a narrative about work routine and home life; can write clear, detailed text on topics related to personal interests, e.g. describing a personal weekend routine (B2).*

Conversation 1

Lorenz Müller ist 26 Jahre alt und Dozent an der Friedrich-Schiller-Universität Jena. Er erzählt, wie sein Tagesablauf an Wochentagen und am Wochenende aussieht.

 1 02.01 **Lorenz Müller, a lecturer at the University of Jena, tells us what a typical day looks like for him. He also mentions what he does at weekends. What does he usually do in the morning after breakfast and what does he say about his hobbies?**

statt/finden	*to take place*
vor/bereiten	*to prepare*
beziehungsweise	*or, alternatively*
laufen	*to walk (coll.), to run*
die Mensa	*refectory, university dining hall*
erledigen	*(here) to finish off, to deal with*
was sonst an Arbeit anfällt	*whatever jobs need doing*
ausgiebig	*thorough, thoroughly*
die Schwiegereltern	*parents-in-law*
liegen/bleiben	*(here) to leave undone*
insofern	*(here) as such*
sich beschäftigen mit	*to concern oneself with*

Mein Tagesablauf beginnt morgens gegen halb acht, wenn ich aufstehe und anschließend frühstücke. Zum Frühstück esse ich normalerweise Brötchen mit Marmelade oder mit Nutella und trinke eine Tasse Kaffee, türkisch.

Meistens gehe ich aber dann erst mittags in die Stadt, in die Universität, weil meine Seminare erst später stattfinden. So habe ich also Zeit, am Vormittag zu Hause am Schreibtisch zu arbeiten, Seminare vorzubereiten, beziehungsweise zu lesen. Zur Arbeit fahre ich meistens mit dem Bus, aber manchmal laufe ich auch in die Stadt – es sind nur zehn Minuten zu Fuß.

Meine Seminare beginnen meistens erst am frühen Nachmittag oder sogar erst am frühen Abend. Mittagspause habe ich zwischen zwölf und zwei. Ich esse dann in der Mensa. Wenn ich keine Seminare habe, komme ich dann am frühen Nachmittag nach Hause, gehe einkaufen oder erledige, was sonst an Arbeit in der Wohnung anfällt. Am Abend lese ich ausgiebig die Zeitung, schaue Nachrichten im Fernsehen, manchmal dann noch einen Film. Gewöhnlich lese ich aber etwas, beziehungsweise höre Radio.

Am Wochenende besuchen wir öfters Freunde, gehen essen, besuchen die Schwiegereltern oder gehen ein wenig spazieren. Aber es muss auch all die Arbeit getan werden, die während der Woche liegen geblieben ist. Es wird gewaschen, sauber gemacht, aufgeräumt.

Hobbys habe ich insofern keine, da glücklicherweise mein Beruf mein Hobby geworden ist. Ich beschäftige mich ausgiebig mit der Literatur und schreibe auch selbst.

2 Beantworten Sie die folgenden Fragen.

a What does he have for breakfast?

b Where does he eat his lunch?

c What does he do when there are no seminars?

d Who does he visit at weekends?

3 Richtig oder falsch? Korrigieren Sie die falschen Aussagen.

a Lorenz Müller steht normalerweise um 8.30 Uhr auf.

b Am Vormittag arbeitet er meistens zu Hause.

c Er fährt immer mit dem Bus zur Arbeit.

d Bis zur Universität ist es weit.

e Abends geht er oft in die Kneipe.

f Literatur ist sein Hobby.

4 Wie heißt das auf Deutsch? Finden Sie im Text die deutschen Wörter für:

   a to start
   b to get up
   c to have breakfast
   d to take place
   e to run/to walk
   f to go shopping
   g to visit

LANGUAGE TIP – PASSIVE

Have you noticed the different passive constructions in the text?

es wird gewaschen	*washing is done; (here) we do the washing*
es wird sauber gemacht	*cleaning is done; (here) we do the cleaning*
es wird aufgeräumt	*clearing-up is done; (here) we do the clearing-up*

For more information about **Das Passiv**, see **Unit 9**.

Language discovery 1

You have already seen this language in action. Can you work out the rules?

1 **Look at the following sentences from Conversation 1. Can you identify the position of the subject and the verb in each sentence? How is it different to English, and what is the reason for this?**

   a Zum Frühstück esse ich normalerweise Brötchen mit Marmelade.
   b Meistens gehe ich aber dann erst mittags in die Stadt.
   c Mittagspause habe ich zwischen zwölf und zwei.
   d Am Wochenende besuchen wir öfters Freunde.

2 **Here are some useful words for describing a sequence of events. Can you put them in the right order, first through fifth?**

anschließend _____ zuerst _____ danach _____ dann _____ zum Schluss _____

1 WORTSTELLUNG *WORD ORDER*

You might remember that in German the verb is usually the second element in a sentence. So, if you start the sentence with a word or phrase other than the subject, the subject has to go straight after the verb. This is called **'subject–verb inversion'**:

1	2 VERB	3 SUBJECT	
Zum Frühstück	trinkt	Lorenz	eine Tasse Kaffee.
Gewöhnlich	liest	er	abends.
Am Wochenende	besuchen	sie	öfters Freunde.

2 WANN UND WIE OFT ... *SAYING WHEN AND HOW OFTEN ...*

Here is a list of adverbs referring to a sequence of events:

zuerst	*(at) first*	**Zuerst** haben wir etwas gegessen.
dann	*then*	**Dann** haben wir uns unterhalten.
danach	*after that, then*	**Danach** haben wir Zeitung gelesen.
als Nächstes	*next*	**Als Nächstes** haben wir Kaffee getrunken.
anschließend	*afterwards*	Wir sind dann **anschließend** ins Theater gegangen.
später	*later*	**Später** haben wir noch einen alten Freund getroffen.
zuletzt	*at last, finally*	**Zuletzt** sind wir wieder nach Hause gegangen.

Here are some words you can use when expressing how often you do certain things:

immer *always*, **meistens** *mostly*, **normalerweise** *normally*, **oft/öfters** *often*, **gewöhnlich** *usually*, **manchmal** *sometimes*, **gelegentlich** *occasionally*, **selten** *seldom, rarely*, **nie** *never*.

Practice 1

1 Wortstellung.

Start these sentences with the italicized word or phrase and make the required changes to the word order.

Beispiel: Ich stehe *um 7.30 Uhr* auf → Um 7.30 Uhr stehe ich auf.

a Ich mache *zuerst* 15 Minuten Yoga.

b Ich trinke Orangensaft *zum Frühstück* und esse ein Croissant mit Marmelade.

c Ich gehe *normalerweise* gegen acht Uhr aus dem Haus.

d Wir arbeiten *meistens* bis 18.00 Uhr.

e Ich besuche *am Wochenende* öfters Freunde oder gehe essen.

f Mein Freund and ich fahren *in den Ferien* zum Windsurfen an den Starnberger See.

2 Sagen Sie es anders.

Replace the expressions in italics with a word that has a similar meaning.

a Er geht *jeden Morgen* joggen. → Er geht _ _ _ _ _ joggen.

b Sie trinkt *nicht oft* Tee. → Sie trinkt _ _ _ _ _ _ Tee.

c *Normalerweise* sind sie pünktlich. → G _ _ _ _ _ _ _ _ _ sind sie pünktlich.

d Sie waren noch *nicht einmal* in der Oper. → Sie waren noch _ _ _ in der Oper.

3 Was macht Herr Müller normalerweise?

Do you remember what Lorenz Müller usually does on a typical day? Put the following phrases in the right sequence.

( ) frühstückt

( ) liest und hört Musik

(a) steht gegen halb acht auf

( ) gibt Seminare an der Universität

( ) fährt oder geht zur Arbeit

( ) arbeitet zu Hause am Schreibtisch

( ) isst in der Mensa

Now retell his daily routine in complete sentences, starting with the following words.

    a *Zuerst steht Herr Müller gegen halb acht auf.*

    b Dann ...

    c Danach ...

    d Anschließend ...

    e Als Nächstes ...

    f Später ...

    g Zuletzt ...

 4 Und Sie?

Talk about your daily routine and say in which order you normally do things. Start your sentences with sequencing words (**zuerst**, **dann**, **danach** ...). Make some notes to prepare your answer, including as much detail as you can. Then, try to speak for at least two minutes without stopping (yes, you can!).

Listen and understand

WAS MACHT FRAU WOLFRAM?

Corinna Wolfram ist 22 Jahre alt und arbeitet als Kellnerin in einer Gaststätte in München. Hören Sie, was sie erzählt.

 1 02.02 **Corinna Wolfram is 22 years old and works as a waitress in a restaurant in Munich. Listen to what she says. Why does she want to brush up her English?**

> **LEARNING TIP**
>
> You do not need to understand all the words to make sense of a conversation. Instead, focus on getting the gist of what's being said. You will understand more details when you listen again, especially if you preview the key vocabulary first. To become a good listener, resist the temptation to read along with the **Listen and understand** transcripts.

Es kommt darauf an, ob ...	*It (all) depends whether ...*
die Frühschicht (-en), die Spätschicht (-en)	*early shift, late shift*
jemandem zur Verfügung stehen	*to be at someone's disposal*
die Scheibe (-n)	*(here) slice*
in Anspruch nehmen	*to take up, make demands on*
auf/frischen	*to freshen up, to brush up on*
höchstens	*at (the) most*
die Mahlzeit (-en)	*meal*
umsonst	*free (of charge)*
die Kochnische (-n)	*kitchenette*

2 Beantworten Sie die Fragen.

    a How long has Corinna lived in Munich?

    b What does she do when she comes home after her late shift?

    c At what time does her late shift start?

    d What is an advantage of working in a restaurant, according to Corinna?

3 Welche Antwort stimmt?

Decide which of the two answers is true.

    a Ihre Gaststätte ist geöffnet

        1 bis um Mitternacht.   **2** bis nach Mitternacht.

    b Wenn sie Spätschicht hat, kommt sie

        1 um eins nach Hause.   **2** gegen eins, halb zwei nach Hause.

    c Zum Frühstück isst sie

        1 eine Scheibe Toast.   **2** eine Scheibe Brot.

    d Sie räumt ihr Zimmer

        1 ab und zu auf.   **2** einmal in der Woche auf.

    e Mit ihrem Freund geht sie gern

        1 schwimmen.   **2** ins Kino.

    f Ihre Eltern sieht sie

        1 höchstens dreimal im Jahr.   **2** höchstens viermal im Jahr.

> **LANGUAGE TIP – HÖREN SIE DAS RICHTIG?**
>
> In der Aufnahme sagt Corinna, sie sieht ihre Eltern „höchstens viermal im Jahr **zu** Weihnachten und **bei** Geburtstagen."
> In Süddeutschland sagt man meistens **zu Weihnachten**, in Norddeutschland **an Weihnachten**.
> Je nach Region kann man auch **zu Geburtstagen**, **an Geburtstagen** oder **bei Geburtstagen** sagen.
> Es gibt hier kein „richtig" oder „falsch" – der Gebrauch hängt von der Region ab.

 4 02.03 **Sagen Sie's auf Deutsch!**

Can you supply the German equivalents for the following phrases which you heard in the last conversation? Listen to confirm your answers and practise imitating the native speaker's intonation.

    a It (all) depends ...

    b around one (o'clock)

    c I'll take a quick shower.

    d a slice of toast

    e now and again

    f four times a year at most

    g at Christmas

    h on birthdays

📖 Reading

1 **Wenn Leute von zu Hause zur Arbeit fahren, heißt das pendeln** *to commute.*
 **Lesen Sie den Text und finden Sie heraus, wie die meisten Deutschen zu ihrem
 Arbeitplatz kommen.**

**Read the following text about how Germans travel to work. Without looking at the
vocabulary first, try to find out how many people travel by car, how many by public
transport and how many by bike.**

Der Weg zur Arbeit
Die meisten nehmen das Auto

Rund vier Prozent der Deutschen können den Arbeitstag stressfrei beginnen,
da sie direkt an ihrem Arbeitsplatz wohnen. Das bedeutet, dass sie nach dem
Frühstück schon im Büro, im Laden oder in der Werkstatt stehen.

Das sind aber die Ausnahmen. Die anderen müssen sich dagegen jeden Morgen
auf den Weg zur Arbeit machen. Die meisten – etwa 60 Prozent – fahren mit
dem Auto. Einige finden es bequemer mit dem Auto, andere wohnen so weit
außerhalb, dass es für sie keine andere Möglichkeit gibt, als den eigenen Wagen
zu benutzen. Mit öffentlichen Verkehrsmitteln – Bahn oder Bus – fahren etwa
13 Prozent zur Arbeit.

Nur neun Prozent gehen zu Fuß zur Arbeit und noch weniger (etwa acht Prozent)
fahren mit dem Fahrrad. Diese Leute haben aber das schöne Gefühl, dass sie
etwas für die Umwelt tun.

Der Weg zur Arbeit ist für viele Menschen weiter geworden. Vor 10 Jahren betrug
die Entfernung von der Wohnung bis zum Arbeitsplatz für 52 Prozent weniger
als 10 km – heute wohnen nur noch 45 Prozent weniger als 10 km von der
Arbeitsstelle entfernt. Jeder Sechste (16,2 Prozent) muss sogar mehr als 25 km
bis zum Arbeitsplatz fahren.

der Laden (-ˆ)	*shop*
die Werkstatt (ˆ-en)	*workshop*
die Ausnahme (-n)	*exception*
außerhalb	*(here) out of town*
die öffentlichen Verkehrsmittel (pl.)	*public transport*
das Gefühl (-e)	*feeling*
die Umwelt	*environment*

2 Lesen Sie den Text noch einmal und beantworten Sie die Fragen.

Now read the text once more and answer these questions.

  a What does the figure of 4% represent?
  b Why do most Germans go to work by car?
  c What sort of feeling do those who don't drive get from walking or bicycling to work?
  d What has changed in the last ten years?
  e What is the problem for about one in six people?

3 Verbinden Sie die Satzteile.

Match both parts of the statements.

  a Etwa 60 Prozent der Deutschen
  b Mit Bus oder Bahn
  c Vier Prozent der Deutschen
  d Neun Prozent
  e Etwa acht Prozent

  1 gehen zu Fuß.
  2 arbeiten an ihrem Wohnort.
  3 fahren mit dem Fahrrad.
  4 fahren mit dem Auto.
  5 fahren etwa 13 Prozent.

Language discovery 2

You have already seen this language in action. Can you work out the rules?

1 Here are a number of separable verbs you have met in the context of a daily routine. Can you identify the part of the verb that can split from the main verb? Do you remember what this part is called?

aufstehen, aufräumen, auffrischen, aussehen, einkaufen, mitmachen, stattfinden, vorbereiten

2 Write out the missing forms of the following verbs. Apart from the different endings what else changes?

	ich	du	Sie	er/sie/es
essen	esse	_____	_____	_____
fahren	_____	_____	fahren	_____
laufen	_____	_____	_____	_____

1 TRENNBARE VERBEN *SEPARABLE VERBS*

Separable verbs consist of a main verb and a prefix that often separates from the main verb:

aufräumen	Sie **räumt** jedes Wochenende ihr Zimmer **auf**.
vorbereiten	Er **bereitet** das Abendessen **vor**.

Commonly used separable prefixes include:

ab-, an-, auf-, aus-, ein-, mit-, nach-, statt-, vor-, zu-

Note that with modal verbs, such as **können**, **müssen**, **wollen**, etc., the separable verb does not split up:

aufräumen	Ich **muss** mein Zimmer **aufräumen**.
vorbereiten	Er **will** das Abendessen **vorbereiten**.

2 VERBEN MIT VOKALWECHSELN *VERBS WITH VOWEL CHANGES*

There are a number of irregular verbs which require a vowel change for the **du** and **er/sie/es** forms in the present tense.

The stem vowel changes of irregular verbs follow certain patterns. The following four are the most frequent:

e → i	essen	ich esse	du **i**sst	er/sie/es **i**sst
e → ie	lesen	ich lese	du **lie**st	er/sie/es **lie**st
a → ä	fahren	ich fahre	du **fä**hrst	er/sie/es **fä**hrt
a → äu	laufen	ich laufe	du **läu**fst	er/sie/es **läu**ft

You'll find a list of common irregular verbs at the end of the book.

Practice 2

1 Wie heißt es richtig?

Supply the correct forms of these irregular verbs.

Beispiel: Morgens _____ Marion immer zwei Scheiben Toast. (essen)

→ Morgens *isst* Marion immer zwei Scheiben Toast.

   a Dann _____ sie die Zeitung auf ihrem iPad. (lesen)

   b Danach _____ sie meistens mit dem Fahrrad zur Arbeit. (fahren)

   c Im Winter _____ sie auch manchmal den Bus. (nehmen)

   d Marion _____ viel mit Kunden im Ausland. (sprechen)

   e Nachmittags _____ sie einer Kollegin mit der neuen Software. (helfen)

   f Nach der Arbeit _____ sie gern Freundinnen. (treffen)

   g Am Wochenende _____ sie oft 10 km oder mehr. (laufen)

2 Trennbare Verben.

Form at least ten separable verbs by adding a prefix from the left circle to a main verb from the right circle. For some verbs there is more than one possibility. Make sure you understand the meaning of the verbs.

Beispiele: *anfangen = to start; anmachen = to switch on*

3 Welche Verben passen?

Complete these sentences using a correct separable verb from the box.

> einladen   fernsehen   abwaschen   vorbereiten
> stattfinden   abräumen   auffrischen   ~~anfangen~~

a Die Seminare *fangen* erst am Nachmittag *an*.

b Am Vormittag _____ er sich auf den Unterricht _____.

c Die Geschirrspülmaschine ist kaputt. Herr und Frau Müller _____ selber

_____.

d Nach dem Essen _____ Frau Wolfram den Tisch _____.

e Das Konzert _____ am Samstag in der Konzerthalle _____.

f Viele Kinder _____ mehr als drei Stunden pro Tag _____.

g Er _____ sehr gern Gäste zu sich nach Hause _____.

h Ich muss mein Deutsch _____.

Conversation 2

Frau Beitz, 78, ist Rentnerin. Sie erzählt über ihren Alltag.

 1 02.04 **Mrs Beitz, a 78 year-old pensioner, talks about her daily routine. What does she do during the day and why doesn't she mind going to bed quite late?**

Wird Ihnen nicht langweilig?	*Don't you get bored?*
gemächlich	*leisurely*
der Ausflug (-¨e)	*excursion, day trip*
die Umgebung (-en)	*surrounding area*
der/die Urenkel/in (-)	*great-grandson/great-granddaughter*
stricken	*to knit*
ich bin gerade dabei, ...	*I'm just (in the process of) ...*
sich etwas an/schauen	*to watch something (e.g. on TV)*
die Nachrichtensendung (-en)	*news (broadcast)*
die Podiumsdiskussion (-en)	*panel discussion*
der Dokumentarfilm (-e)	*documentary (film)*
die Ratesendung (-en)	*panel game*
die Unterhaltungsserie (-n)	*light entertainment programme*

Paul	Frau Beitz, Sie sind Rentnerin und wohnen hier allein. Wird Ihnen nicht manchmal langweilig?
Frau Beitz	Aber nein! Mir wird nie langweilig. Es gibt ja allerhand zu tun. Meistens stehe ich schon um 7 Uhr auf. Ich hole dann ein paar Brötchen von der Bäckerei und koche Kaffee. Ich frühstücke ganz gemächlich – im Sommer sitze ich in der Morgensonne auf meinem Balkon. Anschließend lese ich die Zeitung. Ich interessiere mich nämlich sehr für Politik.
Paul	Sehen Sie auch fern?
Frau Beitz	Ja, aber erst abends und dann nur selten. Während des Tages gehe ich lieber eine von meinen Freundinnen besuchen oder wir gehen zusammen im Stadtpark spazieren. Gelegentlich esse ich in einem Restaurant zu Mittag.
Paul	Haben Sie Familie?
Frau Beitz	Ja, mein Sohn Helmut kommt mich fast immer am Wochenende besuchen. Er wohnt mit seiner Frau in Hamburg, also gar nicht weit weg. Wir machen dann samstags oder sonntags schöne Ausflüge in die Umgebung – mal die Ostseeküste entlang nach Wismar oder Rostock, mal in nördlicher Richtung nach Kiel oder Flensburg.
Paul	Haben Sie irgendwelche Hobbys?
Frau Beitz	Ich stricke gern. Ich bin gerade dabei, einen Pullover für meine Urenkelin zu stricken. Sie ist erst drei Jahre alt und wohnt in Osnabrück. Im März war ich eine Woche dort bei meiner Enkelin und ihrem Mann zu Besuch.
Paul	Und was für Fernsehprogramme schauen Sie sich gerne an?
Frau Beitz	Vor allem Nachrichtensendungen, Podiumsdiskussionen und Dokumentarfilme. An Ratesendungen und Unterhaltungsserien habe ich gar kein Interesse.
Paul	Und wann gehen Sie ins Bett?
Frau Beitz	Normalerweise erst gegen Mitternacht. In meinem Alter braucht man ja nicht mehr so viel Schlaf!

2 Beantworten Sie die Fragen auf Deutsch.

a Was isst Frau Beitz zum Frühstück?

b Was macht sie nach dem Frühstück?

c Wo geht sie mit ihren Freundinnen spazieren?

d Wie oft kommt ihr Sohn zu Besuch?

e Was ist ihr Hobby?

f Was hat sie im März gemacht?

g Was für Fernsehsendungen sieht sie gern?

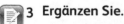 **3 Ergänzen Sie.**

Study the dialogue once more and then complete the missing information.

a Wird Ihnen nicht manchmal ...?

b Meistens stehe ich schon ...

c Im Sommer sitze ich in der Morgensonne ...

d Ich interessiere mich sehr ...

e Gelegentlich esse ich in einem Restaurant ...

f Wir machen samstags oder sonntags Ausflüge ...

g Ich bin gerade dabei, einen Pullover für meine Urenkelin ...

h An Ratesendungen und Unterhaltungsserien habe ich ...

 4 Mein Tagesablauf.

Write a description of your typical weekend from Friday to Sunday night, using the vocabulary and structures covered in this unit.

Comment on your Friday night activities: how do you celebrate the end of the working week? Describe your morning routine at weekends: when you get up, what you have for breakfast, the chores you do at home, etc. Are you more active or relaxed at weekends? Do you prefer to do sport or watch films? Give full details about the activities you do alone, or with friends and family.

Pay special attention to the subject–verb inversion and try to use words such as **zuerst**, **dann**, **danach**, **oft**, **manchmal**, etc. to add fluency and detail.

Here is a reminder of some of the daily activities and expressions covered in this unit.

Daily tasks	In the house	Hobbies, interests
aufstehen	abwaschen	Freunde besuchen
frühstücken	das Zimmer aufräumen	Gäste einladen
Brötchen holen	die Wäsche waschen	Ausflüge machen
zur Arbeit fahren	sauber machen	Nachrichtensendungen
sich unter die	den Tisch abräumen	anschauen
Dusche stellen	Kaffee kochen	sich mit der Literatur
		beschäftigen

Go further with grammar

1 WORTSTELLUNG *WORD ORDER*

Although German word order is relatively flexible, there are some basic rules.

a In **Language discovery 1** you were reminded of **subject–verb inversion** when the sentence starts with a word or phrase other than the subject, so that the verb is the second idea:

1	2	3
Abends	sehe	ich meistens fern.

b Another rule of thumb is TIME (when?) – MANNER (how?) – PLACE (where/where to?):

	TIME	MANNER	PLACE
Ich fahre	morgen	mit dem Wagen	nach Berlin.
Er geht	vor der Arbeit	noch schnell	ins Fitnesscenter.

Of course, not all these elements have to be present at once:

	TIME	MANNER	PLACE
Ich fahre	morgen	–	nach Berlin.
Er geht	–	noch schnell	ins Fitnesscenter.

Sometimes all three elements are present, but one of them moves into first position, so the subject–verb inversion becomes necessary:

TIME	VERB	SUBJECT	MANNER	PLACE
Morgen	fahre	ich	mit dem Wagen	nach Berlin.

2 TRENNBARE UND UNTRENNBARE VERBEN *SEPARABLE AND INSEPARABLE VERBS*

   a In **Language discovery 2** you saw how **separable** verbs work in practice and that commonly used prefixes include :
   ab-, an-, auf-, aus-, ein-, mit-, nach-, statt-, vor-, zu-

   b Note that the following prefixes are always **inseparable**:
   be-, emp-, ent-, er-, ge-, ver-, zer-

besuchen	Am Wochenende **besucht** er seine Schwiegereltern.
erzählen	Frau Beitz **erzählt** über ihren Alltag.

   c There are also some prefixes which can be **separable** or **inseparable**:
   durch-, hinter-, über-, um-, unter-, voll-, wider-, wieder-

Verbs with these prefixes tend to be **separable** when the meaning is more concrete and **inseparable** when they carry a more abstract meaning, e.g.:

   über/setzen   *to ferry over* (separable)
Er **setzte** das Boot an das andere Ufer **über**.

He ferried the boat over to the other bank.

   übersetzen   *to translate* (inseparable)
Sie **übersetzte** den Text ins Deutsche.

She translated the text into German.

   d Stress pattern for separable and inseparable verbs:

   Separable verbs – the stress normally falls on the first syllable:
   aufstehen, **ein**kaufen, **aus**gehen, **um**steigen, **statt**finden

   Inseparable verbs – here the stress is put on the verb stem:
   be**such**en, emp**fehl**en, er**zähl**en, ver**steh**en

3 VERBENDUNGEN IM PRÄSENS *VERB ENDINGS IN THE PRESENT TENSE*

As you saw in **Language discovery 2** there are a number of irregular verbs which have a stem vowel change in the **du** and **er/sie/es** forms.

However, almost all German verbs follow the same pattern of endings in the present tense form. Here is a reminder of the required endings:

ich spiel**e**	wir spiel**en**
du spiel**st**	ihr spiel**t**
Sie spiel**en**	Sie spiel**en**
er/sie/es spiel**t**	sie spiel**en**

Note that there are a number of verbs whose stem ends in **-d** or **-t**. These normally need an extra **-e-** for the 2nd person singular and plural and the 3rd person singular:

arbeiten   ich arbeite   du arbeit**est**   er/sie/es arbeit**et**   ihr arbeit**et**

finden   ich finde   du find**est**   er/sie/es find**et**   ihr find**et**

? Test yourself

Bear in mind that you should carry on working on this unit until you can answer over three-quarters of the questions correctly for all sections of the self-test.

1 Welches Verb passt am besten?

Find the most suitable verb. The first one has been done for you.

> laufen   auffrischen   stellen   machen   ~~besuchen~~   aufräumen   abwaschen
> anschauen   stricken   erledigen   vorbereiten   übersetzen

a Freunde → *besuchen*
b sich unter die Dusche → _____
c das Geschirr _____
d zum Bus → _____
e eine Unterhaltungsserie → _____
f ein Seminar → _____
g das Zimmer → _____
h einen Pullover → _____
i Arbeit → _____
j einen Text → _____
k einen Ausflug → _____
l Deutschkenntnisse → _____

2 Look at the verbs from the previous exercise again. There are five separable verbs. Can you identify them? There are also two verbs which have inseparable prefixes and one verb whose prefix could be separable or inseparable. Do you know which ones they are?

3 Wortstellung.

Put the phrase in brackets into the appropriate position in the main sentence.

Beispiel: Frau Peters frühstückt im Café. (fast jeden Morgen) →

Frau Peters frühstückt fast jeden Morgen im Café.

   a Claudia fährt im Winter mit der U-Bahn. (zur Universität)
   b Kommst du mit ins Kino? (heute Abend)
   c Theo und Anke gehen in der Mittagspause ins Restaurant. (zu Fuß)
   d Manfred fährt nachmittags zu seinem Freund ins Krankenhaus. (mit seinem Auto)
   e Hans Martinek geht oft ins Fitnesscenter. (nach der Arbeit).
   f Frau Tiedke kauft abends noch schnell ein. (im Supermarkt)
   g Die Fuhrmanns wollen nächstes Wochenende eine Radtour machen. (an die Ostsee)

4 Marianne redet mit ihrer Freundin über ihren Tagesablauf.

Setzen Sie die Sätze in die richtige Reihenfolge.

Reconstruct the following dialogue between Marianne (M) and her friend Barbara (B). Start with sentence (f).

   a (B) Ja, ich esse meistens in einem Restaurant eine warme Mahlzeit.
   b (B) Es kommt darauf an, ob ich arbeite oder ob ich frei habe.
   c (M) Und was machst du abends nach der Arbeit?
   d (B) Doch. Ich gehe gern windsurfen. Aber das mache ich am Wochenende oder in den Ferien.
   e (B) Meistens erledige ich, was in der Wohnung an Arbeit anfällt. Manchmal schaue ich auch fern oder stricke.
   f (M) Wie sieht eigentlich dein Tagesablauf aus?
   g (B) Wenn ich arbeite, stehe ich um 7 Uhr auf, wasche mich, frühstücke und fahre mit dem Bus ins Büro.
   h (M) Und wie ist es, wenn du arbeitest?
   i (M) Hast du sonst keine Hobbys?
   j (M) Isst du in der Stadt zu Mittag?

1	2	3	4	5	6	7	8	9	10
f									

5 02.05 Und jetzt Sie!

Follow the prompts and answer questions about your daily routine. Rehearse your answers first, then practise speaking at normal speed. The answers can be heard on the audio.

Bekannte	Wann stehst du eigentlich morgens auf?
Sie	*Tell her that during the week you usually get up at around seven, at weekends mostly at around half past nine.*
Bekannte	Was frühstückst du normalerweise?
Sie	*Say that you normally get rolls from the bakery. Say that you then make coffee and eat rolls with jam and butter, and drink a glass of juice. Say that you also usually read the paper.*
Bekannte	Und wie fährst du zur Arbeit?
Sie	*Say that you mostly go by car, and only seldom by bus.*
Bekannte	Hast du denn auch eine Mittagspause?
Sie	*Tell her that you usually have a lunch break between 12.30 and 13.15. Say that you mostly eat in your company and only occasionally have lunch in a restaurant.*
Bekannte	Und was machst du am Abend, nach der Arbeit?
Sie	*Tell her that you usually watch the news on TV, read a book or listen to the radio.*
Bekannte	Und was machst du gerne am Wochenende?
Sie	*Answer that you sometimes visit friends or your parents, go for a walk occasionally, or do the work that has been left during the week. Say that on Sundays you sometimes make day trips in the surrounding area.*

SELF CHECK

I CAN. . .

- ... talk about my routines, including work and home life.
- ... describe a sequence of events and how often I do things.
- ... understand an article about commuting to work.
- ... apply the principles of German word order.
- ... use separable and inseparable verbs.
- ... describe my personal weekend routine in writing.

3 *Ausbildung oder Studium?*

In this unit you will learn how to:
- ▶ *give facts about education and training.*
- ▶ *talk and write about past events.*
- ▶ *use the present perfect and simple past tenses.*
- ▶ *make and discuss plans for the future.*

CEFR: *Can keep up with an animated discussion between native speakers; can take an active part in informal discussions and put a point across clearly, e.g. explain personal academic background; can scan quickly through complex texts, locating relevant details, e.g. an overview of the German education system (B2).*

Conversation 1

LEHRE ODER STUDIUM?

Birgit spricht mit ihrem Onkel über ihre Arbeit und warum sie nicht studieren wollte.

 1 03.01 **Birgit talks to her uncle, who is visiting from Argentina, about her work and why she didn't want to go to university. She tells him that the number of university graduates is a problem for the German economy: is that because there are too few or too many?**

V die Banklehre (-n)	banking apprenticeship
die Stellung (-en)	job, position
der Akademiker (-)	graduate
das Abitur	school-leaving examination taken at 18+
das Hochschulstudium	study at an institution of higher education
die Wirtschaft (-en)	economy
die Zweigstelle (-n)	branch
zufrieden	satisfied, content

Heinz	Deine Mutter hat mir gesagt, dass du bei der Deutschen Bank eine Lehre machst. Hast du denn nicht studieren wollen?
Birgit	Eigentlich doch. Aber ich musste auch einsehen, dass gerade hier in Deutschland für Akademiker Schwierigkeiten bestehen, Arbeit zu finden. Und ich wollte auf keinen Fall arbeitslos werden. Ich habe mich deshalb um eine Banklehre beworben.
Heinz	Kennst du denn Leute, die studiert haben und nachher keine Stellung gefunden haben?
Birgit	Oh, ja! Sehr viele sogar. Bei uns gibt es eben zu viele Studenten. Es hat ja jeder, der Abitur gemacht hat, das Recht auf ein Hochschulstudium, und die Universitäten sind deswegen überfüllt. Die Wirtschaft kann so viele akademisch qualifizierte Leute einfach nicht aufnehmen.
Heinz	Als ich aber vor drei Jahren hier war, hast du dich – wenn ich mich recht erinnere – für die englische Sprache besonders interessiert. Hast du das denn aufgeben müssen?
Birgit	Aber gar nicht! Jeden Tag mache ich von meinen Englischkenntnissen Gebrauch. Und im Augenblick lerne ich intensiv Italienisch, da ich im Oktober für ein ganzes Jahr zu unserer Zweigstelle in Florenz geschickt werde.
Heinz	Und du bedauerst es wirklich nicht, dass du nicht studiert hast?
Birgit	Doch, ein bisschen! Aber ich bin ehrlich gesagt mit meinem Beruf sehr zufrieden.

2 Beantworten Sie die folgenden Fragen.

a What's the name of the bank where Birgit is doing her training?

b Why did she decide not to pursue a university degree?

c Why is she learning Italian?

d How does she feel about her profession?

V ein/sehen	to recognize, acknowledge
bestehen	to exist
sich bewerben um	to apply for
sogar	even
das Recht auf	the right to
überfüllt	overcrowded
auf/nehmen	to accept, absorb
Gebrauch machen von	to make use of
bedauern	to regret

Deutsche Bank ✎

3 Wie heißt das im Text?

Replace the words in italics with an expression from Conversation 1 conveying a similar meaning.

Beispiel: ich musste *verstehen* → ich musste *einsehen*

   a es *gibt* Schwierigkeiten

   b eine *Arbeit* finden

   c die Universitäten sind *zu voll*

   d die Wirtschaft kann so viele Leute nicht *beschäftigen*

   e ich *nutze* meine Englischkenntnisse

   f ich bin sehr *glücklich*

4 Richtig oder falsch?

Lesen Sie den Dialog noch einmal und korrigieren Sie die falschen Aussagen.

   a Für Akademiker in Deutschland gibt es keine Probleme, eine Arbeit zu finden.

   b Birgit kennt nur wenige Leute, die studiert haben und jetzt arbeitslos sind.

   c Ein Problem ist, dass die deutschen Universitäten zu voll sind.

   d Die deutsche Wirtschaft kann so viele Akademiker nicht beschäftigen.

   e Birgit hat in ihrem Beruf leider keine Möglichkeit, ihre Englischkenntnisse zu nutzen.

> **CULTURE TIP – DIE DUALE AUSBILDUNG** *THE DUAL EDUCATION SYSTEM*
> Die duale Ausbildung in Deutschland verbindet die Lehre in einer Firma mit der Berufsausbildung in einer besonderen Schule, der Berufsschule. Es gibt mehr als 350 Ausbildungsberufe für junge Leute.

Language discovery 1

 You have already seen this language in action. Can you work out the rules?

1 **Can you supply the present perfect forms (past participles) of these verbs? They have all appeared in Conversation 1. Do you know which ones are regular and which ones irregular?**

   a bewerben   Ich habe mich um eine Banklehre _____ .

   b finden   Kennst du Leute, die keine Stellung _____ haben.

   c machen   Jeder, der Abitur _____ hat, darf studieren.

   d studieren   Bedauerst du nicht, dass du nicht _____ hast?

2 **Find out how the following is expressed in Conversation 1. Do you know what this tense is called and when it is normally used in German?**

   a I had to ... _____

   b I wantcd ... _____

   c I was ... _____

ÜBER DIE VERGANGENHEIT SPRECHEN UND SCHREIBEN *TALKING AND WRITING ABOUT THE PAST*

If you want to talk about the past in German, for instance about your education, you normally use the **Perfekt** *present perfect* tense. For writing purposes, for instance reports, newspaper articles or novels, the **Präteritum** or simple past is generally used.

However, there are a number of exceptions. Birgit used the simple past twice when talking about herself:

Aber ich **musste** auch einsehen, dass …

Und ich **wollte** auf keinen Fall arbeitslos werden.

These are modal verbs whose simple past forms are easier to use in speaking than their present perfect alternatives (**ich habe einsehen müssen … , ich habe auf keinen Fall arbeitslos werden wollen.**).

Other examples of verbs which are frequently used in the simple past tense include **sein**, **haben** and **geben**:

Ich **war** letzte Woche krank.

Ich **hatte** eine Erkältung.

Es **gab** nichts zu essen.

Here is a short reminder on how the present perfect and simple past tenses are formed. For a detailed overview, see the **Go further with grammar** section.

1 DAS PERFEKT *THE PRESENT PERFECT TENSE*

Here are a few important points to remember:

▶ regular verbs normally form the past participle by adding **ge-** to the front and **-t** to the end: **machen** → **gemacht**

▶ the past participle of irregular verbs often has a vowel change and ends in **-en**: **finden** → **gefunden**

▶ some verbs are formed with **sein**, not **haben**: **gehen** → **ich bin gegangen**

2 DAS PRÄTERITUM *THE SIMPLE PAST TENSE*

The most important features are:

▶ regular verbs usually form the past simple by adding the appropriate ending to the stem:
ich mach**te**, du mach**test**, Sie mach**ten**, er/sie/es mach**te,**

wir mach**ten**, ihr mach**tet**, Sie mach**ten**, sie mach**ten**

▶ irregular verbs normally have a stem vowel change and the following endings:
ich sah, du sah**st**, Sie sah**en**, er/sie/es sah,

wir sah**en**, ihr sah**t**, Sie sah**en**, sie sah**en**

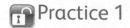

Practice 1

1 Mehr über Birgit.

Birgit has written a short text about herself for a youth magazine. Complete her sentences using the most appropriate verb from the box, in the simple past tense

> bewarb   ging   arbeitete   wusste   fand
> wurde   machte   sollte   begann   bekam
> war   lernte ... kennen

Blog	Add post

Ich **(a)** _____ in Lübeck geboren. Dort **(b)** _____ ich auch in die Schule. Mit 18 Jahren **(c)** _____ ich mein Abitur. Ich **(d)** _____ nicht, ob ich studieren oder eine Lehre machen **(e)** _____. Das **(f)** _____ keine leichte Entscheidung. Schließlich **(g)** _____ ich mich bei einigen Banken und **(h)** _____ auch einen Ausbildungsplatz bei der Deutschen Bank. Vor etwa einem Jahr **(i)** _____ ich meine Lehre. In den ersten sechs Monaten **(j)** _____ ich meistens in unserer größten Bank im Stadtzentrum. Danach **(k)** _____ ich auch andere Zweigstellen _____. Das **(l)** _____ ich sehr interessant. Diesen Oktober werde ich für ein Jahr nach Florenz gehen. Ich freue mich schon darauf.

2   Wie heißen die Partizipien?

Do you remember how the so-called past participles (the verb form used in the present perfect tense) go?

    a arbeiten → *gearbeitet*
    b studieren → _____
    c bewerben → _____
    d passieren → _____
    e verbringen → _____
    f gehen → _____
    g werden → _____
    h fahren → _____
    i besuchen → _____
    j beenden → _____

Which four of these verbs take sein in the present perfect tense?

3 Was hat Martin gemacht?

How would Martin Klostermann talk about his education and training? Put the following sentences in the appropriate tense, keeping in mind the points made in Language discovery 1.

Beispiel: Ich/in Karlsruhe/aufwachsen. → *Ich bin in Karlsruhe aufgewachsen.*

   a Dort/ich/auch die Schule/besuchen.

   b Mit 17 Jahren/ich/meine Schule/abschließen.

   c Dann/ich/ein Jahr für ein soziales Projekt mit Kindern/arbeiten.

   d Anschließend/ich/mich/um eine Lehre als Hotelfachmann/bewerben.

   e Es/geben/viele Bewerber,/aber/ich/haben/Glück.

   f Ich/dürfen/auch drei Monate/in Berlin /arbeiten.

   g Das /eine gute Erfahrung/für mich /sein /und ich /auch viele neue Sachen /lernen.

   h Vor einem halben Jahr/ich/meine Lehre/beenden.

4 Und Sie?

Talk about your education. Say where you were born, where you grew up and went to school, and when you graduated. Explain what you did afterwards (whether you started work, did further training courses, studied at university, etc.) and what you are doing at the moment. Make some notes to prepare your answers, including as much detail as you can. Then, try to speak for two minutes without stopping.

Reading

DAS DEUTSCHE BILDUNGS– UND AUSBILDUNGSSYSTEM

1 The article gives a short overview about the German education system. Without looking at the vocabulary first, can you find out:

   a the age when children in Germany first go to school?

   b the number of years education is compulsory?

   c how long it typically takes to qualify as a teacher?

Das deutsche Bildungs- und Ausbildungssystem

In Deutschland, wie in anderen Ländern, gehen viele Kinder in ihren ersten Jahren in einen Kindergarten. Das ist aber nicht obligatorisch. Erst mit sechs Jahren muss man zur Schule gehen. Diese erste Schule, die man vier Jahre lang besucht, heißt Grundschule. Nach der Grundschule wird meistens entschieden, in welchen Schultyp ein Kind anschließend geht.

Da die Bildung in Deutschland Sache der verschiedenen Bundesländer ist, gibt es unterschiedliche Bildungssysteme. Aber in der Regel gibt es nach der Grundschule drei verschiedene Schultypen – die Hauptschule, die Realschule und das Gymnasium. Die Hauptschule führt mit 15 oder 16 Jahren zum Hauptschulabschluss und ist beruflich orientiert. Die Realschule führt mit 16 Jahren zur mittleren Reife und ist oft der Beginn einer mittleren Karriere in der Wirtschaft oder im öffentlichen Dienst. Das Gymnasium bietet eine akademische Bildung und führt mit 18 oder 19 Jahren zum Abitur, das man traditionellerweise braucht, wenn man studieren möchte.

In einigen Bundesländern findet man alle drei Bildungsmöglichkeiten unter einem Dach in der sogenannten Gesamtschule.

In Deutschland muss man 12 Jahre lang zur Schule gehen. Nach neun Jahren (in manchen Ländern 10 Jahren) darf man die Vollzeitschule verlassen. Man beginnt dann meistens eine Lehre im Handwerk oder in der Industrie, die dann zu einem bestimmten Beruf, wie z.B. Kfz-Mechaniker/in, Schreiner/in, Friseur/in oder Industriekaufmann/-kauffrau führt. Neben der Lehre muss man auch eine Schule, die sogenannte Berufsschule, besuchen, meistens einmal pro Woche.

Mit dem Abitur hat man theoretisch das Recht, an einer Universität oder Hochschule zu studieren. In der Praxis gibt es heutzutage für viele Fächer ein Quotensystem. Das Studienjahr hat zwei Semester – das Wintersemester und das Sommersemester.

Wer zum Beispiel Lehrer werden möchte, muss meistens neun Semester studieren und legt am Ende das Staatsexamen ab.

Die deutschen Universitäten bieten Bachelor- und Masterkurse an. Wie in anderen Ländern auch dauert das Bachelorstudium meistens drei Jahre und das Masterstudium noch ein bis zwei Jahre.

V	
das Bundesland (-̈er)	*federal state*
in der Regel	*normally, as a rule*
sogenannt	*so-called*
das Handwerk	*trade, craft*
Kfz-Mechaniker/in (-)/in (-nen)	*car mechanic*
der/die Schreiner (-)/in (-nen)	*carpenter*
der/die Industriekaufmann/frau (-̈er/-en)	*industrial business management assistant*
das Quotensystem (-e)	*quota system*

das Staatsexamen (-)	state examination (a degree that is also a teaching qualification)
ab/legen	to sit, take (an exam)
der Abschluss (-¨e)	leaving examination

2 Beantworten Sie die Fragen.

a In the German system, how many types of school normally follow on from primary school (**Grundschule**)?

b What kind of jobs do people often take after finishing the **Realschule**?

c What sort of curriculum do students follow at the **Gymnasium**?

d What is special about the **Gesamtschule**?

e What kind of formal schooling must people also follow when they do an apprenticeship?

3 Welches Wort passt zu welcher Definition?

> Kindergarten   Staatsexamen   Hauptschule   Realschule
> Gymnasium   Abitur   Berufsschule   Grundschule

a Können Kinder besuchen, bevor sie in die Schule gehen: _____

b Dorthin müssen alle Kinder gehen: _____

c Führt oft zu einer Lehre im Handwerk oder in der Industrie: _____

d Der Abschluss dort heißt mittlere Reife: _____

e Dort macht man das Abitur: _____

f Muss man besuchen, wenn man eine Lehre macht: _____

g Braucht man, wenn man studieren möchte: _____

h Ein Abschluss, den man an der Universität macht: _____

4 Eine Zusammenfassung.

Now write a short summary of the German education system by completing the sentences with the information from the reading you have just done.

a In Deutschland gehen die Kinder mit sechs Jahren ...

b Nach der Grundschule gibt es ...

c Insgesamt müssen die Kinder mindestens ...

d Wenn man studieren möchte, braucht man ...

e Das Studienjahr hat ...

f Das Studium dauert ...

5 Wie ist das Bildungssystem in Ihrem Land?

Now using the prompts from the last exercise, give a short overview about the system in your country. Make some notes to prepare your answers and include as much detail as you can.

Conversation 2

STUDIUM – UND WAS DANN?

Ilona, eine Chemiestudentin, sucht einen Platz in der Mensa und lernt Vera kennen, die Anglistik studiert.

 1 03.02 **Ilona, a Chemistry student who is looking for a seat in the cafeteria meets Vera, a student of English language and literature. For which ministry does Ilona want to work and what is she worried about?**

Ilona	Ist hier noch frei?
Vera	Ja, bitte schön. Ich studiere Anglistik im vierten Semester. Was studierst du?
Ilona	Chemie. Isst du jeden Tag hier in der Mensa zu Mittag?
Vera	Nein. Es kommt darauf an, ob ich zu einem Seminar oder zu einer Vorlesung muss. Womöglich arbeite ich zu Hause und esse dann auch da zu Mittag.
Ilona	Du hast aber Glück! Wir Chemiestudenten müssen jeden Tag ins Labor. Versuche durchführen kann man eigentlich nur im Labor. Bald bin ich aber mit dem Studium fertig. Ende nächsten Semesters will ich das Staatsexamen ablegen.
Vera	Und was möchtest du dann werden?
Ilona	Ich werde mich um eine Stellung beim Umweltministerium bewerben. Die Konkurrenz ist zwar ziemlich stark, aber vielleicht schaffe ich es trotzdem. Und du, was hast du vor?
Vera	Ich möchte Gymnasiallehrerin für Englisch werden. Bis ich mit dem Studium fertig bin, wird hoffentlich wieder Nachfrage nach Lehrern bestehen.
Ilona	Hast du auch in England studiert?
Vera	Ja, ich habe vor zwei Jahren ein Jahr in Canterbury studiert. Es hat ungeheuer viel Spaß gemacht.

die Anglistik	*English language and literature*
die Vorlesung (-en)	*lecture*
womöglich	*(here) when(ever) possible*
der Versuch (-e)	*(here) experiment*
durch/führen	*to conduct, carry out*
Was möchtest du werden?	*Would would you like to become?*
das Umweltministerium	*Ministry of the Environment*
die Konkurrenz	*competition*
schaffen	*to manage (coll.)*
fertig sein mit etwas	*to have finished with something*
die Nachfrage (-n)	*demand*
ungeheuer	*huge(ly); immense(ly)*

2 Richtig oder falsch? Korrigieren Sie die falschen Aussagen.

   a Vera studiert Anglistik im ersten Semester.
   b Chemie-Studenten müssen meistens im Labor arbeiten.
   c Ilona will in einem Jahr das Staatsexamen ablegen.
   d Sie wird sich beim Finanzministerium bewerben.
   e Vera möchte Englischlehrerin werden.
   f Sie hofft, dass die Situation für Lehrer besser sein wird.

CULTURE TIP – HOCHSCHULEN IN DEUTSCHLAND

Die älteste Hochschule in Deutschland ist die Universität Heidelberg. Sie wurde 1386 gegründet. Bekannt sind auch die Universitäten von Jena und Tübingen, wo zum Beispiel der Astronom Johannes Kepler studiert hat.

Johannes Keppler (1571-1630)

Insgesamt studieren etwa 2,5 Millionen Menschen in Deutschland. Die meisten Universitäten werden vom Staat finanziert und es gibt keine Studiengebühren (fees). Es gibt aber auch Privathochschulen wie die Universität Witten-Herdecke oder die European Business School in Schloss Reichartshausen. Mehr als 37% eines Jahrgangs gehen heutzutage an eine Hochschule.

---

3 03.03 **Sagen Sie's auf Deutsch!**

Can you say the following in German? In most instances, you'll have to make changes to the original sentences from Conversation 2. Try it before you listen for the answers.

   a Is this seat free?
   b I have been studying English literature and linguistics for one and a half years.
   c Aren't you lucky!
   d At the end of the next semester I intend to take my final exam.
   e And what would you like to be?
   f And what are your plans?
   g I would like to teach English in a grammar school.
   h It was great fun.

Language discovery 2

 You have already seen this language in action. Can you work out the rules?

1 **Look at these two sentences from Conversation 2. Can you work out which verb is used to construct the future tense in German?**

   a Ich werde mich um eine Stellung beim Umweltministerium bewerben.

   b Bis ich mit dem Studium fertig bin, wird hoffentlich wieder Nachfrage nach Lehrern bestehen.

2 **Which words/expressions are used to indicate that these sentences refer to future events?**

   a Bald bin ich aber mit dem Studium fertig.

   b Ende nächsten Semesters will ich das Staatsexamen ablegen.

DIE ZUKUNFT *THE FUTURE*

Now that you have revised the past tenses, it is time to look at ways of talking about the future in German, e.g. career or other plans.

The future tense in German is formed by using **werden** together with the infinitive form of the relevant verb which goes to the end of the sentence:

Ich **werde** dich **besuchen**.   *I will visit you.*

Wirst du nach England **fahren**?   *Will you go to England?*

However, it is quite common to use the present tense to refer to the future, especially if this is indicated by an expression of time:

Ich bin **bald** fertig.   *I'll be ready soon.*

Fährst du **im Sommer** nach England?   *Are you going to England this summer?*

Frequently used expressions to indicate future events include: **morgen** (*tomorrow*), **übermorgen** (*the day after tomorrow*), **später** (*later*), **bald** (*soon*), **nächste Woche** (*next week*), **nächsten Monat** (*next month*), **in 14 Tagen** (*in a fortnight*), **in den kommenden Monaten** (*in the coming months*), **in der Zukunft** (*in the future*)

Note that **werden** on its own means *to become*:

Was möchtest du **werden**?   *What do you want to be (i.e. become)?*

For more information about the future tense, see the **Go further with grammar** section in this unit.

# Practice 2

1 Was werden die Leute machen?

Beantworten Sie die Fragen, indem Sie *werden* benutzen. Remember the rules on word order that you learned in Unit 2.

Beispiel: Wann macht Andrea ihr Examen? (im Juni) → *Sie wird im Juni ihr Examen machen.*

  a Wann kommt Peter in die Schule? (nächsten Sommer)
  b Um wie viel Uhr fängt das Seminar an? (um 16.00 Uhr)
  c Wer hält die Vorlesung? (Frau Dr. Martini)
  d Bei welcher Firma macht Susanne ihre Lehre? (bei der Telekom)
  e Wo machen Lisa und Annette ihren Sprachkurs? (in Madrid)
  f Wann fängt Thomas seinen neuen Job an? (in zwei Wochen)

2 Sagen Sie es anders – Zeitausdrücke.

Replace the expressions with a word conveying the same meaning:

  a in zwei Tagen: _____
  b der Monat nach Oktober: _____
  c in den nächsten Monaten: in den _____ Monaten
  d in 14 Tagen: in zwei _____
  e es dauert nicht mehr lange: _____
  f im Juni, Juli, August: im _____
  g am Samstag, am Sonntag: am _____

3 03.04 **Sagen Sie es einfacher!**

Hilda and Werner are telling their friends what they're going to do in the coming weeks. They're using the future tense to express their plans. As the same ideas can be expressed using the present tense, change the sentences and then listen to check your answers.

Beispiel: Morgen werden wir um sechs Uhr aufstehen. → *Morgen stehen wir um sechs Uhr auf.*

  a Morgen werden wir unsere Eltern besuchen.
  b Am Dienstag werde ich im Garten arbeiten.
  c Demnächst werden wir das Haus renovieren lassen.
  d Ich werde bald mit meinem Englischkurs anfangen.
  e Im Oktober werden wir nach England fahren.
  f Im September wird Martin in die Schule kommen.
  g In zwei Wochen werde ich meinen Job als Bedienung anfangen.
  h Übermorgen werde ich zum Friseur gehen.
  i Am Wochenende werden wir zum Windsurfen gehen.
  j Übrigens, das Abendessen wird gleich fertig sein!

4 Meine Zukunftspläne.

What about your future plans? Talk about some of the things that you are planning to do. Use the prompts to get you started and remember that you can use both the future and present tense.

Morgen werde ich ...
Am Wochenende ...
Nächsten Montag muss ich ...
In zwei Wochen ...
Letzten Sommer haben wir in Italien verbracht, diesen Sommer ...
In den kommenden Monaten ...
Zu Weihnachten ...

Go further with grammar

1 VERGANGENHEITSFORMEN IM DEUTSCHEN *PAST TENSES IN GERMAN*

1.1 Present perfect tense

To form the present perfect tense use the appropriate form of **haben** or **sein** together with the past participle of the required verb.

Regular verbs

As you saw in **Language discovery 1**, past participles of regular verbs are normally formed by putting **ge-** in front of the stem and **-t** at the end:

hör-en	ich habe **ge**hör**t**
spiel-en	ich habe **ge**spiel**t**

Irregular verbs

The past participles of most irregular verbs have **ge-** at the front and **-en** at the end. The stem also changes in many cases:

ess-en	ich habe **ge**gess**en**
sing-en	wir haben **ge**sung**en**

Important points

   a Haben or **sein**?

Although most verbs need **haben** in the present perfect tense, there are quite a few important verbs which form their present perfect tense with **sein**. **Sein** is being used with:

▶ verbs indicating motion from one place to another, including **abfahren**, **fliegen**, **gehen**, **joggen**, **kommen**, **laufen**, **schwimmen**, **springen**:
   Ich **bin** ins Kino **gegangen**.

- verbs indicating a change of state (**aufwachen**, **wachsen**, **werden**, **sterben**):
  Die Bevölkerung von L.A. **ist gewachsen.**

- a few frequently used verbs: **bleiben, sein, passieren**:
  Was **ist passiert?**

  Wie lange **bist** du **geblieben**?

  b Separable verbs

  The past participles of separable verbs, whether regular or irregular, have the **-ge-** in between the separable particle and the verb:

  abholen → ab**ge**holt   abfahren → ab**ge**fahren

  c Past participles with no **ge-** in front

  The past participles of inseparable verbs (see Unit 2) do not take **ge-**:

  bezahlen → **be**zahlt   **ver**stehen → **ver**standen

  Verbs ending in **-ieren** also fall into this category:

  telefon**ieren** → telefoniert

1.2 Präteritum The simple past tense

Regular verbs

To form the simple past tense of regular verbs, take the stem and add the appropriate endings:

spiel-en → **spielten**

ich spiel**te**	wir spiel**ten**
du spiel**test**	ihr spiel**tet**
Sie spiel**ten**	Sie spiel**ten**
er/sie/es spiel**te**	sie spiel**ten**

Irregular verbs

Irregular verbs usually have a change in the stem vowel and add the following endings. Note that there are no endings for **ich** and **er/sie/es**:

fahr-en → **fuhren**

ich fuhr	wir fuhr**en**
du fuhr**st**	ihr fuhr**t**
Sie fuhr**en**	Sie fuhr**en**
er/sie/es fuhr	sie fuhr**en**

1.3 Points to watch out for

Mixed verbs

There are a number of verbs (e.g. **bringen, denken, wissen, kennen**), often referred to as **mixed verbs**, which have a change in the vowel but take the endings of the regular verbs, both in the present perfect tense and in the simple past:

Example: denken: Ich habe oft an Sie **gedacht**. → Er **dachte** viel an seine Familie.

Additional -e

Note that if the stem of the regular verb ends in **-t**, **-n** or **-d**, you normally have to add an extra **-e** before the relevant ending:

Regular verbs: **antworten** → ich **antwortete** → **geantwortet**
regnen → es **regnete** → **geregnet**

For irregular verbs this applies to the **du** and **ihr** forms only:
finden → du **fandest**;   **halten** → du **hieltest**

Vowel change

Irregular verbs in the perfect and simple past tenses often follow a pattern. The following vowel changes are common:

1 ei – i – i   schn**ei**den – schn**i**tt – geschn**i**tten
          r**ei**ten – r**i**tt – ger**i**tten
2 i – a – u   f**i**nden – f**a**nd – gef**u**nden
          tr**i**nken – tr**a**nk – getr**u**nken
3 ei – ie – ie   bl**ei**ben – bl**ie**b – gebl**ie**ben
          schr**ei**ben – schr**ie**b – geschr**ie**ben
4 ie – o – o   fl**ie**gen – fl**o**g – gefl**o**gen
          z**ie**hen – z**o**g – gez**o**gen
5 e – a – o   st**e**rben – st**a**rb – gest**o**rben
          spr**e**chen – spr**a**ch – gespr**o**chen

2 DAS FUTUR *THE FUTURE TENSE*

The future tense in German is formed with the present tense of **werden** together with the infinitive of the verb in question:

ich **werde spielen**   wir **werden spielen**
du **wirst spielen**   ihr **werdet spielen**
Sie **werden spielen**   Sie **werden spielen**
er/sie/es **wird spielen**   sie **werden spielen**

The future tense has rather limited use in German and the present tense is used more widely than it is in English to refer to future time:

Morgen um diese Zeit sind wir in Berlin.   *This time tomorrow, we'll be in Berlin.*
Wann sagst du mir, ob du kommst?   *When will you tell me whether you'll be coming?*

It is certainly possible to use the future tense in most instances where a time in the future is being referred to, and this also applies to the example sentences above:

Morgen um diese Zeit werden wir in Berlin sein.
Wann wirst du mir sagen, ob du kommen wirst?

Nevertheless, the present tense is usually preferred so long as the context makes the time reference clear.

The future tense tends to be used for:

a predictions

Heute wird es nicht mehr regnen.	*It won't rain any more today.*
Das wirst du bereuen!	*You'll regret that!*

b promises

Ich werde dir morgen im Geschäft helfen.	*I'll help you in the shop tomorrow.*
Ich werde nicht zu spät kommen.	*I won't be late.*

c firm intentions

Ich werde im Sommer in Italien arbeiten.	*I'll work in Italy in the summer.*
Ich werde heute Abend mitkommen.	*I'll come along this evening.*

d probability

Er wird wohl heute Abend ankommen.	*He'll probably arrive this evening.*
Anna wird wohl krank sein.	*Anna must be ill.*

Note that **wohl** is often used with the future tense to express probability.

? Test yourself

Bear in mind that you should carry on working on this unit until you can answer well over 75% of the questions correctly in all sections of the tests.

1 Welches Verb passt am besten?

> studieren bewerben machen kennenlernen
> besuchen ablegen schreiben treffen
> diskutieren beenden durchführen bestehen

a eine Ausbildung → *machen*
b sich bei einer Firma → _____
c an einer Universität → _____
d Versuche → _____
e sich mit Freunden → _____
f die Lehre → _____
g ein Seminar → _____
h Nachfrage → _____
i über ein Thema → _____
j eine Examensarbeit → _____
k ein Staatsexamen → _____
l neue Leute → _____

2 Wie heißt es richtig?

Supply the correct form of **werden** to form the future tense.

- **a** Morgen _____ es regnen.
- **b** _____ ihr wieder Urlaub in den Bergen machen?
- **c** Er _____ wohl in den kommenden Monaten viel arbeiten müssen.
- **d** Wann _____ die Besucher am Wochenende kommen?
- **e** Sophie _____ wohl wieder zu spät kommen.
- **f** Ich _____ euch bei den Hausaufgaben helfen.
- **g** _____ du bald deine Ausbildung anfangen?

3 Marcos Ausbildung und Job.

Put the following sentences in the **Präteritum** (*simple past tense*).

Beispiel: Marco ist mit sieben Jahren in die Schule gegangen. →

Marco ging mit sieben Jahren in die Schule.

- **a** Mit 16 Jahren hat er seinen Schulabschluss gemacht.
- **b** Als Teenager hat er sich schon für Elektronik interessiert.
- **c** Nach der Schule hat er eine Ausbildung als Elektroniker angefangen.
- **d** Die Ausbildung hat dreieinhalb Jahre gedauert.
- **e** Nach der Ausbildung hat er sich bei Siemens beworben und hat zunächst im IT-Bereich gearbeitet.
- **f** Nach ein paar Jahren ist er in den Energiebereich gewechselt.
- **g** Bald ist er Abteilungsleiter geworden und hat ein Team von 25 Leuten geleitet.

4 03.05 Und jetzt Sie!

You talk to a friend about your career plans after doing the **Abitur**. Complete the dialogue with the help of the English prompts.

Freund	Was hast du denn eigentlich nach dem Abitur vor?
Sie	*Tell him that you have applied for a place to study biology at the University of Heidelberg.*
Freund	Das ist eine gute Universität. Und wie lange dauert das Studium?
Sie	*Tell him that a bachelor degree normally takes three years. Say afterwards one can do a masters. That takes one or two years.*
Freund	Und weißt du schon, in welchem Bereich du danach arbeiten willst?
Sie	*Say you are not sure yet. Perhaps you can work for the Ministry of the Environment or a big international firm. But you would not like to become a teacher.*
Freund	Und was macht eigentlich deine Schwester Marion?
Sie	*Say that two years ago she started a banking apprenticeship. Say that she is very content with her position. Last year she worked in London for three months. She had a lot of fun.*

I CAN...
● ... give facts about my education and training.
● ... talk and write about past events.
● ... use the present perfect and simple past tense.
● ... make and discuss my plans for the future.
● ... understand a text about the German education system.

4 Aus der Arbeitswelt

In this unit you will learn how to:

▶ *talk about jobs and occupations.*

▶ *discuss the positive and negative aspects of work.*

▶ *understand and format a standard CV.*

▶ *link sentences and ideas using conjunctions.*

▶ *use commas according to German punctuation rules.*

CEFR: *Can read reports about contemporary issues and identify attitudes and viewpoints, e.g. a professional's explanation of her working conditions (B2); can write in an appropriate style for a specific audience, e.g. writing a personal résumé (C1).*

Conversation 1

WAS SIND SIE VON BERUF?

In der folgenden Höraufnahme unterhalten sich Herr Vlado Krause und Frau Monika Kubig auf einem Flug von Stuttgart über ihre Reiseziele und ihre Berufe.

 1 04.01 **Study the vocabulary first, and then listen to the conversation. What do Vlado and Monika both like about their jobs?**

Ich habe dort geschäftlich zu tun.	*I've got business to do there.*
der Bauingenieur (-e)/-in (-nen)	*civil engineer*
staunen über	*to be amazed at*
die Minderheit (-en)	*minority*
genau(er) hinschauen	*to take a close(r) look*
der leitende Angestellte (-n)	*executive manager*
die Werkzeugmaschine (-n)	*machine tool*
sich etwas vor/stellen	*to imagine something*
her/stellen	*to produce*
die Verhandlung (-en)	*negotiation*
bloß	*only, just*
der Zeitmangel	*lack of time*
die Geschäftsreise (-n)	*business trip*
in Anspruch nehmen	*to take up (time)*

Vlado Krause	Wohin fliegen Sie? Nach Budapest?
Monika Kubig	Nein, nach Wien. Und Sie?
Vlado Krause	Ich fliege nach Budapest. Ich habe dort geschäftlich zu tun. Machen Sie Urlaub in Wien?
Monika Kubig	Nein. Ich gehe zu einem Ingenieurkongress. Ich bin nämlich Bauingenieurin.
Vlado Krause	Was?! Da muss ich aber staunen! Bauingenieur habe ich mir immer als Männerberuf vorgestellt.
Monika Kubig	Ach, nein. Wir bilden zwar immer noch nur eine kleine Minderheit, aber Frauen gibt es schon seit mehreren Jahren in diesem Beruf.
Vlado Krause	Ja, wenn man so ein bisschen genauer hinschaut, findet man heutzutage Frauen in fast jedem Beruf.
Monika Kubig	Und was sind Sie von Beruf, wenn ich fragen darf?
Vlado Krause	Ich bin leitender Angestellter bei einer Firma, die Werkzeugmaschinen herstellt. Ich fliege nach Budapest, um Verhandlungen mit einer ungarischen Firma zu führen.
Monika Kubig	Und wie gefällt Ihnen Ihr Beruf?
Vlado Krause	Eigentlich habe ich nur selten genügend Zeit, mir diese Frage zu stellen! Ich bin jetzt seit sieben Jahren bei der Firma Pfauter beschäftigt und bin im Allgemeinen sehr zufrieden. Bloß möchte ich etwas mehr Zeit haben für meine Frau und meine Kinder.
Monika Kubig	Zeitmangel ist ja eines der größten Probleme, wenn man berufstätig ist. Und Geschäftsreisen nehmen natürlich viel Zeit in Anspruch.
Vlado Krause	Sicher, aber für mich ist das Reisen einer der attraktivsten Aspekte meiner Arbeit.
Monika Kubig	Für mich auch.

2 Richtig oder falsch?

a Vlado Krause is surprised that Monika Kubig is a civil engineer.

b Because of time pressure he is not happy with his job.

c Monika Kubig says that there are many female civil engineers.

d She thinks that lack of time is one of the biggest problems when working.

3 Beantworten Sie die Fragen.

a Was macht Monika Kubig in Wien?

b Wie lange arbeitet Vlado Krause schon bei seiner Firma?

c Was stellt die Firma her?

d Warum fliegt er nach Budapest?

e Was wünscht er sich?

f Was ist für Monika Kubig der Nachteil von Geschäftsreisen?

4 Wie heißt das im Text?

Finden Sie für die Wörter in *kursiv* die Ausdrücke im Text mit den gleichen Bedeutungen.

Beispiel: Machen Sie *Ferien?* → Machen Sie *Urlaub?*

a *ein Beruf für Männer*

b eine Minderheit *sein*

c etwas *produzieren*

d Verhandlungen *leiten*

e bei einer Firma *angestellt sein*

f *im Großen und Ganzen*

g *nicht genug Zeit*

> **CULTURE TIP – FRAUEN UND DER ARBEITSMARKT**
>
> In Deutschland sind etwa 17,5 Millionen Frauen berufstätig, das sind etwa 70% aller Frauen zwischen 20 und 64 Jahren. Dies ist mehr als der EU-Durchschnitt von 60%. Doch gibt es Unterschiede beim Geld – Frauen verdienen im Durchschnitt 22% weniger als Männer und nur circa 25% der Top-Positionen sind von Frauen besetzt. Seit ein paar Jahren gibt es in Deutschland einen Girl's Day - an diesem Tag können Mädchen einen „typischen Männerberuf" kennen lernen.

Language discovery 1

 You have already seen this language in action. Can you work out the rules?

1 What words are missing in these two sentences from Conversation 1? What function do they serve?

a Wir bilden zwar immer noch nur eine kleine Minderheit, _____ Frauen gibt es schon seit mehreren Jahren in diesem Beruf.

b Ich bin jetzt seit sieben Jahren bei der Firma Pfauter beschäftigt _____ bin im Allgemeinen sehr zufrieden.

2 What do you notice about the position of the verbs in the clauses introduced by the conjunctions wenn, dass, weil or obwohl?

a Und was sind Sie von Beruf, wenn ich fragen darf?

b Ich finde, dass die meisten Leute sehr offen sind.

c Meistens gehe ich aber dann erst mittags in die Universität, weil meine Seminare erst später stattfinden.

d Sie hat eine Lehre gemacht, obwohl sie eigentlich studieren wollte.

WIE MAN SÄTZE VERBINDET (1) *LINKING SENTENCES (1)*

1 COORDINATING CONJUNCTIONS

It is important to know how to link sentences in German. Here are some useful words:

aber	*but*	**sondern**	*but (after a negative statement)*
denn	*for, since, because*	**und**	*and*
oder	*or*		

These words, called coordinating conjunctions, are normally used to join sentences which could also stand on their own:

Ich bin bei der Firma Pfauter beschäftigt. Ich bin im Allgemeinen sehr zufrieden. →
Ich bin bei der Firma Pfauter beschäftigt **und** ich bin im Allgemeinen sehr zufrieden.

Petra kommt aus Köln. Sie lebt in L.A. → Petra kommt aus Köln, **aber** sie lebt in L.A.

Kai ist nicht Deutscher. Er ist Schweizer. → Kai ist nicht Deutscher, **sondern** er ist Schweizer.

Note: when using these conjunctions the word order normally doesn't change, i.e. the verb in the second clause remains the second element in the clause.

2 SUBORDINATING CONJUNCTIONS

As you saw in **Language discovery 1**, there is also another group of conjunctions in German which sends the verb to the end of the clause. They include:

da	*since (because)*	**obwohl**	*although*
dass	*that*	**weil**	*because*
ob	*whether*	**wenn**	*when, whenever, if*

Subordinating conjunctions normally introduce subordinating clauses which can't stand on their own and depend on a main clause:

Ich finde, **dass** die meisten Leute sehr offen sind.

Mit der Arbeitszeit ist sie zufrieden, **da** sie um 17.00 Uhr Feierabend hat.

Ich weiß noch nicht, **ob** ich morgen **kommen kann**.

Mir macht mein Job Spaß, **obwohl** ich oft lange **arbeiten muss**.

As you can see from the last two examples, when there is more than one verb in a subordinate clause (for instance a modal verb + infinitive), the modal verb is in the final position.

For more details on conjunctions and clauses, see the **Go further with grammar** section at the end of this unit.

Practice 1

1 Bilden Sie lange Sätze.

Join the following sentences together by using und, aber, oder, denn or sondern.

  a Monika Kubig kommt aus Stuttgart. Sie ist Bauingenieurin.
  b Sie fährt nach Wien. Sie möchte einen Kongress besuchen.
  c Vlado Krause ist kein Ingenieur. Er ist leitender Angestellter.
  d Seine Arbeit gefällt ihm. Er lernt viele neue Dinge.
  e Er reist viel. Geschäftsreisen nehmen viel Zeit in Anspruch.
  f Machen Sie jetzt die nächste Übung? Möchten Sie eine Pause machen?

2 Verbinden Sie die Satzteile. Match both parts of the statements.

a Max fährt oft nach London, ...

b Zeitmangel ist ein Problem, ...

c Sie mag ihren Job, ...

d Geschäftsreisen sind attraktiv, ...

e Frau Martini ist nicht sicher, ...

f Vlado spricht auf Englisch, ...

1 obwohl sein Kunde auch Deutsch kann.

2 weil er dort geschäftlich zu tun hat.

3 obwohl sie viel Zeit in Anspruch nehmen.

4 ob sie zu dem Kongress fahren kann.

5 wenn man arbeitet.

6 weil sie sehr kreativ sein kann.

3 Herr Johnson lernt Deutsch. Warum eigentlich?

Schreiben Sie, warum Herr Johnson Deutsch lernt. Benutzen Sie **weil**.

Beispiel: Seine Großeltern stammen aus Österreich. → *Herr Johnson lernt Deutsch, weil seine Großeltern aus Österreich stammen.*

a Er ist geschäftlich oft in München.

b Er muss Verhandlungen auf Deutsch führen.

c Er interessiert sich für die deutsche Kultur.

d Er trinkt gern deutsches Bier.

e Seine Freundin kommt aus Berlin.

f Er möchte vielleicht einmal in Deutschland oder Österreich leben.

4 Und Sie? Warum lernen Sie Deutsch?

Think of at least four reasons why you are learning German. Make some notes and prepare your answer. Use the following prompts to give a brief speech:

> Ich lerne Deutsch weil, ...
> Außerdem lerne ich Deutsch, weil ...
> Ein anderer Grund ist, dass ich ...
> Darüber hinaus lerne ich Deutsch, weil ...

LANGUAGE TIP – DENN/WEIL

Denn und **weil** bedeuten beide *because*. Vorsicht: bei **denn** bleibt das Verb in Position 2, bei **weil** geht es ans Ende:

Ich lerne gern Deutsch, **denn** ich **finde** es ist eine schöne Sprache.

Ich lerne gern Deutsch, **weil** ich es eine schöne Sprache **finde**.

Listen and understand

WAS MACHST DU JETZT FÜR EINE ARBEIT?

Im folgenden Dialog begegnen sich Gerd und Heiko zum ersten Mal nach ihrer Studienzeit. Hören Sie sich den Dialog an und beantworten Sie die Fragen.

1 04.02 **What does Heiko say about the students he teaches and what does Gerd find tiring about his job?**

 was für ein(e/n)   *what kind of (coll.)*
unterrichten   *to teach, instruct*
fleißig   *hard-working*
etwas nötig haben   *(here) to need something*
die Bezahlung (-en)   *pay*
das Heim (-e)   *home*
körperlich/geistig behindert   *physically/mentally disabled*
der Sozialpädagoge (-n)/   *person with a degree in*
  die Sozialpädagogin (-nen)   *social education*
der Vertrag (-¨e)   *contract*
befristet   *(here) fixed-term*
verlängern   *to extend*

2 Hören Sie den Dialog noch einmal und unterstreichen Sie die richtigen Antworten.

   a Heiko unterrichtet im Moment Spanisch/Deutsch/Französisch als Fremdsprache.

   b Seine Arbeit gefällt ihm im Allgemeinen gut/sehr gut/nicht.

   c Was ihm nicht gefällt, ist die Bezahlung/Arbeitszeit/Arbeitsatmosphäre.

   d Eigentlich möchte er Hauptschullehrer/Realschullehrer/Gymnasiallehrer werden.

   e Gerd ist Sozialarbeiter/Sozialpädagoge/Soziologe von Beruf.

   f Er arbeitet in einem Heim für körperlich und geistig behinderte Kinder/Jugendliche/ Erwachsene.

   g Er hat einen befristeten Vertrag für zwei Monate/zehn Monate/zwölf Monate.

CULTURE TIP – DIE POPULÄRSTEN BERUFE

	Jungen	Mädchen
1	Kraftfahrzeugmechatroniker*	Bürokauffrau
2	Industriechemiker	Kauffrau im Einzelhandel
3	Kaufmann im Einzelhandel	Medizinische Fachangestellte
4	Anlagenmechaniker für Sanitär-, Heizungs- und Klimatechnik	Friseurin
5	Koch	Zahnmedizinische Fachangestellte
6	Elektroniker für Energie- und Gebäudetechnik	Industriekauffrau
7	Metallbauer	Fachverkäuferin im Lebensmittelhandwerk
8	Kaufmann im Groß- und Außenhandel	Kauffrau für Bürokommunikation
9	Maler und Lackierer	Verkäuferin
10	Mechatroniker*	Hotelfachfrau

*Mechaniker + Elektroniker = Mechatroniker
Statistisches Bundesamt, Datenreport.

3 Welche Antwort passt?

  a Lange nicht gesehen! Wie geht's dir?

    1 Ihm geht's nicht so gut.

    2 Ich unterrichte Deutsch.

    3 Gut, danke.

  b Und wie gefällt dir deine Arbeit?

    1 Sie macht ihr viel Spaß.

    2 Im Allgemeinen sehr gut.

    3 Da sie es nötig haben, so schnell wie möglich die deutsche Sprache zu erlernen.

  c Und was machst du eigentlich zurzeit?

    1 Wie du weißt, bin ich ja Sozialpädagoge.

    2 Ich möchte Gymnasiallehrer für Deutsch und Englisch werden.

    3 Ich arbeite zurzeit in einem Heim für körperlich und geistig behinderte Kinder.

  d Und was hast du danach vor?

    1 Das ist schon anstrengend.

    2 Ich weiß noch nicht genau.

    3 Im Moment gibt es relativ viele Jobs für Sozialpädagogen.

 4 04.03 **Sagen Sie's auf Deutsch!**

Which German phrases were used in the last conversation to say the following? Check your answers and pronunciation on the audio.

  a Long time no see!

  b What kind of work are you doing at the moment?

  c in general

  d They need to ...

  e if that is the case ...

  f as you know

  g I really enjoy it.

Reading

EIN LEBENSLAUF

1 **Read Maria Schrader's CV. Can you work out what the terms Persönliche Daten, Berufspraxis, Praktika, Hochschulausbildung, Schulausbildung, besondere Kenntnisse and EDV would be on an English CV?**

der Schwerpunkt (-e)	*focus, main area/subject*
angewandt	*applied*
die Gesamtnote (-n)	*final mark, classification*
die Diplomarbeit (-en)	*dissertation*
die Bewältigung (-en)	*(here) coping with*
die Personalabteilung (-en)	*HR department, personnel*
Personalberater/in (-, -nen)	*HR, personnel consultant*
stellvertretende	*(here) deputy*
Personalleiter/in (-, -nen)	*Head of HR*

Lebenslauf

Persönliche Daten:	Schrader, Maria Berndstr. 7 24310 Hamburg Tel.: 030/4567352 geb. am 1.04.1985 in München verheiratet, 1 Kind
Berufspraxis:	
9/2010– 7/2012 7/2012 – 6/2014 seit 7/2014	Personalberaterin bei Unilever, Hamburg Stellvertretende Personalleiterin bei Unilever, Hamburg Personalleiterin bei Hapag-Lloyd, Hamburg
Praktika:	
2006 2008	Personalabteilung Springer Jacoby, München Marketingabteilung Otto-Versand, Hamburg
Hochschulausbildung:	
10/2004–6/2009	Universität Hamburg Studium der Psychologie Schwerpunkt: Angewandte Psychologie Abschluss als Diplom-Psychologin Gesamtnote: 1 Thema der Diplomarbeit: Die Bewältigung interpersoneller Stresssituationen am Arbeitsplatz
Schulausbildung:	
1991–1995 1995–2004	Grundschule, München Schiller-Gymnasium, München Abschluss: Abitur (2,1)
Besondere Kenntnisse:	
EDV Fremdsprachen	Textverarbeitung (MS Word) Tabellenkalkulation (Excel) PowerPoint Englisch – sehr gut Französisch – sehr gut Japanisch – Anfängerkenntnisse
Interessen und Hobbys:	
Hamburg, 17.1. 2015	Musik, Kochen, Motorradfahren

2 Lesen Sie den Lebenslauf von Maria noch einmal und beantworten Sie die Fragen.

a In was für einer Position arbeitet Maria im Moment?

b Wo arbeitete sie nach ihrem Studienabschluss?

c Was und wie lange studierte sie?

d Was war ihre Gesamtnote an der Universität?

e Wo verbrachte Maria ihre Kindheit?

f Wie gut ist ihr Japanisch?

CULTURE TIP – LEBENSLAUF

Für einen Lebenslauf in Deutschland braucht man – anders als zum Beispiel in Großbritannien oder den USA – ein Foto. Unter persönlichen Daten gibt man das Geburtsdatum und den Familienstand an, oft auch die Anzahl der Kinder. Am Ende steht der Ort, das Datum und die Unterschrift.

---

3 Welches Wort fehlt?

Maria has written a short version of her CV for her social media page. Can you supply the missing information?

Blog   `Add post`

Ich bin am 1. April 1985 in München **(a)** _____. Mit sechs Jahren kam ich in die
(b) _____. Mein **(c)** _____ machte ich 2004 auf dem Schiller-Gymnasium. Nach
der Schule begann ich gleich ein **(d)** _____ der **(e)** _____ in Hamburg. Mein
(f) _____ war Angewandte Psychologie. In meiner **(g)** _____ beschäftigte ich mich
mit der Bewältigung von Stresssituationen am **(h)** _____. Daneben machte ich auch zwei
(i) _____ bei Springer Jacoby und dem Otto-Versand. Nach dem Studium arbeitete ich für
vier Jahre bei Unilever, zunächst als **(j)** _____, dann als **(k)** _____ Personalleiterin.
Seit Juli 2014 bin ich **(l)** _____ bei Hapag Lloyd. In meiner **(m)** _____ höre ich gern
Musik, koche gern und **(n)** _____ Motorrad.

---

4 Mein Lebenslauf.

Write your own CV in German, using all the headings from Maria's CV which apply to your situation (**Persönliche Daten**, **Berufspraxis**, **Praktika**, **Hochschulausbildung**, **Schulausbildung**, **Besondere Kenntnisse**, **EDV**). If you did an apprenticeship or vocational training use **Ausbildung**.

Conversation 2

FRAU ANDRESEN ERZÄHLT VON IHREM BERUF

 1 04.04 **Frau Andresen ist Grafikdesignerin und erzählt von ihrem Beruf. Hören Sie, was sie sagt, und beantworten Sie die Fragen.**

    a What kind of company does she work for?

    b Does she work part-time or full-time?

der Auftrag (-¨e)	order
aus/tauschen	to exchange
der Termindruck	(pressure of meeting) deadlines
gründen	to found, to establish
die Verantwortung (-en)	responsibilty

Mein Name ist Claudia Andresen und ich arbeite als Grafikdesignerin bei einer PR-Firma. Ich fange morgens meistens so gegen neun Uhr an und mache dann um halb fünf, fünf Feierabend. Wenn wir wichtige Aufträge haben, dann arbeite ich natürlich auch mal länger, wenn es sein muss auch mal am Wochenende, aber im Allgemeinen ist das eigentlich selten.

Die Arbeitsatmosphäre ist generell sehr gut. Wir sind insgesamt fünf Grafikdesigner und -designerinnen und arbeiten sehr eng in einem Team zusammen. Da wir über viele Dinge ähnlich denken und alle Sinn für Humor haben, verstehen wir uns ganz gut.

Mir gefällt an meinem Job, dass ich sehr kreativ sein kann. Es ist eigentlich nie langweilig oder Routine, da wir immer an neuen Projekten arbeiten. Außerdem mag ich die Arbeit im Team sehr gern, das heißt, dass wir uns austauschen und über Ideen sprechen. Was mir nicht gefällt, ist der Termindruck, unter dem wir oft arbeiten müssen. Wenn wir wichtige Deadlines haben – und die haben wir sehr oft – dann ist es schon sehr stressig.

Mit der Bezahlung bin ich sehr zufrieden. Ich verdiene etwa 3000,– Euro brutto im Monat. Bevor ich hier in der Firma angefangen habe, habe ich einige Jahre als Teilzeitkraft gearbeitet, ohne richtiges Urlaubsgeld, Weihnachtsgeld und ohne Kranken- und Rentenversicherung. Als Vollzeitkraft bekommt man das natürlich alles.

Mein Traum für die Zukunft ist es, mich in ein paar Jahren selbstständig zu machen und meine eigene Firma zu gründen. Dann habe ich noch mehr Verantwortung und vielleicht auch mehr Stress, aber das wäre eine gute Herausforderung für mich.

2 Beantworten Sie die Fragen.

 a Wie ist die normale Arbeitszeit von Claudia?

 b Wie ist die Arbeitsatmosphäre?

 c Nennen Sie mindestens zwei Dinge, die sie an ihrem Job mag.

 d Was mag sie nicht?

 e Wie viel verdient sie?

 f Was möchte sie in ein paar Jahren machen?

3 Wie heißt das auf Deutsch?

In the text are lots of useful words for talking about work and working conditions.
Find the German expressions and words for the following:

 a part-time employee

 b full-time employee

 c holiday pay

 d extra month's salary (at Christmas)

 e pension scheme

 f self-employed

 g a challenge

4 Lesen Sie den Text noch einmal und ergänzen Sie.

 a Claudia Andresen arbeitet bei ...

 b Ihre Kollegen haben alle Sinn .....

 c Ihr Beruf ist nie ...

 d Mit ihrer Bezahlung ist sie ...

 e Ihr gefällt nicht, wenn sie unter ...

 f Als Vollzeitkraft bekommt man Urlaubsgeld, Weihnachtsgeld und hat eine ...

 g In der Zukunft möchte sie sich ...

 h Das ist für sie eine ...

Language discovery 2

You have already seen this language in action. Can you work out the rules?

1 Can you restore the word order in the clauses introduced by wenn or bevor?

 a wichtige / Wenn / haben / wir / Aufträge, arbeite ich natürlich auch mal länger.

 b wichtige / wir / Wenn / Deadlines / haben, ist es schon sehr stressig.

 c habe / der / Bevor / ich /in / hier / angefangen / Firma, habe ich einige Jahre als Teilzeitkraft gearbeitet

2 Comma or no comma? Add one in the following sentences, if it is needed. If you are not sure, look at Conversation 2 again.

 a Mein Name ist Claudia Andresen und ich arbeite als Grafikdesignerin bei einer PR-Firma.

 b Mir gefällt an meinem Job dass ich sehr kreativ sein kann.

1 WIE MAN SÄTZE VERBINDET (2) *LINKING SENTENCES (2)*

You saw in **Language discovery 1** that subordinating conjunctions such as **wenn**, **weil** or **obwohl** introduce a subordinate clause and send the verb to the end. Another of these prepositions is **bevor** *before*.

When you start a sentence with one of these conjunctions the verb goes to the end of the first clause, while the second clause starts with the verb:

Bevor er Sänger **war**, **arbeitete** er bei einer Versicherung.
Wenn wir wichtige Deadlines **haben, ist** es schon sehr stressig.
Weil seine Freundin aus Berlin **kommt, lernt** Herr Johnson Deutsch.
Obwohl sie unter Termindruck **arbeiten muss, mag** Claudia ihren Job.

As you can see from the last sentence, when there are two verbs in a subordinate clause (for instance a modal verb + infinitive), the modal verb follows the infinitive.

For more details, see the **Go further with grammar** section at the end of this unit.

2 ZEICHENSETZUNG: KOMMAS *PUNCTUATION: COMMAS*

Commas are important in written German. They are used to separate a main clause and a subordinate clause, as you saw in several of the previous examples:
Mir gefällt an meinem Job, dass ich sehr kreativ sein kann.
Wenn wir wichtige Deadlines haben, ist es schon sehr stressig.

But avoid overusing commas. There is a temptation to put a comma after the introductory phrase in such sentences as:
Am Nachmittag arbeitet er meistens bis 17 Uhr.

No comma is needed here, as there is no subordinate clause.

Also think twice about using commas before **und** and **oder**. There should normally be no comma, even if they combine two main clauses:
Sie arbeitet als Designerin **und** ihre Firma liegt im Stadtzentrum.
Macht Carsten eine Ausbildung **oder** studiert er?

However, there is normally a comma before **aber**:
Ich arbeite auch mal länger, **aber** im Allgemeinen ist das selten.

Practice 2

1 Komma oder kein Komma?

Do these sentences need a comma or not?
   a Und was sind Sie von Beruf wenn ich fragen darf?
   b Ich bin seit fast zehn Jahren verheiratet und wir haben zwei Kinder.
   c Die Konkurrenz ist stark aber vielleicht schaffe ich es ja trotzdem.
   d Diese Leute haben das schöne Gefühl dass sie etwas für die Umwelt tun.
   e Hobbys habe ich insofern keine da mein Beruf mein Hobby geworden ist.
   f In den Ferien möchte ich gern mit dem Mazda bis nach Italien fahren.

2 Was passt besser: weil oder obwohl?

Join the two sentences together by using weil or obwohl. Make any necessary changes to the word order.

Beispiel: Monika Kubig mag ihren Beruf. Sie kann viel reisen. → *Monika Kubig mag ihren Beruf, weil sie viel reisen kann.*

    a Vlado Krause fliegt oft nach Budapest. Er hat dort geschäftlich zu tun.

    b Claudia gefällt ihr Beruf. Sie muss oft unter Termindruck arbeiten.

    c Sie arbeitet gern im Team. Ihre Kollegen haben alle Sinn für Humor.

    d In der Zukunft möchte sie sich selbstständig machen. Das bedeutet mehr Stress.

    e Claudia möchte ihre eigene Firma gründen. Dies ist eine Herausforderung.

3 And now rewrite the sentences, starting with a weil or obwohl clause.

Beispiel: *Weil sie viel reisen kann, mag Monika Kubig ihren Beruf.*

    a _____

    b _____

    c _____

    d _____

    e _____

 4 Mein Job.

Now talk about the pros and cons of your work, real or imagined, using the vocabulary and structures covered in this unit. Make some notes to prepare your answers using some or all of the prompts. Then speak for at least two minutes.

> Ich bin ... von Beruf.
> Meine normale Arbeitszeit ist von ... bis ...
> Ich mag meinen Job, weil ...
> Was ich nicht mag ist, dass ...
> Die Arbeitsatmosphäre ist ...
> Meine Kollegen sind ...
> Obwohl mir meine Arbeit im Allgemeinen (nicht) gefällt, ...
> In der Zukunft möchte ich ...

Try including some of these phrases in your discussion of the positive and negative aspects of your work.

Positiv	Negativ
Ich habe früh Feierabend und kann Zeit mit meiner Familie verbringen.	Ich muss oft nachts oder am Wochenende arbeiten.
Mit der Bezahlung bin ich sehr zufrieden.	Was mir nicht gefällt, ist die Bezahlung.
Es ist eigentlich nie langweilig oder Routine.	Wenn wir Deadlines haben, ist es stressig.
Die Arbeitsatmosphäre ist gut.	Was ich nicht mag, ist der Termindruck.
Ich kann kreativ sein.	Zeitmangel ist ein Problem.
Es ist interessant, ich lerne viel.	Als Teilzeitkraft bekommt man oft kein Urlaubsgeld.

Go further with grammar

1 KONJUNKTIONEN *CONJUNCTIONS*

As you saw in the **Language Discoveries** there are two main groups of conjunctions, one that does not affect the word order (including **und** and **aber**) and the other which sends the verb or verbs to the end of the clause.

Those in the first group are called **coordinating conjunctions** and those in the second group are called **subordinating conjunctions**.

If two sentences are joined together with a subordinating conjunction (such as *because* or *although*), one clause becomes the main clause (**Hauptsatz**) and the other the subordinate clause (**Nebensatz**):

Sentence 1: **Er blieb zu Hause.**

Sentence 2: **Er war krank.**

Er blieb zu Hause, weil er krank war.

Main clause   Subordinate clause

As you saw earlier, subordinating conjunctions have the effect of sending the finite verb (the verb which takes different endings) to the end of the subordinate clause:

Main clause	Subordinate clause
Ich musste um 6 Uhr aufstehen,	**obwohl** ich sehr müde **war**.
Wir werden zu Hause bleiben,	**weil** es stark **regnet**.
Er konnte nicht kommen,	**weil** er arbeiten **musste**.

It is quite common for the subordinate clause to begin the sentence. When this happens, the finite verb has to come at the beginning of the main clause:

Subordinate clause	Main clause
Wenn ich ihn sehe,	**ist** er immer allein.
Als sie 18 war,	**lebte** sie in Australien.
Weil es stark regnet,	**werden** wir zu Hause bleiben.

Here is a list of subordinating conjunctions which appear quite frequently in German:

als	*when (with past tense)*	**ob**	*whether*
bevor	*before*	**obwohl**	*although*
bis	*until*	**seitdem**	*since*
damit	*so that*	**sobald**	*as soon as*
da	*since (because)*	**während**	*while*
dass	*that*	**wenn**	*when/if*
nachdem	*after*		

Note that there is always a comma between the main clause and the subordinate clause.

You may notice a tendency in colloquial German to not always put the finite verb at the end of the sentence or clause when using **weil**:

Ich konnte nicht kommen, weil ich arbeitete bis spät.

2 BERUFSTITEL *JOB TITLES*

It is common in German to give job titles in both the male and the female forms and not simply to subsume females under male job titles. Here are some examples:

Arzt – Ärztin *doctor*; **Busfahrer – Busfahrerin** *bus driver*

Manager – Managerin *manager*; **Rechtsanwalt – Rechtsanwältin** *solicitor*

As you can see, **-in** is usually added for the female form and some words also require an umlaut.

There are only a few exceptions to this pattern. The most common are:

Krankenpfleger – Krankenschwester, Kaufmann – Kauffrau

The words for civil servants and employees don't follow the usual pattern:

Beamter – Beamtin, Angestellter – Angestellte

If the male profession title ends in **e**, this is dropped in the female form:

Sozialpädagoge – Sozialpädagogin, Psychologe - Psychologin

When a group of people consists of both males and females, it is common to refer to them collectively using the feminine plural, but with a capital I, e.g. **StudentInnen**, **KollegInnen**.

 Test yourself

The Arbeitsagentur acts as a job centre and also deals with claims for employment-related benefits.

1 Berufe.

  a In this unit you met a number of professions and German job titles. Can you remember how to say *civil engineer*, *executive*, *employee* and *civil servant*? Do you know what the following professions are in English? If you are not sure, check your answers in the key.

Aktienhändler	Journalist	Personalberater
Apotheker	Juwelier	Rechtsanwalt
Architekt	Klempner	Reiseleiter
Arzt	Kellner	Schauspieler
Bauarbeiter	Koch	Schriftsteller
Bauingenieur	Krankenpfleger	Sozialarbeiter
Beamter	Künstler	Tierarzt
Büroangestellter	Landwirt	Übersetzer
Dolmetscher	Lehrer	Verkäufer
Elektriker	Makler	Werbetexter
Friseur	Metzger	Wirt
Informatiker	Modedesigner	Zahnarzt

  b You have probably realized that all job titles here are given in the masculine form. For the feminine form you normally simply add -in, but can you find the following:

    1 Five words where an umlaut is also needed?

    2 Three words which have a different feminine form, not just a feminine ending?

2 Und wer macht was?

Finden Sie die passenden Berufe.

Beispiel: sie schreibt Computerprogramme → *Informatikerin*

(a) Sie schneidet Haare: _____; **(b)** sie behandelt Patienten: _____; **(c)** er repariert zum Beispiel Toiletten, Heizungen: _____; **(d)** sie unterrichtet Kinder: _____; **(e)** er bedient in einem Restaurant: _____; **(f)** sie verkauft zum Beispiel Aspirin oder Nasensprays: _____; **(g)** er übersetzt Texte: _____; **(h)** er arbeitet auf einem Bauernhof: _____; **(i)** sie berät Leute mit psychischen Problemen: _____; **(j)** sie handelt an der Börse: _____; **(k)** sie entwirft die Pläne für ein Gebäude: _____.

3 Konjuntionen.

Choose an appropriate conjunction from the box to link the sentences logically.

| da   ob   während   obwohl   wenn   seitdem |

Beispiel: Sie möchte als Designerin arbeiten. Ihr Studium ist beendet. (sobald) →
  Sie möchte als Designerin arbeiten, sobald ihr Studium beendet ist.

  a Zeitmangel ist oft ein Problem. Man ist berufstätig.
  b Carsten hört gern klassische Musik. Er checkt seine E-Mails.
  c Pia und Tim sind gestresst. Sie haben viele Deadlines.
  d Er hat einen befristeten Vertrag. Er arbeitet lange bei der Firma.
  e Sie wissen noch nicht. Sie bekommen den Auftrag.
  f Sie ist zufriedener. Sie macht regelmäßig Yoga und Pilates.

 4 04.05 Und jetzt Sie!

When Anna meets her old friend Anke, they exchange information about work. Play Anna's part and complete the dialogue with the help of the English prompts.

Anke	Hallo, Anna. Lange nicht gesehen! Sag mal, was bist du jetzt von Beruf?
Sie	*Tell her that you are a building engineer (civil engineer), that you are generally satisfied with your occupation, that you especially like the travelling, but that one of the biggest problems is the lack of free time. Ask her what she is doing now.*
Anke	Ich war fünf Jahre lang leitende Angestellte bei einer Kleiderfabrik, die aber leider nicht mehr konkurrenzfähig war. Deshalb bin ich im Moment arbeitslos.
Sie	*You say that you imagine that to be very difficult. Ask her what she intends to do.*
Anke	Beim jetzigen Wirtschaftsklima ist es schwer, eine Stellung zu finden. Ich möchte deshalb einen Computerkurs machen, und hoffe, dass ich dann bessere Chancen habe.
Sie	*You say that this is a good idea, and that currently a lot of jobs are offered which require knowledge in that field. Wish her good luck.*
Anke	Vielen Dank!

SELF CHECK

I CAN. . .

○	... talk about jobs and occupations.
○	... discuss the positive and negative aspects of work.
○	... understand and format a standard CV in German.
○	... link sentences and ideas using conjunctions.
○	... use commas according to German punctuation rules.

5 Interessieren Sie sich für Kultur?

In this unit you will learn how to:
▶ *talk about your interests, likes and dislikes.*
▶ *discuss different ways of spending your free time.*
▶ *use prepositions correctly with certain verbs.*
▶ *form clauses with zu + infinitive.*

CEFR: *Can explain a viewpoint on a topical issue, e.g. giving personal reasons for liking or disliking certain art forms or sports; can read articles and reports concerned with contemporary problems, e.g. a text about the demographic and economic aspects of Munich (B2).*

Conversation 1

MARION, DER KULTURMENSCH

Marion und Cornelia unterhalten sich darüber, was sie in ihrer Freizeit machen und was ihre Interessen und Hobbys sind.

 1 05.01 **Marion and Cornelia talk about their interests and hobbies. Study the vocabulary first, and then listen to the conversation. Which of the following items are not mentioned by the two women?**

a new films	**b** modern plays	**c** ballet
d classical music	**e** art exhibitions	**f** poetry

vor/ziehen	*to prefer*
ehrlich gesagt	*quite honestly*
sich begeistern für	*to be enthusiastic about*
die Vorliebe (-n)	*preference*
auf dem Laufenden sein	*to be informed, up to date*
an/gehen	*(here) to concern*
der Untertitel (-)	*subtitle*
auf/polieren	*to brush up*
selbstverständlich	*naturally*
schätzen	*(here) to appreciate*
abgesehen von	*apart from*
sowohl ... als auch	*as well as*

Marion	Übrigens, Cornelia, ich habe zwei Karten für die Oper am Samstagabend. Hast du nicht Lust mitzukommen?
Cornelia	Das ist ja sehr nett von dir, Marion, aber ehrlich gesagt interessiert mich die Oper nicht besonders. Ich bin zwar schon kulturinteressiert, aber im Allgemeinen ziehe ich sportliche Aktivitäten vor.
Marion	Ach, komm, du musst doch auch mal was anderes sehen als immer nur den Sportplatz! Ich meine, ich habe natürlich Verständnis dafür, wenn jemand Sport machen will, aber ich persönlich kann mich dafür gar nicht begeistern. Sport hat mich eigentlich schon immer gelangweilt.
Cornelia	Und was sind deine Vorlieben?
Marion	Nun ja, ich interessiere mich eben für alles, was mit Kultur zu tun hat – in einer Großstadt wie München gibt es da ja alle Möglichkeiten. Ich bin gerne auf dem Laufenden, was die neuesten Filme, Theaterproduktionen und so weiter angeht. Was ich auch ganz toll finde, ist, dass hier so viele Filme in der Originalsprache mit Untertiteln gegeben werden. Da kann ich wenigstens auch meine Sprachkenntnisse aufpolieren!
Cornelia	Und magst du nur moderne Theaterstücke?
Marion	Selbstverständlich schätze ich auch die Klassiker wie Goethe und Schiller. Abgesehen davon besuche ich auch regelmäßig Ausstellungen – letzten Sonntag war ich in der großen Impressionisten-Ausstellung, einfach fantastisch. Hier wird ja so viel Interessantes und Aufregendes geboten!
Cornelia	Interessierst du dich auch für Musik?
Marion	Sicherlich! Ich mag sowohl klassische als auch moderne Musik. Letzten Monat war ich erst wieder auf einem Konzert von Herbert Grönemeyer.

2 Beantworten Sie die Fragen.

  a How does Cornelia react when Marion asked her to go to the opera?
  b What does Marion like to keep informed about?
  c Why does she like watching films in the original language?
  d What kind of exhibition did she see?

> **CULTURE TIP – HERBERT GRÖNEMEYER**
>
> Herbert Grönemeyer ist ein bekannter deutscher Musiker, Musikproduzent und Komponist. Er begann seine Karriere als Schauspieler in dem Film „Das Boot". Mit über 13 Millionen in Deutschland verkauften CDs ist er einer der kommerziell erfolgreichsten Musiker im deutschsprachigen Raum. Daneben engagiert sich Grönemeyer auch für soziale Zwecke, unter anderem für Afrika und gegen Armut. Vom Magazin „Time Magazine" wurde er als „European Hero" ausgezeichnet.
> Mehr auf: www.groenemeyer.de

3 Richtig oder falsch? Korrigieren Sie die falschen Aussagen.

  a Cornelia ist kulturinteressiert, treibt aber lieber Sport.
  b Marion interessiert sich auch für Sport.
  c Sie sagt, dass man in München nicht viel machen kann.
  d Sie sieht gern Filme in der Originalsprache.
  e Die Impressionisten-Ausstellung fand Marion nicht besonders gut.
  f Vor einem Monat war sie auf einem Konzert.

4 Vorlieben und Abneigungen.

A number of common expressions used to indicate preferences and dislikes appear in Conversation 1. Read through it again, and find the German expressions which mean the following:

  a I am interested in everything that …
  b What I find great is …
  c I appreciate the classics like …
  d In general, I prefer …
  e That doesn't interest me.
  f Sport has always bored me.

Language discovery 1

 You have already seen this language in action. Can you work out the rules?

  1 What English preposition stands for *über* in denken/sprechen/schreiben/erzählen *über* etwas?

  2 Supply the missing prepositions (um/für) in these sentences. What do you observe about usage compared to English?
   a Ich interessiere mich _____ alles, was mit Kultur zu tun hat.
   b Ich habe mich deshalb _____ eine Banklehre beworben.

  3 Match the sentence parts and, for each completed statement, then give the German equivalent of the reflexive pronouns (*myself*, *yourself*, etc.).

a Ich freue		**1** uns auf den Feierabend.
b Freust du		**2** sich auf seinen Urlaub?
c Freut Boris		**3** mich auf das Wochenende.
d Wir freuen		**4** dich auf die Sommerferien?

  ich → *mich* du → _____ er/sie/es → _____ wir → _____

1 VERBEN UND PRÄPOSITIONEN *VERBS AND PREPOSITIONS*

Many German verbs, like English verbs, are followed by a preposition. It is important to learn these verbs together with their preposition, as the German and English are often different:

Ich interessiere mich **für** Musik.	*I am interested **in** music.*
Ich bewerbe mich **um** eine neue Stelle.	*I am applying **for** a new job.*

Here are some common examples:

sich ärgern über	*to be annoyed about*
sich erinnern an	*to remember*
denken an	*to think of, to think about*
sich freuen auf	*to look forward to*

sich freuen über	*to be pleased about*
glauben an	*to believe in*
nachdenken über	*to think thoroughly about something or somebody, to reflect on*
träumen von	*to dream of*
sich verstehen mit	*to get along with somebody*
warten auf	*to wait for*

You might have noticed that many of the verbs are reflexive, i.e. they include the reflexive pronouns **mich**, **sich**, **uns**, etc. For example:

Ich freue **mich** auf den Urlaub.   *I am looking forward to the holiday.*

Note that prepositions such as **auf**, **an** and **über**, which can be followed either by the accusative or dative case, usually require the accusative in verb + preposition constructions:

Sie erinnert sich gern **an ihren ersten** Freund.

Ich muss **über die** Sache nachdenken.

Prepositions which normally take the dative case do so in this instance, too:

Wir unterhielten uns lange **mit der** Sängerin.

Ich habe heute Nacht **von dem** Konzert geträumt.

Note that in a negative statement **nicht** comes after the verb and the reflexive pronoun (if there is one), and before the preposition:

Sie glaubt **nicht** an Ufos.

Er interessiert sich **nicht** für moderne Musik.

For more details see the **Go further with grammar** section at the end of this unit.

2 REFLEXIVE VERBEN *REFLEXIVE VERBS*

In German, many of the verbs which are followed by a preposition are reflexive. Here is an overview of the accusative reflexive pronouns you'll normally need to use with these verbs:

ich → **mich** (*myself*)
Sie → **sich** (*yourself*)
du → **dich** (*yourself*)
er/sie/es → **sich** (*himself, herself, itself*)

wir → **uns** (*ourselves*)
Sie → **sich** (*yourselves*)
ihr → **euch** (*yourselves*)
sie → **sich** (*themselves*)

 Practice 1

1 Reflexivpronomen. What reflexive pronoun is missing?

    a Interessiert ihr _____ für Opernmusik?

    b Nina hat _____ ein neues Smartphone und Tablet gekauft.

    c Wir freuen _____ auf die Filmpremiere.

    d Tom und Merlin ärgern _____ über die hohen Eintrittspreise.

    e Hast du _____ auf der Party gut amüsiert?

2 Verbinden Sie die Satzteile. Match both parts of the statements.

a	Frau Beitz interessiert sich sehr	**1**	mit ihren Kollegen.
b	Birgit bewirbt sich	**2**	an das letzte Gespräch.
c	Er erinnerte sich	**3**	von ihrer eigenen Firma.
d	Vlado Krause freut sich	**4**	über ihre Reiseziele.
e	Er und Monika Kubig unterhalten sich	**5**	auf seine Familie.
f	Claudia Andresen versteht sich gut	**6**	für Politik.
g	Sie spricht mit ihnen	**7**	um eine Banklehre.
h	Claudia träumt	**8**	über ihr neues Projekt.

3 Verben und Präpositionen. Supply the missing prepositions.

a sich interessieren: *für*　　　　　　**f** sich verstehen: _____

b sich erinnern: _____　　　　　**g** sprechen: _____ / _____

c denken: _____　　　　　　　　**h** träumen: _____

d sich bewerben: _____　　　　　**i** warten: _____

e sich unterhalten: _____ / _____

Note that **sich unterhalten** and **sprechen** can have two prepositions: **mit** when you address a person directly, and **über** when you speak about someone or something: Ich habe **mit** Barbara **über** das Konzert gesprochen.

4 Wie heißen die Fragen?

When asked her opinion on various matters, this is what Frau Andresen said. But what were the questions? Find an appropriate question for each answer.

Beispiel: Nein, ich interessiere mich nicht für Mode. Mode finde ich langweilig. →
　　　　　　Interessieren Sie sich für Mode?

a Ja, ich ärgere mich über das Wetter. Das ist im Allgemeinen schrecklich.

b Ja, ich verstehe mich gut mit meinen Kollegen, weil wir alle sehr gut zusammen arbeiten.

c Ufos? Nein, ich glaube nicht an Ufos. Das ist doch Quatsch.

d Ja, ich interessiere mich sehr für Kunst, besonders schätze ich abstrakte Malerei.

e Nein, für Techno-Musik kann ich mich nicht begeistern, weil sie viel zu laut ist.

f Ja, ich freue mich auf die Ferien, da ich für 14 Tage nach Mallorca fahre.

5 Was antworten Sie?

Go through the questions you asked in Exercise 4 again, but this time answer them for yourself. Make some notes and prepare your answers. Justify your opinion with examples and extend your answers to two or three sentences. Then, practise the questions and answers out loud.

Beispiel: Interessieren Sie sich für Mode? Ja, ich interessiere mich sehr für Mode. Ich bin gern auf dem Laufenden, was die neusten Modetrends angeht. Ich ziehe mich gern modisch an und mag besonders die Sachen von jungen Designern.

Listen and understand

PLÄNE FÜR DEN SOMMER

Sebastian und Jochen, zwei Schüler, unterhalten sich über ihre Vorlieben und Abneigungen und was sie in den Sommerferien machen wollen.

 1 05.02 **Sebastian und Jochen, both in their last year at school, talk about their personal preferences and what they are planning to do during their summer break. What kind of lessons do they each plan to take?**

sich an/melden	*to register, enrol*
der Durchschnitt (-e)	*average*
durch/fallen	*to fail (a test or exam)*
der Deckel (-)	*(here) coll. for driving licence*
der Tanzkurs (-e)	*dancing lessons, dancing class*
ein/treten	*(here) to join (a club)*
die Hochzeit (-en)	*wedding*
der Schritt (-e)	*step*
die Gelegenheit (-en)	*opportunity*
eingebunden	*tied*
etwas vor/ziehen	*to prefer something*

2 Was stimmt?

Hören Sie sich den Dialog noch einmal an und unterstreichen Sie die richtigen Antworten.

    a Sebastian sagt, im Durchschnitt braucht man 10/20/25 Stunden, wenn man einen Führerschein macht.

    b Jochen möchte seinen zweiten/dritten/vierten Tanzkurs machen.

    c Danach möchte er in einen Tanzclub eintreten und auf Turnieren/Wettkämpfen/Tanzabenden tanzen.

    d Außer Tanzen singt/segelt/schwimmt er noch in seiner Freizeit.

    e Er sagt, es ist eine gute Gelegenheit, neue Menschen/Leute/Personen kennenzulernen.

    f Sebastian meint, es würde ihm nicht gefallen, so eingebunden/gebunden zu sein.

    g Er zieht es vor, seine Freizeit individuell/frei/flexibel zu gestalten.

> **CULTURE TIP – VEREINE/ *CLUBS IN DEUTSCHLAND***
> Vereine spielen eine große Rolle in Deutschland. Viele Leute arbeiten dort als ehrenamtliche Mitarbeiter (*volunteers*). Insgesamt sind etwa 23 Millionen Menschen in Deutschland in einem Sportverein. Die folgenden Sportarten haben die meisten Mitglieder:
>
> | | | | |
> |---|---|---|---|
> | 1 | Fußball | 5 | Leichtathletik |
> | 2 | Turnen | 6 | Handball |
> | 3 | Tennis | 7 | Wandern |
> | 4 | Sportschießen | 8 | Reiten |

3 Welche Antwort passt?

    a Also, was hast du eigentlich so geplant?

        1 Sie werden im Sommer nach Griechenland fahren.

        2 Ich werde meinen Führerschein anfangen.

        3 Das ist übrigens dem Peter passiert.

b Wie viele Stunden brauchst du denn?

    1 Heute Abend um 7 Uhr.

    2 Es fängt am Sonntag an.

    3 Na ja, 20 ist so der Durchschnitt.

c Hast du denn eine Partnerin für den Kurs?

    1 Ja, du kennst doch die Sybille, oder?

    2 Vielleicht den Marco.

    3 Ja, den Kurs mache ich alleine.

d Da muss man doch ziemlich oft trainieren, oder?

    1 Nein! Das glaube ich dir nicht.

    2 Ach, aber außer dem Tanzen mache ich eigentlich nichts weiter.

    3 Aber das wäre mir ehrlich gesagt zu viel.

4 Welches Verb passt am besten?

Complete the sentences with the appropriate word from the box.

eintreten	~~machen~~	gehen	interessieren	halten
durchfallen	besuchen	aufpolieren	treiben	

a einen Tanzkurs → *machen*

b sich für moderne Kunst → _____

c bei einem Examen → _____

d in einen Verein → _____

e Sport → _____

f Sprachkenntnisse → _____

g Ausstellungen → _____

h auf Turniere → _____

i sich fit → _____

 Reading

EINE STADT MIT VIEL KULTUR

1 Read the following text about Munich. Without looking at the vocabulary first, can you find out:

    a what is expensive in Munich?

    b how significant Munich is in the publishing industry?

    c the name of a famous city landmark?

München – Weltstadt mit Herz

Sie gilt als eine Weltstadt mit Herz und nach einer Umfrage der Zeitschrift Focus ist sie die Stadt, in der die meisten Deutschen leben möchten: München, mit mehr als 1,37 Millionen Einwohnern die drittgrößte Stadt Deutschlands. Ein Ort zum Wohlfühlen, der viel Lebensqualität bietet – Alpenblick, Biergärten, große Seen in unmittelbarer Nähe, elegante Shopping-Boutiquen. Der Nachteil: Neben Düsseldorf hat München die höchsten Miet- und Immobilienpreise der Bundesrepublik – ein Quadratmeter kostet mehr als £10,20.

Wirtschaftlich ist München ein Renner: Heimatstadt für BMW, Siemens, viele Banken, Versicherungen, Modefirmen und Brauereien. Täglich pendeln 450 000 Menschen. Und auch für Bücher ist München von Bedeutung: Es ist die größte Verlagsstadt in Europa.

Kein Wunder, dass München viele Touristen anlockt: 102 Millionen Tagesbesucher und über 12 Millionen Übernachtungen hat die Stadt pro Jahr. Viele kommen auch wegen des kulturellen Angebotes - mehr als 60 Museen und 70 Theater bietet die Stadt. Ein Tipp: Das Deutsche Museum, das jährlich von einer Millionen Menschen besucht wird.

Andere Attraktionen sind die Marienkirche, das Wahrzeichen der Stadt, der Englische Garten, einer der größten städtischen Gärten, das BMW-Museum und die Bavaria-Filmstudios, wo unter anderem berühmte Filme wie *Das Boot* oder *Die unendliche Geschichte* gedreht wurden. Und nicht zuletzt das Oktoberfest, das größte Bierfest der Welt. Es findet meistens von Mitte September bis Anfang Oktober statt.

die Umfrage (-n)	*survey*
ein Ort zum Wohlfühlen	*a place to feel at home in*
der Nachteil (-e)	*disadvantage*
der Renner (-)	*(here) hit, success*
pendeln	*to commute*
die Bedeutung (-en)	*importance, significance*
der Verlag (-e)	*publishing company*
an/locken	*to attract*

2 Sind die folgenden Aussagen richtig oder falsch? Korrigieren Sie die falschen Aussagen.

    a München ist die beliebteste Stadt in Deutschland.

    b Sie ist die zweitgrößte Stadt der Bundesrepublik.

    c Ökonomisch hat München keine Probleme.

    d Jährlich kommen 10 Millionen Besucher nach München.

    e Das Oktoberfest ist das größte Bierfest der Welt.

    f Es findet nur im Oktober statt.

3 Can you say in English what the following figures refer to?

    a 10,20

    b über 60

    c über 70

    d 450 000

    e 1,37 Million

    f über 12 Millionen

    g 102 Millionen

Conversation 2

Helga and Peter Schneider unterhalten sich mit Birgit über ihre Hobbys und was man in der Freizeit machen kann.

1 05.03 **Hören Sie sich den Dialog an und beantworten Sie die Fragen:**

    a Why can't Helga and Peter go to Birgit's party?

    b What wouldn't be to Birgit's taste?

    c What does Peter mention as the positive aspects of being in a club?

der Kegelclub (-s)	*bowling club*
etwas aus/fallen lassen	*to skip something, give something a miss*
sich aus/schließen	*to exclude oneself, not to take part in something*
gesellig	*sociable*
Das wäre nicht nach meinem Geschmack.	*That would not be to my taste.*

Birgit	Hallo, ihr beiden. Habt ihr nächstes Wochenende schon was vor? Alex und ich geben eine große Party.
Helga	Toll, da kommen wir gern, nicht wahr, Peter?
Peter	Vielen Dank für die Einladung, Birgit, aber nächstes Wochenende sind Helga und ich mit dem Kegelclub in England, in unserer Partnerstadt. Hast du das etwa vergessen, Helga?
Birgit	Könnt ihr das denn nicht mal ausfallen lassen? Wir haben doch so lange schon nicht mehr zusammen gefeiert.
Helga	Ich weiß, Birgit. So ein Pech! Es tut uns ja auch wirklich leid, aber das ist schon seit Wochen geplant. Und du weißt ja, wie das ist in so einem Club – da kann man sich schlecht ausschließen, wenn solche Veranstaltungen organisiert werden. Das sagt uns auch nicht immer zu.
Birgit	Habt ihr denn nie daran gedacht auszutreten? Also, ich hätte davon schon längst genug. Da kann man sich ja gar nichts anderes mehr vornehmen außer Kegeln.
Peter	Das ist eigentlich das Einzige, was uns beiden nicht so gut gefällt. Aber es hat auch unheimlich viele Vorteile.
Helga	Ja, das stimmt. Ich mag ganz besonders die gesellige Seite. Kegeln ist immer lustig und man trifft öfters neue Leute, besonders wenn man auf Turniere geht.
Birgit	Was, auf Turniere geht ihr auch noch? Da ist doch bestimmt eure ganze Freizeit verplant. Das wäre ganz und gar nicht nach meinem Geschmack. Ich habe gerne auch mal Zeit für mich selbst. So sehr eingebunden zu sein, würde mir überhaupt nicht gefallen.
Peter	Aber du darfst auch nicht vergessen, dass der Club viele interessante Unternehmungen organisiert, die uns beiden doch viel Spaß machen. Denk doch nur mal an die Städtereisen, die wir schon unternommen haben – und schließlich ist es ja auch eine sportliche Betätigung, die man bis ins hohe Alter betreiben kann.

die Partnerstadt (¨-e)	*twin town*
sich etwas vor/nehmen	*to plan something*
das sagt uns nicht zu	*that is not to our liking*
aus/treten aus (+ dat.)	*to leave (a club, society, etc.)*
das Turnier (-e)	*tournament*
von etwas genug haben	*to have enough of something*
verplanen	*to book fully, to plan every minute*
die Betätigung (-en)	*activity*
betreiben	*to do (esp. sport), to pursue*

2 Richtig oder falsch? Korrigieren Sie die falschen Aussagen.

a Birgit und Alex geben in zwei Wochen eine große Party.

b Helga und Peter bekommen Besuch von Keglern aus England

c Weil sie in einem Club sind, können sie sich nicht ausschließen.

d Helga gefällt es besonders, dass man beim Kegeln dieselben Leute trifft.

e Birgit sagt, sie braucht Zeit für sich selber.

f Helga und Peter haben noch nie eine Städtereise mit dem Club unternommen.

3 Positiv und negativ …

Lesen Sie den Text noch einmal und ergänzen Sie die folgenden vier positiven und vier negativen Aussagen.

Positiv	Negativ
a Es hat auch unheimlich …	**a** Also, ich hätte davon schon …
b Ich … die gesellige Seite.	**b** Das ist das einzige, was …
c Kegeln ist immer …	**c** Das wäre ganz und gar nicht nach …
d Der Club organisiert viele Unternehmungen, die …	**d** So eingebunden zu sein, würde …

4 05.04 **Sagen Sie's auf Deutsch!**

a Have you made any plans for the coming weekend?

b Splendid, we'd love to come.

c Can't you skip that for once?

d What a pity!

e That is not always to our liking.

f Well, I would have had enough of that long ago.

g That would not be at all to my taste.

Language discovery 2

You have already seen this language in action. Can you work out the rules?

1 Look at the following questions involving verbs and prepositions. Can you figure out how the question word is formed in German, when asking: *What are you interested in? What are you dreaming of?* **or** *What are you thinking of?*

a Wofür interessierst du dich?

b Wovon träumst du?

c Worüber denkst du nach?

2 Which word is missing from these sentences?

a Hast du Lust, mit ins Theater _____ gehen?

b Sebastian meint, es würde ihm nicht gefallen, so eingebunden _____ sein.

c Er zieht es vor, seine Freizeit flexibel _____ gestalten.

1 VERBEN UND PRÄPOSITIONEN – FRAGEN *VERB + PREPOSITIONS – FORMING QUESTIONS*

Yes/No questions involving verb and prepositions are formed by putting the verb at the beginning:

Interessieren Sie sich für Sport?

Ärgern Sie sich über das Wetter?

Most open-ended questions are constructed by using **wo(r)** + the relevant preposition:

sich interessieren **für** ...	**Wofür** interessieren Sie sich?
sich ärgern **über** ...	**Worüber** ärgerst du dich?
denken **an** ...	**Woran** denkst du?

Note that the letter **-r** is added if the preposition starts with a vowel.

When specifically referring to a person, the question starts with the relevant preposition, followed by the appropriate form of **wer**:

denken an	An **wen** denkst du?	*Who(m) are you thinking of?*
träumen von	Von **wem** hast du geträumt?	*Who(m) did you dream of?*

The form of **wer** depends on the case required by the preposition, hence **wen** (accusative) or **wem** (dative).

2 ZU + INFINITIV *ZU + INFINITIVE CONSTRUCTIONS*

A number of expressions that are often used to talk about hobbies, leisure time, etc., require **zu** + infinitive:

Ist es teuer, in die Oper **zu gehen**?   *Is it expensive to go to the opera?*

Er hat keine Zeit **zu kommen**.   *He doesn't have the time to come.*

As you can see, **zu** + infinitive go to the end of the sentence or clause. The second part of the sentence also needs to be separated from the main clause by a comma, unless it consists only of **zu** + infinitive, as in the second example.

Verbs that often need **zu** + infinitive are: **beabsichtigen** *to intend*, **aufhören** *to stop*, **hoffen** *to hope*, **vornehmen** *to plan something*, **vorziehen** *to prefer*, **versuchen** *to try*.

Many expressions which consist of a verb + adjective are also often followed by an infinitive + **zu**:

Es ist möglich, ...	*It is possible ...*
Es ist wichtig, ...	*It is important ...*

The same applies to expressions which consist of a verb + noun:

Ich habe (keine) Lust, ...	*I (don't) fancy ...*
Es macht Spaß, ...	*It is fun ...*

Practice 2

1 Wie heißen die Fragen?

Form questions using question words starting with wo(r). Use the du-form.

Beispiel: sich erinnern an → *Woran erinnerst du dich?*

    a sich freuen auf → _____

    b glauben an → _____

    c nachdenken über → _____

    d sich erinnern an → _____

    e warten auf → _____

    f suchen nach → _____

    g sich unterhalten über → _____

2 Was bedeutet das auf Englisch?

Match the German expressions which are often followed by infinitive + zu to their English equivalents.

a Es ist unmöglich, ...		**1** I intend ...
b Es ist wichtig, ...		**2** It's no fun ...
c Ich habe große Lust, ...		**3** It's crazy ...
d Es macht keinen Spaß,...		**4** It's time ...
e Es ist Zeit, ...		**5** It's important ...
f Es ist verrückt, ...		**6** I prefer ...
g Ich ziehe es vor, ...		**7** It's impossible ...
h Ich beabsichtige, ...		**8** I really fancy ...

3 Antworten Sie.

Complete the answers to the following questions by using a zu + infinitive construction.

Beispiel: Fährst du im Sommer nach Griechenland? → *Ja, ich hoffe, im Sommer nach Griechenland zu fahren.*

    a Geht ihr heute Abend tanzen? Nein, wir haben keine Lust, ...

    b Willst du eigentlich bald deinen Führerschein machen? Ja, ich habe vor, ...

    c Kann man dort auch ein Bier trinken? Nein, dort ist es nicht möglich, ...

    d Geht ihr nachher noch ins Restaurant? Ja, wir haben Lust, ...

    e Bekommt man noch Karten für das Konzert? Nein, es ist unmöglich, ...

    f Möchtest du deine Freizeit lieber selbst gestalten? Ja, ich ziehe es vor, ...

4 Was ich mag (👍). Was ich nicht mag (👎).

Write about your personal likes and dislikes on your social media page. What do you find interesting? What bores you and what do you get annoyed about? Are you looking forward to anything in particular?

Write at least three sentences for each heading, using the vocabulary and structures covered in this unit.

Blog	Add post

Wofür ich mich interessiere (👍) *Ich interessiere mich für...*

_____

_____

Was ich langweilig finde (👎) Ich finde es sehr langweilig...

_____

_____

_____

Worüber ich mich ärgere (👎) Ich ärgere mich zum Beispiel über...

_____

_____

_____

Worauf ich mich freue (👍) Ich freue mich sehr...

_____

_____

_____

Go further with grammar

1 VERBEN UND PRÄPOSITIONEN *VERBS AND PREPOSITIONS*

In **Language discovery** 1, you were introduced to verbs that are followed by a preposition. Here is a list of the most common ones and the case they require:

an	denken an (acc.)	*to think of/about*
	sich erinnern an (acc.)	*to remember*
	glauben an (acc.)	*to believe in*
	schreiben an (acc.)	*to write to*
auf	sich freuen auf (acc.)	*to look forward to*
	warten auf (acc.)	*to wait for*
bei	sich entschuldigen bei (dat.)	*to say sorry to*
für	sich entschuldigen für (acc.)	*to say sorry for*
	sich interessieren für (acc.)	*to be interested in*
	sich begeistern für (acc.)	*to be enthusiastic about*

mit	aufhören mit (dat.)	to stop something
	sprechen mit (dat.)	to talk to
	telefonieren mit (dat.)	to phone
nach	fragen nach (dat.)	to ask about
	suchen nach (dat.)	to look for
über	nachdenken über (acc.)	to think about
	sich ärgern über (acc.)	to get annoyed about
	sich freuen über (acc.)	to be pleased about
	sprechen über (acc.)	to talk about
um	sich bewerben um (acc.)	to apply for
von	träumen von (dat.)	to dream of, about

Note that prepositions such as **an**, **auf** and **über**, which can be followed by either the accusative or dative case, usually take the accusative in a verb + preposition expression:

Ich schreibe an meinen Bruder.   *I'm writing to my brother.*

As you might have noticed, some verbs also go with more than one preposition and change their meaning depending on the preposition used:

Ich freue mich auf den Film.   *I'm looking forward to the film.*
Ich freue mich über mein Geschenk.   *I'm pleased about my present.*

Verbs can also take more than one preposition at a time:
Ich habe **mit** Herrn Schmidt **über** das Theaterstück gesprochen.

For more information about **prepositions and cases**, see **Unit 7**.

2 PRÄPOSITIONALPRONOMEN *PREPOSITIONAL PRONOUNS*

If you reply to a question which contains a verb + preposition, you don't have to repeat the whole phrase. Look at the examples:

Hat er **nach** Ihrem Namen gefragt? → Nein, er hat nicht **danach** gefragt.

Interessieren Sie sich **für** Sport? → Nein, ich interessiere mich nicht **dafür**.

Note that you can put **da(r)-** in front of most prepositions when you want to say *in it, on it, about it*, etc. and replace the noun with a so-called prepositional pronoun:

Erinnern Sie sich **an** dieses Buch? → Ja, ich erinnere mich sehr gut **daran**.

Ärgerst du dich **über** moderne Musik? → Nein, ich ärgere mich nicht **darüber**.

The prepositional pronoun can in most cases also go at the beginning of a phrase:

Hat er **nach** Ihrem Namen gefragt? → Nein, **danach** hat er nicht gefragt.

3 ZU + INFINITIVSÄTZE *ZU + INFINITIVE CLAUSES*

As you saw in **Language discovery 2**, **zu** is often needed to create an infinitive clause, as in:
Ich versuche, noch Karten **zu** bekommen.

Apart from a number of verbs, many expressions which consist of a verb + noun or a verb + adjective are often followed by an infinitive + **zu**. In particular, the phrases **Ich habe ...** and **Es ist ...** signal the use of a **zu** + infinitive clause:
Ich habe große Lust, einen Tanzkurs **zu** machen.
Es ist Zeit, nach Hause **zu** gehen.
Es ist verrückt, so viel Sport **zu** treiben.
Ist es nicht langweilig, den gleichen Film noch einmal **zu** sehen?

Note also the useful German construction **um ... zu ...** *in order to*, in which **zu** + infinitive is used:

Sie treibt viel Sport, **um** fit **zu** bleiben.	*She is doing a lot of sport (in order) to stay fit.*
Ich fliege nach Budapest, **um** Verhandlungen mit einer ungarischen Firma **zu** führen.	*I'm flying to Budapest (in order) to conduct negotiations with a Hungarian firm.*

As you can see, **um** goes at the beginning of the clause and the **zu** + infinitive at the end.

⑦ Test yourself

1 Dafür, daran usw.

Answer these questions, using the prompts in brackets. After either **Ja** or **Nein** you should start your answer with the appropriate combination of **da(r)** + preposition.

Beispiele: Interessieren Sie sich für Fußball? (Nein – gar nicht)→
Nein, dafür interessiere ich mich gar nicht.

Erinnerst du dich an meine 18. Geburtstagsparty? (Ja – sehr gut!)→
Ja, daran erinnere ich mich sehr gut!

   a Freust du dich auf deinen Urlaub in Spanien? (Ja – sehr)
   b Erinnern Sie sich an meine erste Ausstellung? (Nein – leider nicht)
   c Bewerben Sie sich um die Stelle? (Ja – bestimmt)
   d Ärgerst du dich über das englische Wetter? (Nein – überhaupt nicht)
   e Interessierst du dich für Musik? (Ja – ungeheuer)
   f Hast du dich nicht über deine Geschenke gefreut? (Nein – ganz und gar nicht!)

2 Was kann man auch sagen?

Welche Ausdrücke haben eine ähnliche Bedeutung?

a Ich bin kulturinteressiert.
b Das hat mich schon immer gelangweilt.
c Das würde mir nicht gefallen.
d Ich bin gern auf dem Laufenden.
e Das schätze ich sehr.
f Das ist das Einzige, was uns nicht gefällt.
g Ich habe kein Verständnis dafür.

1 Ich weiß gern, was so passiert.
2 Das ist eine Sache, die wir nicht mögen.
3 Das verstehe ich nicht.
4 Ich interessiere mich für Kultur.
5 Das mag ich nicht.
6 Das fand ich schon immer langweilig.
7 Das ist mir viel wert.

3 05.05 Und jetzt Sie!

Übernehmen Sie die folgende Rolle und sprechen Sie mit Hilfe der englischen Hinweise über Ihre Freizeitaktivitäten. Benutzen Sie die Vokabeln, die in dieser Lektion vorgekommen sind. Die Antworten hören Sie auf der Höraufnahme.

Markus	Was machst du denn gerne in deiner Freizeit?
Sie	*Tell him that you have been swimming for a club for eight years, and that you are also a member of a bowling club.*
Markus	So viel Sport – das wäre ganz und gar nicht nach meinem Geschmack! Da ist doch bestimmt deine ganze Freizeit verplant!
Sie	*Tell him that sometimes you think that it is a little bit too much. However, you think it has a lot of advantages.*
Markus	Was gefällt dir denn so gut daran?
Sie	*Tell him that you meet a lot of people, you also keep fit and you get to see a lot of new places when going to tournaments with the clubs.*
Markus	Interessierst du dich denn gar nicht für Kultur?
Sie	*Tell him that you are interested in culture, but that you prefer sports.*
Markus	Magst du denn zum Beispiel klassische Musik oder Malerei?
Sie	*Tell him that, quite honestly, you prefer modern music, and that you also like to go to the cinema.*
Markus	Naja, jeder nach seinem Geschmack!

SELF CHECK

	I CAN. . .
○	... talk about my interests, likes and dislikes.
○	... discuss the ways I spend my free time.
○	... use prepositions correctly with certain verbs.
○	... form clauses with **zu** + infinitive.
○	... understand a text about Munich.
○	... write a blog about what I like or dislike.

6 Und wie ist Ihre Meinung?

In this unit you will learn how to:
▶ *talk about health matters and staying fit.*
▶ *ask for and express opinions.*
▶ *recognize short forms in colloquial German.*
▶ *agree and disagree.*
▶ *use modal verbs.*
▶ *use the genitive case correctly.*

CEFR: *Can understand long and complex factual texts, e.g. a health blog about the causes of stress (C1); can explain a viewpoint on a topical issue and argue the pros and cons of various options, e.g. discussing a no-smoking policy (B2).*

Conversation 1

RAUCHEN IN DER ÖFFENTLICHKEIT – PRO UND CONTRA

Elke und Jochen diskutieren über ein Rauchverbot in der Öffentlichkeit.

 1 06.01 **Study the vocabulary first, and then listen to the conversation in which Elke and Jochen discuss the pros and cons of a smoking ban in public. What is Jochen's position – is he in favour or against a ban?**

die Öffentlichkeit (-en)	*public*
ganz und gar nicht	*not at all*
die Forderung (-en)	*demand*
rein	*pure, clean*
das Abgas (usually pl. die Abgase)	*exhaust fumes*
das Recht auf	*the right to*
Da ist bestimmt 'was dran.	*There's certainly something in that.*
Es gibt nur noch ein Unrecht mehr.	*Two wrongs don't make a right.*
verpesten	*to pollute, foul up*
sich Sorgen machen um	*to worry about*

Elke	Bist du der Meinung, dass das Rauchen in der Öffentlichkeit verboten werden sollte?
Jochen	Ganz und gar nicht! Ich finde, die Antiraucherfanatiker sind schon zu weit gegangen mit ihren neurotischen Forderungen.
Elke	Was hältst du also von dem Argument, dass jeder das Recht haben sollte, reine Luft zu atmen?
Jochen	Das ist ja ein Witz! Ich als Radfahrer muss die ganzen Abgase von den vielen Autos einatmen. Wo bleibt denn da mein Recht auf reine Luft?
Elke	Da ist bestimmt 'was dran. Aber es gibt nur noch ein Unrecht mehr, wenn man sowohl Zigarettenrauch als auch Autoabgase atmen muss.
Jochen	Das ist mir egal. Solange die Autofahrer meine Luft verpesten, bestehe ich auf meinem Recht, auch in der Öffentlichkeit zu rauchen.
Elke	Und machst du dir um deine Gesundheit keine Sorgen?
Jochen	Nee, eigentlich nicht. Mir macht das Rauchen unheimlich viel Spaß.

2 Richtig oder falsch? Korrigieren Sie die falschen Aussagen.

   a Elke fragt, ob das Rauchen in der Öffentlichkeit verboten werden sollte.

   b Jochen denkt, dass die Forderungen der Antiraucher richtig sind.

   c Er selber ist auch Nichtraucher.

   d Über die Autofahrer beschwert er sich aber nicht.

   e Elke sagt, es ist nicht richtig, wenn man Zigarettenrauch und Abgase einatmet.

   f Jochen macht sich große Sorgen um seine Gesundheit.

3 06.02 **Sagen Sie's auf Deutsch!**

Can you say these sentences in German? They all appeared in the conversation.

   a Not at all!

   b You must be joking!

   c There may well be something in that.

   d I don't care.

   e I really enjoy smoking.

Language discovery 1

You have already seen this language in action. Can you work out the rules?

1 Match the German questions with their English equivalent. Which ones are formal, which ones are less formal?

   a Was denkst du über … ?

   b Wie ist deine Ansicht über … ?

   c Glaubst du, dass … ?

   d Bist du der Meinung, dass … ?

   1 Do you believe that … ?

   2 Are you of the opinion that … ?

   3 What is your view on … ?

   4 What do you think of … ?

2 Look at these two phrases from Conversation 1. In sentence a, what is the unabridged form of *'was*? In sentence b, what is the standard German word for *nee*?

a Da ist bestimmt 'was dran.

b Nee, eigentlich nicht.

1 NACH MEINUNGEN FRAGEN UND MEINUNGEN ÄUSSERN *ASKING ABOUT AND EXPRESSING OPINIONS*

In German there are a number of ways of asking about and expressing opinions. Some you probably already know; here are the most common ones:

Glauben Sie, dass ... ?	*Do you believe that ... ?*
Wie finden Sie ... ?	*What do you think of ... ?*
Was denken Sie über (+ acc.) **... ?**	*What do you think about ... ?*
Was halten Sie von (+ dat.) **... ?**	*What do you think of ... ?*
Wie ist Ihre Meinung/Ansicht über ... ?	*What's your opinion/view on ... ?*
Sind Sie der Meinung/Ansicht, dass ... ?	*Are you of the opinion/view that ... ?*

Note that you could of course use the **du** form for the questions, e.g. **Wie findest du ...?** **Wie ist deine Meinung über ... ?**

Ich finde, .../Ich denke, .../Ich meine, ...	*I think ...*
Ich glaube, ...	*I believe ...*
Ich bin der Meinung/Ansicht, dass ...	*I am of the opinion/view that ...*
Meiner Meinung/Ansicht nach ...	*In my opinion ...*

Note the gradual increase in formality for both the questions and the answers.

Some commonly used phrases to express agreement or disagreement are:

Das stimmt./Das stimmt nicht.	*That's right./That's not right.*
Da haben Sie recht./Da haben Sie unrecht.	*You are correct./You are wrong (about this).*
Da bin ich (ganz) Ihrer Meinung.	*I am (completely) of the same opinion.*
Da bin ich (ganz) anderer Meinung.	*I've got (quite) a different opinion (on that).*
Da stimme ich mit Ihnen überein.	*I agree with you there.*
Da muss ich widersprechen.	*I have to disagree (with you) there.*

Note that **überein/stimmen** means *to agree* and **widersprechen** is *to disagree*.

2 UMGANGSSPRACHLICHES DEUTSCH *COLLOQUIAL GERMAN*

As in English, it's quite common in spoken informal German to drop certain letters and to combine words. Frequently abridged words include **es**, **etwas** and **das**:

Das **war es**. → Das **war's**.

Sagen **Sie es** auf Deutsch. → Sagen **Sie's** auf Deutsch?

Da ist **etwas** dran. → Da ist **'was** dran.

Kannst du mir **etwas** mitbringen? → Kannst du mir **'was** mitbringen?

Was **soll das**? → Was **soll's**?

Was **kostet das**? → Was **kostet's**?

Conversation 1 also contains a number of emotionally charged expressions used to state or to react to an opinion:

nee	*no* (colloquial for **nein**)
Das ist ja ein Witz!	*You must be joking!*
Das ist mir egal.	*I don't care.*

Similar phrases include:

Das ist ja Quatsch!	*What nonsense!*
Was für ein Blödsinn!	*What drivel!*
Red keinen Müll!	*Don't talk rubbish!*
Jetzt reicht's mir aber.	*Now I've had enough.*

Practice 1

1 Umgangssprache. Shorten these sentences as in the example.

Beispiel: Wie geht es? → *Wie geht's?*

   a Mach das nochmal.

   b Gib das her!

   c Habt ihr etwas Schönes unternommen?

   d Jetzt wird es ernst.

   e Hast du das verstanden?

   f Morgen wird es regnen.

   g Das war es.

2 Sagen Sie es höflicher!

Find a more polite way to react to the following statements. There is often more than one possibility.

Beispiel: – A: Rauchen sollte verboten werden.

         – B: Das ist ja ein Witz! → *Da bin ich anderer Meinung!/Da muss ich widersprechen!*

   a – A: Autoabgase sind auch sehr gefährlich.

      – B: Das stimmt.

   b – A: Man sollte weniger mit dem Auto fahren.

      – B: Da ist bestimmt 'was dran.

   c – A: Wir sollten alle mit dem Fahrrad zur Arbeit fahren.

      – B: Was für ein Blödsinn!

   d – A: Ich finde, du gehst zu weit mit deinen Forderungen.

      – B: Ach was! Ganz und gar nicht.

   e – A: Aber Rauchen ist doch ungesund, findest du nicht?

      – B: Das stimmt leider.

   f – A: Jeder sollte das Recht auf reine Luft haben.

      – B: Na ja, das ist richtig.

Kinder mögen es rauchfrei!

Machen Sie mit - schützen Sie Kinder vor dem Passivrauchen!

 uicc
global cancer control

AKTIONSBÜNDNIS NICHTRAUCHEN
www.tabakkontrolle.de   www.abnr.de   www.krebshilfe.de

 Helfen.
Forschen.
Informieren.

3 Was fehlt hier? Ergänzen Sie die folgenden Fragen.

 a _____ findest du eigentlich Deutsch?

 b _____ denkst du _____ d_____ Politik der Regierung?

 c Was halten Sie _____ d_____ Idee, mehr Sport zu treiben?

 d _____ Sie _____ Meinung, dass Sie gesund leben?

 e Stimmen Sie mit mir _____, dass es schwer ist, das Rauchen aufzugeben?

 f _____ ist Ihre An_____ über ein Rauchverbot in der Öffentlichkeit?

 4 Und Sie? Wie ist Ihre Meinung?

Go through the questions you asked in Exercise 3 again, but this time answer them for yourself. Make some notes to justify your opinion with examples. Then, practise the questions and answers out loud. For the last question include some of these pros and cons:

Rauchverbot in der Öffentlichkeit	
Dafür 👍	**Dagegen** 👎
Jeder sollte das Recht haben, reine Luft zu atmen. Es ist doch klar, dass Passivrauchen ungesund ist. Vor allem Kinder und schwangere Frauen würden geschützt.	Die Anti-Raucher sind schon viel zu weit gegangen. Solange die Autofahrer die Luft verpesten, kann ich auch rauchen. Die Freiheit des Einzelnen wird eingeschränkt.

 # Reading

STRESS UND WORK-LIFE-BALANCE

1 Read the following health blog about how Germans deal with stress. Without looking at the vocabulary first, can you find out:

 a what the main cause of stress is?

 b what sort of people experience burn-out?

 c what the two main health problems associated with stress are?

Add post

Deutsche haben mehr Stress

Fast sechs von zehn Deutschen empfinden ihr Leben als stressig - jeder Fünfte steht sogar unter Dauerdruck. Das zeigt eine neue Studie der Techniker Krankenkasse (TK).

Und der Stresslevel steigt: Mehr als 50% der Deutschen haben das Gefühl, dass ihr Leben in den letzten drei Jahren stressiger geworden ist. Besonders betroffen sind Menschen zwischen 35 bis 45 Jahren. Oft müssen sie sich nicht nur um ihre Karriere und Kinder, sondern auch um die eigenen Eltern kümmern.

Abgearbeitet

Der größte Stressfaktor für die Menschen ist der Job. Zwei Drittel der Berufstätigen fühlen sich in ihrem Job gestresst. Doch schon an zweiter Stelle stehen die hohen Ansprüche der Menschen an sich selbst. "Nicht immer sind äußere Umstände der Grund für die Anspannung, oft ist es auch eine Frage der inneren Einstellung", sagt Dr. Jens Baas, Chef der TK. Als alarmierend nennt er allerdings die Tatsache, dass sich bereits 40 Prozent der Berufstätigen abgearbeitet fühlen, jeder dritte sogar ausgebrannt.

"Ein stressfreier Arbeitsplatz ist eine Utopie - und auch kein erstrebenswertes Ziel", erklärt Baas. Stress sei nicht per se negativ. Wichtig ist, dass man über genügend Ressourcen verfügt, die man dem Stress entgegensetzen kann. Und vielen gelingt dies auch: Jeder zweite Berufstätige sagt, dass Stress ihn motiviert, jeder fünfte läuft unter Druck sogar erst richtig zu Hochform auf.

Die Work-Life-Balance muss stimmen

Es ist selten die Arbeitslast im Job allein, die den Stresspegel in die Höhe treibt. Kritisch wird es, wenn soziale Faktoren wie Konflikte mit Kollegen oder dem Chef hinzukommen. Oder wenn aufgrund von privatem Stress der Ausgleich neben der Arbeit fehlt. Dies ist besonders oft bei berufstätigen Eltern der Fall. "Es ist die Work-Life-Balance, die insgesamt stimmen muss", sagt Baas.

Ständig erreichbar sein

Eine Herausforderung für die Work-Life-Balance ist, dass sich Arbeit und Freizeit immer schlechter trennen lassen. Vier von zehn Berufstätigen geben an, dass sie ständig erreichbar sind, jedem dritten gelingt es auch nach Feierabend und am Wochenende nicht, richtig abzuschalten. Und "always on", stets im Bereitschaftsmodus zu sein, geht auf Dauer an die Substanz.

Die Studie zeigt auch: Je höher der Stresslevel, desto mehr Beschwerden haben die Menschen. Die häufigsten Krankheiten für Gestresste sind Rückenschmerzen und Erschöpfung. Dann folgen Schlafstörungen, Gereiztheit und Kopfschmerzen.

(Adapted from Techniker Krankenkasse)

der Dauerdruck (no pl.)	*constant pressure*
sich kümmern um	*to take care of, to look after*
der Anspruch ("-e)	*demand, aspirations*
die Anspannung (-en)	*tension, strain*
die inneren Einstellung (-en)	*inner attitude*
abgearbeitet	*worn out*
ausgebrannt	*burnt out*
erstrebenswert	*desirable, worth striving for*
der Ausgleich (-e)	*balance*
erreichbar	*to be able to be contacted*
ab/schalten	*to disconnect, to switch off*
die Erschöpfung (-en)	*exhaustion, fatigue*
die Gereiztheit (no pl.)	*edginess, irritability*

2 Richtig oder falsch? Korrigieren Sie die falschen Aussagen auf Englisch.

   a On average, Germans feel less stressed than three years ago.

   b The age group most affected by stress is the young.

   c 'Being too demanding with yourself' is the second biggest cause of stress.

   d Stress is always a negative force.

   e Working parents usually find it more difficult to get the work-life balance right.

   f It has become easier to separate work and leisure time.

   g 40% of working people find it difficult to disconnect from work.

CULTURE TIP – GESUNDHEITSVERSORGUNG *HEALTH CARE*

Die Gesundheitsversorgung in Deutschland ist auf einem sehr hohen Standard. Die meisten Deutschen gehören einer gesetzlichen Krankenkasse an (*statutory health insurance scheme*), wie zum Beispiel der Allgemeinen Ortskrankenkasse (AOK) oder der Techniker Krankenkasse (TK). Daneben gibt es auch zahlreiche Privatkrankenkassen.

Menschen, die länger krank sind, können oft eine Kur machen. Die Krankenkassen übernehmen einen großen Teil der Kosten. Der Name der meisten Kurorte beginnt mit „Bad", wie zum Beispiel Bad Gandersheim oder Bad Harzburg. Der bekannteste Kurort in Deutschland ist Baden-Baden.

Herzlich willkommen in Bad Gandersheim!

Stadt **Bad Gandersheim**

Wohlfühlen leicht gemacht

Bad Gandersheim ist einer der vielen deutschen Kurorte. Sein Heilbad bietet Linderung bei Rheuma, Kreislaufstörungen, usw.

---

3 Wie heißt das im Text?

Finden Sie für die Wörter in kursiv die Ausdrücke im Text mit den ähnlichen Bedeutungen.

Beispiel: Der Stresslevel wird *höher*. → Der Stresslevel steigt.

   a jeder Fünfte steht sogar unter *permanentem Druck*

   b oft ist es eine *Charakterfrage*

   c die hohen *Erwartungen* der Menschen an sich selbst

   d ein stressfreier Arbeitsplatz ist *nicht realistisch*

   e Wichtig ist, dass man über genügend *Kräfte* verfügt, …

   f es fehlt *die Balance*

   g jedem dritten gelingt es nicht *sich richtig zu entspannen*

   h sie sind *die ganze Zeit* erreichbar

4 Verbinden Sie die Satzteile. Match both parts of the statements to summarize the main points of the article.

a Mehr als 50% haben das Gefühl,
b Der größte Stressfaktor
c An zweiter Stelle stehen
d Nicht immer sind äußere Umstände
e Es ist selten die Arbeitslast allein,
f Arbeit und Freizeit
g Vier von zehn Leuten geben an,
h Stets im Bereitschaftsmodus zu sein,
i Je höher der Stresslevel,

1 der Grund für die Anspannung.
2 dass sie ständig erreichbar sind.
3 geht auf Dauer an die Substanz.
4 dass ihr Leben stressiger geworden ist.
5 ist der Job.
6 die Ansprüche der Menschen an sich selbst.
7 desto mehr Gesundheitsprobleme gibt es.
8 lassen sich immer schlechter trennen.
9 die den Stresspegel in die Höhe treibt.

Listen and understand

NACHRICHTENSENDUNG

Die folgende Audioaufnahme ist ein Auszug aus einer Nachrichtensendung.

1 06.03 **Listen to an excerpt from a news programme. What is the main topic under discussion?**

a drug abuse.   b alcoholism.   c problems in the health service.

die Ärztekammer (-)	*chambers of doctors*
hin/weisen auf	*to point out*
unbemerkt	*unnoticed*
an/wachsen	*to grow, increase*
der Folgeschaden (¨)	*harmful effect*
der Missbrauch (-¨e)	*abuse*
die Leberzirrhose (-n)	*cirrhosis of the liver*
der Hirnabbau	*brain damage (lit. brain reduction)*
die Einschätzung (-en)	*estimation*
verkennen	*to fail to appreciate/recognize*

2 Beantworten Sie die Fragen.

a Wo fand der Kongress der deutschen Ärztekammer statt?
b Wovor warnte der Präsident der Ärztekammer?
c Wie hoch ist die Zahl der Alkoholtoten im Vergleich zu den Drogentoten?
d Wie viele Alkoholkranke gibt es in Deutschland?
e Was sind oft die Folgen von Alkoholmissbrauch?

3 Nach oben oder nach unten? Do the following verbs indicate an increase or decrease?

a ansteigen
b fallen
c anwachsen
d in die Höhe treiben
e sinken
f abnehmen
g sich steigern

4 Hören Sie die Audioaufnahme noch einmal und ergänzen Sie die fehlenden Wörter.

Auf einem **(a)** _____ in Berlin hat der Präsident der deutschen **(b)** _____ gestern vor den Gefahren des stark zunehmenden **(c)** _____ gewarnt. Er wies darauf hin, dass das Problem **(d)** _____ von der **(e)** _____ ständig anwachse. Die **(f)** _____ der Alkoholtoten liege etwa zehnmal so **(g)** _____ wie die der Drogentoten. **(h)** _____ gebe es in Deutschland anderthalb bis zwei Millionen Alkoholkranke. Auch die Folgeschäden jahrelangen **(i)** _____, wie **(j)** _____zirrhose, **(k)** _____ abbau und verschiedene **(l)** _____erkrankungen werden nach seiner **(m)** _____ von den meisten Menschen **(n)** _____.

Language discovery 2

You have already seen this language in action. Can you work out the rules?

1 The following phrases show examples of the genitive case. What are the various forms for the definite article? What changes take place for masculine and neuter nouns?

masculine: Die Folgen **des Alkoholmissbrauchs** betreffen viele Menschen.

feminine: Sie ist **der Meinung**, dass es schwer ist, von der Arbeit abzuschalten.

neuter: Es ist eine Frage **des Geldes**.

plural: Der Name **der Kurorte** in Deutschland beginnt meistens mit „Bad".

2 How would you say in German: *You must not park here.*

  a Hier können Sie nicht parken.

  b Hier müssen Sie nicht parken.

  c Hier dürfen Sie nicht parken.

1 DER GENITIV *THE GENITIVE CASE*

The genitive case refers to the concept of possession or ownership, corresponding to the English *'s* or the preposition *of*:

Das sind Tims Laufschuhe.   *These are Tim's running shoes.*

Der Präsident des Vereins   *The president of the club*

The forms of the articles and possessives used in genitive constructions are relatively easy to remember:

masculine: **es**	**des** Bruders	**eines** Bruders	**meines** Bruders
feminine: **er**	**der** Freundin	**einer** Freundin	**seiner** Freundin
neuter: **es**	**des** Kindes	**eines** Kindes	**ihres** Kindes
plural: **er**	**der** Kurorte	–	**unserer** Kurorte

Masculine and neuter nouns normally change in the genitive:

one-syllabus nouns usually add **-es**: des Kind**es**, des Geld**es**;

longer nouns only add **-s**: des Bruder**s**, des Missbrauch**s**.

Feminine and neuter noun endings are not affected by this.

To indicate possession it's quite common in German to add **-s** to the names of people, cities or countries. However, unlike English, there is normally no apostrophe:

Jamie **Olivers** neuer Bestseller	*Jamie Oliver's new bestseller*
New **Yorks** Parks	*New York's parks*
Deutschlands Dichter und Denker	*Germany's poets and thinkers*

The genitive is often used in more formal contexts, for instance in news programmes or when asking or giving opinions in a formal way, as you saw earlier in this unit:

Sind Sie der Meinung ...?

Ich bin der Ansicht ...

The use of the genitive is decreasing in modern usage. In spoken, and sometimes even in written German, it is replaced with **von** + dative:

die Gesundheit meines Bruders → der Gesundheit **von meinem** Bruder

die Abgase der vielen Autos → die Abgase von **den vielen** Autos

2 MODALVERBEN *MODAL VERBS*

Especially in the context of health or fitness it is important to know how to say what one *can do, must do, can't do, mustn't do*, etc.

The verbs which express these functions are called modal verbs. In German they are: **können** *to be able to/can*, **dürfen** *to be allowed to/may*, **müssen** *to have to/must*, **sollen** *ought to/should*, **wollen** *to want to*

Note that the German equivalent of *must not* is **dürfen** + **nicht** or **kein**:

Hier **darf** man **nicht** rauchen.	*Here one mustn't smoke (no smoking allowed).*
Sie **dürfen keinen** Alkohol trinken.	*You mustn't drink any alcohol.*

Ich muss nicht in German means	*I don't have to*:
Ich **muss nicht** mit dem Fahrrad zur Uni fahren, ich kann auch mit der Straßenbahn fahren.	*I don't have to go to the university by bike. I can go by tram, too.*

The modal verbs in German are quite irregular. For an overview of modal verbs in the present and past simple tense, see the **Go further with grammar** section.

Practice 2

1 Üben Sie Endungen im Genitiv.

Add the appropriate endings. Note that at times none is needed.

   a Die Gefahren d_____ Rauchen_____ sind bekannt.

   b Die Tochter mein_____ Bruder_____ ist Mitglied in einem Tennisclub.

   c Der Trainer d_____ Fußballmannschaft_____ hat viel Erfahrung.

   d Der Vater ihr_____ Mann_____ war ein bekannter Sportler.

   e Ich bin da ganz dein_____ Meinung_____.

   f Mein_____ Erachten_____ sind die Preise für den Fitnessclub viel zu hoch.

   g Die Namen mein_____ beiden Brüder_____ willst du wissen?

2 Sagen Sie es anders. Rewrite the sentences by using a genitive construction.

Beispiel: Die Anzahl von den Fitnessclubs hat zugenommen. → *Die Anzahl der Fitnessclubs hat zugenommen.*

    a Die Lehrerin von dem Kurs hat lange in Kalifornien gelehrt.

    b Die Ansprüche von den Menschen an sich selber sind manchmal sehr hoch.

    c Die Unternehmungen von unserem Verein machen uns viel Spaß.

    d Geschäftsreisen sind ein angenehmer Aspekt von ihrem Beruf.

    e Das kulturelle Angebot von München ist wirklich aufregend.

    f Baden-Baden ist der bekannteste Kurort von Deutschland.

3 Wie heißt es richtig? Setzen Sie die richtige Verbform ein.

Beispiel: Hier _____ ihr nicht parken. (dürfen) → *Hier dürft ihr nicht parken.*

    a _____ man hier rauchen? (dürfen)

    b _____ ihr mir sagen, was das kostet? (können)

    c Was? Er _____ nicht schwimmen? (können)

    d Meine Ärztin sagt, ich _____ mehr Sport treiben. (sollen)

    e Ich _____ ja gesünder leben, aber das ist nicht so einfach. (wollen)

    f _____ du morgen mitkommen? (können)

    g Ihr _____ mitkommen, wenn ihr _____, aber ihr _____ nicht. (können/wollen/müssen)

Conversation 2

SUSANNE HÄLT SICH FIT

Susanne tut viel für ihre Gesundheit. Sie ist sehr sportlich und Mitglied in einem Schwimmclub.

1 06.04 **Hören Sie, was sie erzählt und beantworten Sie die Fragen.**

    a How old was Susanne when she started swimming?

    b Why does she never get bored with swimming?

    c What does she believe a swimming regime is good for?

betreiben	*to pursue (hobbies, etc.)*
der Schwimmunterricht (-e)	*swimming lessons*
je nach	*depending on*
der Wettkampf (-¨e)	*competition*
ausgepumpt	*exhausted*
an etwas gewöhnt sein	*to be used to something*
der Kreislauf*	*(here) circulatory system*
etwas in Schwung bringen	*to get something going*
das Gelenk (-e)	*joint*
belasten	*to strain*

(*) This aspect of health is mentioned much more frequently in German than in English. A common diagnosis by German doctors is **Kreislaufstörungen** (lit.) *circulatory disturbances.*

Martina	Sag mal, Susanne, wie lange betreibst du denn dieses Hobby schon?
Susanne	Also, meine Eltern haben mich schon mit fünf Jahren zum Schwimmunterricht geschickt, so dass ich natürlich in der Schule eine der Besten im Schwimmunterricht war. Meine Lehrerin hat mir dann geraten, in einen Schwimmclub einzutreten.
Martina	Und seit wann schwimmst du für diesen Club?
Susanna	Seit zehn Jahren schon.
Martina	Wie oft trainierst du denn da pro Woche?
Susanne	Am Anfang trainiert man zweimal pro Woche eineinhalb Stunden. Dann, je nach Alter und Leistung, steigert sich das Trainingsprogramm: dreimal, viermal, fünfmal pro Woche. Und natürlich auch längere Trainingszeiten.
Martina	Ist dir das denn niemals langweilig geworden?
Susanne	Überhaupt nicht. Erstens trainiert man ja mit den anderen Schwimmern zusammen und hat somit viel Spaß, und zweitens kommen dann auch die verschiedenen Wettkämpfe dazu. Da weiß man, wofür man trainiert hat. Auch wenn man nicht immer gewinnt.
Martina	Bist du denn da nicht oftmals ziemlich ausgepumpt?
Susanne	Eigentlich nicht. Das Trainingsprogramm steigert sich ja langsam, so dass ich jetzt daran gewöhnt bin, fünfmal pro Woche zu trainieren. Außerdem ist Schwimmen natürlich auch eine gute Methode, sich gesundheitlich fit zu halten. Es bringt den Kreislauf in Schwung und ist der Sport, der die Gelenke am wenigsten belastet und dabei alle Muskeln des Körpers trainiert.

2 Beantworten Sie die Fragen.

a Wer hat Susanne geraten, in einen Schwimmclub einzutreten?
b Wie lange schwimmt sie schon für ihren Club?
c Wie viele Stunden hat sie am Anfang trainiert?
d Trainieren die Schwimmer alleine?
e Wie oft trainiert sie im Moment?
f Wozu ist Schwimmen eine gute Methode?
g Warum ist Schwimmen gut für die Muskeln?

3 Was gehört zusammen? Form compound nouns by joining the words from the two columns. Make sure you know what all the words mean. The articles below may help you choose the appropriate second part of the noun.

Beispiel: a *der Schwimmclub (swimming club)*

a	der Schwimm	programm
b	der Wett	schmerzen
c	die Trainings	club
d	die Kreislauf	zeiten
e	das Trainings	störungen
f	die Rücken	versorgung
g	der Drogen	unterricht
h	die Gesundheits	missbrauch
i	der Schwimm	kampf

4 Nach Meinung von Susanne, was sind die wichtigsten Vorteile, wenn man Schwimmen als Sport betreibt? Lesen Sie den Text noch einmal und ergänzen Sie.

Soziale Aspekte	Gesundheitliche Aspekte
Man trainiert *mit anderen Schwimmern zusammen.* Man hat viel ... Dann kommen noch die ... Da weiß man, ...	Es ist eine gute Methode, ... Es bringt den Kreislauf ... Beim Schwimmen belastet man ... Außerdem trainiert man alle ...

5 Meine Work-Life-Balance.

Your friend Ulla has just started a new job and feels very stressed. She would like to know how you handle pressure. Answer her questions in an email, using the vocabulary and structures covered in this unit.

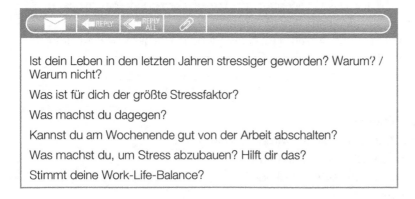

Ist dein Leben in den letzten Jahren stressiger geworden? Warum? / Warum nicht?

Was ist für dich der größte Stressfaktor?

Was machst du dagegen?

Kannst du am Wochenende gut von der Arbeit abschalten?

Was machst du, um Stress abzubauen? Hilft dir das?

Stimmt deine Work-Life-Balance?

Go further with grammar

1 MODALVERBEN *MODAL VERBS*

As you are probably aware, modal verbs in German form a group of their own and do not behave like other verbs. The five most important modal verbs are mentioned in **Language discovery 2**. There is one more that you also need to know: **mögen** *to like*.

Here are their present tense forms:

	dürfen *may*	können *can*	mögen *like (to)*
ich, er/sie/es	darf	kann	mag
du	darfst	kannst	magst
wir, Sie, sie	dürfen	können	mögen
ihr	dürft	könnt	mögt

	müssen *must*	sollen *ought (to)*	wollen *want (to)*
ich, er/sie/es	muss	soll	will
du	musst	sollst	willst
wir, Sie, sie	müssen	sollen	wollen
ihr	müsst	sollt	wollt

And here are the simple past tense forms:

	dürfen *may*	können *can*	mögen *like (to)*
ich, er/sie/es	durfte	konnte	mochte
du	durftest	konntest	mochtest
wir, Sie, sie	durften	konnten	mochten
ihr	durftet	konntet	mochtet

	müssen *must*	sollen *ought (to)*	wollen *want (to)*
ich, er/sie/es	musste	sollte	wollte
du	musstest	solltest	wolltest
wir, Sie, sie	mussten	sollten	wollten
ihr	musstet	solltet	wolltet

Note that for talking about the past, modal verbs usually take the simple past tense form; they occur very seldom in the present perfect tense. However, you do need to know the past participles of modal verbs. Fortunately, they are fairly straightforward:

gedurft	gekonnt	gemocht
gemusst	gesollt	gewollt

Modal verbs can sometimes be used on their own:

Du **kannst** sehr gut Deutsch.	*You can (speak) German very well.*
Birgit **wollte** gestern nach Berlin.	*Birgit wanted (to go) to Berlin yesterday.*
Ich hab's **gekonnt!**	*I was able (to do) it!*

But they usually need a second verb which is at the end of the sentence or clause:

Karin und Gerd **mussten** gestern Abend   *Karin and Gerd had to work at the office*
  bis 22 Uhr im Büro **arbeiten**.   *until 10 p.m. last night.*

To express *would like/should like* you use **möchten**, the subjunctive form of **mögen**:

Möchtet ihr heute Abend bei uns essen?   *Would you like to eat at our place tonight?*

Ich **möchte** im Sommer nach   *I'd like to fly to New York in the summer.*
  New York fliegen.

There is more on modal verbs and the subjunctive form in **Unit 7**.

2 DER GENITIV *THE GENITIVE CASE*

Speakers tend to use different kinds of language or 'registers' depending on the degree of formality required in a given situation. In this unit, the news programme about alcoholism is a good example of a more formal register. You can tell by the use of the genitive case:

Auf einem Kongress in Berlin hat der Präsident **der deutschen Ärztekammer** vor den Gefahren **des zunehmenden Alkoholismus** gewarnt.

Other examples of the genitive from this unit include formal ways of asking for and expressing opinions:

Sind sie **der Ansicht**, dass … ?

Ich bin ganz **Ihrer Meinung** …

Although the use of the genitive is in decline, it appears frequently in a number of expressions, such as:

Am Anfang des Filmes …   *At the beginning of the film …*
In der Mitte des Spieles …   *In the middle of the match …*
Am Ende des Monats …   *At the end of the month …*
Eines Morgens/Eines Abends … *One morning/One evening …*

The genitive is also commonly used in street names, special events and professional titles or roles:

Straße des 17. Juni   *17th June Street (in Berlin)*
der Fall der Mauer   *the fall of the (Berlin) wall*
Welttag des Buches   *World Book Day*
der Präsident des Festivals   *the festival's president*

Furthermore, genitive constructions are required after a few prepositions, including **statt** *instead of*, **trotz** *in spite of*, **während** *during* and **wegen** *due to*. For more information on prepositions, see **Unit 8**.

Remember that there are two main patterns in the genitive case: masculine and neuter forms of articles or possessives end in **-es**, while the feminine and plural end in **-er**:

(masc.) das Auto **meines** Bruders   (fem.) der Bruder **meiner** Freundin
(neuter) die Mutter **des** Kindes   (pl) das Haus **der** Eltern

There is normally an additional noun ending for masculine and neuter nouns (**-s** or **-es**).

As explained in **Language discovery 2**, instead of using the genitive, you can often use **von** + dative. The effect is then less formal.

3 MEINUNGEN – MEHR BEISPIELE *EXPRESSING OPINIONS – MORE EXAMPLES*

Agreeing

Da stimme ich mit Ihnen überein.	*I agree with you there.*
Ich teile Ihre Meinung.	*I share your opinion.*
Darüber sind wir uns einig.	*We're in agreement on that.*

Disagreeing

Da muss ich widersprechen.	*I have to disagree (with you) there.*
Hier gehen unsere Meinungen auseinander.	*On this point we beg to differ.*
Da liegst du völlig falsch!	*You're quite wrong there!*

Conceding a point before going on to put a counterargument

Das mag wohl sein, aber ...	*That may well be, but ...*
Das sehe ich schon ein, aber ...	*I do see that, but ...*
Sicher, aber ...	*Sure, but ...*

Expressing lack of opinion or indifference

Das ist mir (alles) egal.	*It's all the same to me.*
Das ist mir alles wurscht.	*I (really) couldn't care less.*
Na und?	*So what?*

? Test yourself

1 Wie heißt das auf Deutsch?

How would you say the following in German? For the questions, use the **Sie**-form.

    a What is your opinion of ... ?
    b What do you think of ... ? (Give two or three possibilities.)
    c Do you believe that ...?
    d I am of the opinion that ...
    e I agree with you.
    f I have to contradict you on that.
    g You must be joking.
    h Sure, but ...

2 Welches Modalverb passt?

Choose a suitable modal verb to complete the sentences, and pay attention to the verb tense that is required. Sometimes there may be more than one possibility.

Beispiel: Als Kind _____ Herr Petermann unbedingt Arzt werden. → *Als Kind wollte Herr Petermann unbedingt Arzt werden.*

a Früher _____ sie keine Produkte mit Weizen essen.

b Es ist die Work-Life-Balance, die stimmen _____.

c Heutzutage _____ viele Berufstätige am Wochenende nicht mehr richtig abschalten.

d Vor 20 Jahren _____ man noch in fast allen Restaurants rauchen.

e Weil er Konflikte mit den Kollegen hatte, _____ er seine Arbeit nicht mehr.

f Wegen des schlechten Wetters _____ der Marathonlauf abgesagt werden.

g Man braucht Ressourcen, die man dem Stress entgegensetzen _____.

3 Formell oder informell?

Match the pairs of sentences with a similar meaning. Then decide which of the two is less formal.

a	Das hast du zum Teil recht.	**1**	Das war's.
b	Das ist vollkommen falsch.	**2**	Ich bin erschöpft.
c	Jetzt reicht's mir aber.	**3**	Das ist Blödsinn.
d	Ich bin ausgepumpt.	**4**	Das ist genug.
e	Ich bin ziemlich gestresst.	**5**	Das stimmt.
f	Das ist mir egal.	**6**	Da ist bestimmt 'was dran.
g	Das sind wir uns einig.	**7**	Ich stehe unter Dauerdruck.
h	Das ist das Ende.	**8**	Das ist mir wurscht.

 4 06.05 Und jetzt Sie!

Anita und Jürgen talk about the health risks related to smoking and drinking. Complete the dialogue with the help of the English prompts. Note that the German word here for *cut back* is **gedrosselt**.

Jürgen	Sag mal, Anita, warum hast du denn plötzlich das Rauchen aufgegeben?
Anita	*Tell him that you were concerned about your health. Also, your husband is allergic to smoke.*
Jürgen	Stört es dich jetzt, wenn andere Leute in der Öffentlichkeit rauchen?
Anita	*You say 'yes, very much'. Tell him that you think smoking should be forbidden in public places.*
Jürgen	War es nicht schwierig, den guten Vorsatz durchzuhalten?
Anita	*You say 'yes'. Ask him whether he has cut back on his alcohol consumption.*
Jürgen	Ein wenig. Aber ich möchte es ganz aufgeben.
Anita	*Ask him if he had been concerned about the harmful effects of alcohol abuse.*
Jürgen	Ja. Das war auch der Grund, warum ich mich entschlossen habe, vollkommen aufzuhören.

SELF CHECK

I CAN. . .

- ... talk about health matters and staying fit.
- ... ask people for their opinions and express my own.
- ... recognize short forms in colloquial German.
- ... agree or disagree with others using various degrees of formality.
- ... use modal verbs.
- ... use the genitive case in set phrases and to indicate belonging.
- ... understand a health blog about what the causes of stress are.
- ... argue the pros and cons of a no-smoking policy.

7 Berlin ist eine Reise wert

In this unit you will learn how to:

▶ *make travel arrangements and polite requests.*
▶ *understand and give directions.*
▶ *talk about Berlin and its attractions.*
▶ *use prepositions with the appropriate cases.*
▶ *nuance your speech with indirect questions.*

CEFR: *Can write clear and detailed descriptions on a range of subjects, e.g. an overview of one's home town (B2); can sustain a monologue with detailed descriptions, e.g. recount a weekend in a foreign city (B2); can read in detail about complex and abstract topics, if given the chance to read several times, e.g. an online article about tourism trends in Berlin (C1).*

Conversation 1

WAS KOSTET EIN FLUG NACH BERLIN?

Silke möchte nächste Woche nach Berlin fliegen. Sie ist in einem Reisebüro und fragt, wann es Flüge gibt und was sie kosten.

 1 07.01 **Listen to the conversation in which Silke enquires about flights to Berlin. When does she want to fly and what is the problem with the return flight on Monday morning?**

Ich hätte gern gewusst …	(lit.) I would have liked to know …
sonnabends	on Saturdays (Sonnabend *is frequently used in North Germany instead of* Samstag)
nach/sehen	to have a look, to look up
dann müsste ich wissen …	then I would have to know …
die Ankunft (-ˮe)	arrival
schlimm	bad, severe
der Hin- und Rückflug (-ˮe)	return flight

Silke	Guten Tag. Ich hätte gern gewusst, ob es abends nach 18.00 Uhr Flüge nach Berlin gibt.
Frau Jahn	Sonntags bis freitags kann man um 19.20 Uhr nach Berlin Tegel fliegen. Sonnabends ist der letzte Flug um 14.20 Uhr. An welchem Tag wollen Sie denn fliegen?
Silke	Am kommenden Freitag, wenn es geht. Um wie viel Uhr kommt die Maschine in Berlin Tegel an?
Frau Jahn	Um 20.25 Uhr. Ich sehe mal auf dem Computer nach, ob noch Plätze frei sind. (Sie sieht auf dem Computer nach.) Ja, Sie haben Glück, es sind noch Plätze frei. Für wie viele Personen?
Silke	Für mich alleine. Dann müsste ich auch noch wissen, ob ich Sonntagabend oder Montag früh zurückfliegen könnte.
Frau Jahn	Also, sonntagabends startet der letzte Flug um 17.40 Uhr und montags ist der erste Flug um 6.50 Uhr – Ankunft um 8.00 Uhr.
Silke	Mmh. 8.00 Uhr am Flughafen. Dann wäre ich erst gegen 9.00 Uhr im Büro. Aber ich glaube, das wäre nicht so schlimm, wenn ich noch vorher mit meiner Chefin rede. Was kostet der Hin- und Rückflug?

2 Beantworten Sie die Fragen.
  a Um wie viel Uhr geht sonnabends der letzte Flug nach Berlin?
  b Und wann während der Woche?
  c Wann kommt die Maschine in Berlin an?
  d Wann möchte Silke zurückfliegen?
  e Was muss sie noch tun, wenn sie am Montagmorgen fliegt?

3 Wie heißt das im Text? Finden Sie für die Wörter in kursiv die Ausdrücke im Text mit den gleichen Bedeutungen.

Beispiel: am *nächsten* Freitag → *am kommenden Freitag*
  a wenn es *möglich ist*
  b *das Flugzeug*
  c *es gibt noch Plätze*
  d *geht* der letzte Flug
  e das wäre *kein Problem*
  f *Wie teuer ist ...*

Language discovery 1

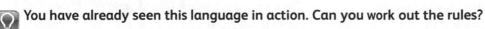

You have already seen this language in action. Can you work out the rules?

1 Look at the conversation again. Which phrases are used to make these questions more polite?
  a _____, ob es abends nach 18.00 Uhr Flüge nach Berlin gibt.
  b _____, ob ich Sonntagabend oder Montag früh zurückfliegen könnte.

2 Which of these sentences indicate that the action may or may not happen?

a Das ist nicht so schlimm.

b Dann wäre ich erst gegen 9.00 Uhr im Büro.

c Nächste Woche habe ich mehr Zeit.

d Wenn Silke mehr Zeit hätte, würde sie länger in Berlin bleiben.

1 INDIREKTE FRAGEN *INDIRECT QUESTIONS*

A polite way to ask a question in German – for instance when you make inquiries at the travel agent's – is to use an indirect question, as in the following examples:

direct: **Was kostet der Flug?**

indirect: **Können Sie mir sagen, was der Flug kostet?**

direct: **Wann kommt die Maschine an?**

indirect: **Wissen Sie, wann die Maschine ankommt?**

As you can see, an indirect clause is often preceded by an introductory question, e.g. **Können Sie mir sagen, …? Wissen Sie, …?**

Indirect questions add a soft touch and avoid the abruptness of asking question after question or having to say *please* all the time.

Direct questions which start with a verb instead of a question word (**wo**, **wann**, **was**, etc.) use **ob** when transformed into indirect questions:

direct: Gibt es einen Flug nach 19.00 Uhr?

indirect: Wissen Sie, **ob** es einen Flug nach 19.00 Uhr gibt?

Note that in indirect clauses, the verb is usually placed in last position.

To sound even more polite, it's customary to use a subjunctive form in the introductory clause:

Könnten Sie mir sagen, … ?   Ich **hätte** gern gewusst, … ?

It is also common to use the indirect structure to reply politely to a request:

Wissen Sie, wie ich zum Bahnhof komme?

Es tut mir leid, ich weiß nicht, wie Sie zum Bahnhof kommen.

2 KONJUNKTIV II (TEIL 1) *IMPERFECT SUBJUNCTIVE (PART 1)*

You might have wondered what form the verbs **wäre** and **hätte** are. They are examples of the subjunctive form called **Konjunktiv II**.

Konjunktiv II is often used for these purposes:

a hypothetical situations to indicate what might happen:

Dann **wäre** ich erst gegen   *Then I wouldn't be at the office till*
9.00 Uhr im Büro.   *about 9.00 a.m.*

b to add a degree of politeness:

Könnten Sie mir helfen?   *Could you help me?*

As you have seen, **Konjunktiv II** forms often introduce indirect questions:

Könnten Sie mir sagen, wie spät es ist?   *Could you tell me what time it is?*

Verbs that are frequently used in the subjunctive include **haben**, **sein**, **werden** and the modal verbs. You are probably already familiar with **möchten**, the subjunctive form of **mögen**.

For more details, including how to construct **Konjunktiv II**, see the **Go further with grammar** section.

 Practice 1

1 Üben Sie Konjunktiv II.

Ergänzen Sie die Sätze mit dem passenden Verb aus der Box.

> möchtet   hätte   könnten   wäre   dürften
> würde   könntest   müsstest   hätten

a Ich _____ gern zwei Eintrittskarten für das Aquarium.

b Dann _____ wir endlich mehr Zeit.

c Entschuldigung, _____ du mir deinen Pullover leihen?

d Sag mal, _____ du nicht schon längst im Bett sein?

e Frau Hakan, _____ wir Sie um einen Rat fragen?

f Wenn ihr _____, _____ wir morgen einen Ausflug machen.

g Wenn ich Sie _____, _____ ich mehr Sport treiben.

2 Können Sie es höflicher sagen?

Setzen Sie das Verb in kursiv in die Konjunktiv II-Form.

Beispiel: *Kann* ich Montag früh zurückfliegen? → *Könnte ich Montag früh zurückfliegen?*

a *Ist* es möglich, die Spätmaschine zu nehmen?

b Ich *muss* noch mal mit dem Reisebüro sprechen.

c *Hast* du Lust, mit ins Kino zu kommen?

d Wissen Sie, wie teuer es *ist*, mit dem Taxi zu fahren?

e *Darf* ich Ihr Handy benutzen?

f *Können* Sie mir sagen, wo man in Berlin gut ausgehen kann?

3 Indirekte Fragen.

You are spending a weekend in Berlin and are trying to find your way around. Re-formulate the following questions using Entschuldigung, könnten Sie mir sagen, ... or Entschuldigung, wissen Sie, ... and an indirect question.

Beispiel: Wo ist der nächste Supermarkt? → *Entschuldigung, könnten Sie mir sagen, wo der nächste Supermarkt ist?*

a Wie weit ist es bis in die Stadtmitte?

b Was kostet eine Tageskarte für die U-Bahn?

c Wie komme ich am schnellsten nach Charlottenburg?

d Gibt es hier in der Nähe eine Touristeninformation?

e Ist das hier vorne eigentlich die Gedächtniskirche?

f Wo befindet sich die nächste öffentliche Toilette?

g Wo kann man hier in der Nähe gut essen gehen?

4 Und Sie?

While on a visit in Germany you decide to go from Munich to Berlin by train. You stop by the station the day before to plan your trip. You want to find out:

▶ if there is a departure tomorrow morning at about 9 a.m.

▶ when the train arrives in Berlin.

▶ how much the trip costs.

▶ If you need to change trains on the way.

▶ if there is a **Speisewagen** (*dining car*) and whether the train has **WLAN-Zugang** (*Wi-Fi connection*).

Challenge yourself by asking questions using introductory clauses such as **Ich hätte gern gewusst, ... Und wissen Sie, ... Könnten Sie mir noch sagen, ... Dann würde ich noch gern wissen, ...**

Then, try to add more questions of your own.

Listen and understand

UND WIE KOMME ICH ZU MEINEM HOTEL?

Am Flughafen Tegel in Berlin fragt Silke an der Information, wie sie am besten zu ihrem Hotel kommt.

 1 07.02 At the information desk at Tegel Airport, Silke asks for the best way to get to her hotel. Why is it better to go by bus and where can she buy a ticket?

das Gepäck	*luggage*
Es lohnt sich (nicht).	*It's (not) worth it.*
circa	*about*
die Bushaltestelle (-n)	*bus stop*
lösen	*to buy, obtain (a ticket)*

2 Beantworten Sie die Fragen.

   a Mit welcher Buslinie soll Silke fahren?

   b Wann lohnt es sich, mit dem Taxi zu fahren?

   c Wie kann sie vom Bahnhof Zoo zu ihrem Hotel fahren?

   d Wie weit ist es?

   e Wie soll Silke von der Information zur Bushaltestelle gehen?

> **CULTURE TIP**
>
> **mit der 109** – The gender is feminine, as this is an abbreviation for **die Buslinie 109**.
> **Bahnhof Zoo** is short for **Bahnhof Zoologischer Garten**, a major intersection of the mainline railway, the **U-Bahn** and the **S-Bahn** in Berlin.

3 **Hören Sie den Dialog noch einmal und unterstreichen Sie die richtige Antwort.**

   a Silke sagt: „Ich habe/hatte/hätte eine Frage, bitte."

   b Mit dem Taxi wäre es ungefähr/mindestens/etwa das Zehnfache.

   c Es lohnt sich vielleicht/bestimmt/wahrscheinlich, mit einem Taxi zu fahren.

   d Ihr Hotel liegt in der Güntherstraße/Goethestraße/Güntzelstraße.

   e Die Bushaltestelle ist circa 50 Meter geradeaus auf der linken/rechten Seite.

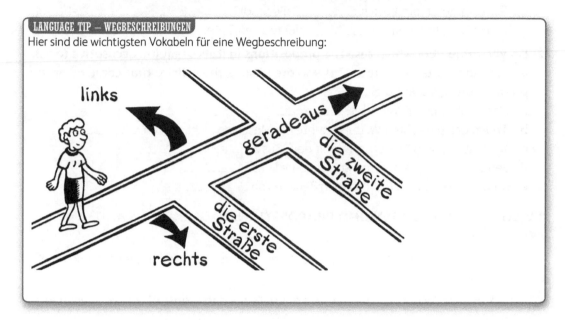

LANGUAGE TIP — WEGBESCHREIBUNGEN
Hier sind die wichtigsten Vokabeln für eine Wegbeschreibung:

4 **Was gehört zusammen?**

Form compound nouns connected with transport by joining the words from the two columns. Make sure you know what all the words mean. Remember that the articles below may help you choose the appropriate second part of the noun.

Beispiel: *h die Flugverbindung (flight connection)*

a	der Bahn	automat
b	der Taxi	ticket
c	die Bus	hafen
d	die U-Bahn	mittel
e	das Tages	haltestelle
f	die öffentlichen Verkehrs	verbindung
g	der Flug	stand
h	die Flug	station
i	der Fahrkarten	hof

Language discovery 2

You have already seen this language in action. Can you work out the rules?

1 What prepositions are needed in these sentences?

    a Ich hätte gern gewusst, ob es abends einen Flug _____ Berlin gibt.

    b _____ Flughafen fahren Sie mit der 109 bis _____ Bahnhof.

    c Wie komme ich am besten _____ die Stadt?

    d Die Haltestelle sehen Sie _____ der rechten Seite.

2 Do you remember which case the prepositions in italics require: accusative (acc.), dative (dat.) or genitive (gen.)? If you are unsure, the articles that come after the prepositions give you a clue.

    a Was zahlt man *für* das Ticket? _____

    b *Wegen* des schlechten Wetters konnte die Maschine nicht starten. _____

    c Am besten und billigsten ist es, *mit* dem Bus zu fahren. _____

    d Gehen Sie *durch* den Ausgang hier vorne links. _____

    e Er hat viel *von* dem Nachtleben in Berlin erzählt. _____

1 WEGBESCHREIBUNGEN UND PRÄPOSITIONEN *DIRECTIONS AND PREPOSITIONS*

When giving or asking for directions, prepositions are very important. Here are some points to remember:

When asking for a location or building you normally need to use **zu**, often in conjunction with **bis** *until*:

Wie komme ich **zum** Bahnhof?

Gehen Sie **bis zur** Kreuzung.

If you actually intend to go into a building or enter a location, and if you refer to an area, use **in**:

Gehen wir **ins** Kino?

Ich gehe **ins** Stadtzentrum.

Wir fahren **in die** Vorstadt.

To say on the right-/left-hand side, use **auf**:

Das Rathaus liegt **auf** der rechten Seite.

Don't forget that you use **nach** for most towns, cities and countries.

2 PRÄPOSITIONEN UND FÄLLE *PREPOSITIONS AND CASES*

You probably remember that prepositions require a certain case:

accusative: **bis, durch, für, gegen, ohne, um, entlang**

dative: **aus, bei, mit, nach, seit, von, zu, gegenüber, außer**

genitive: **(an)statt, trotz, während, wegen**

There are also a number of prepositions, the so-called **Wechselpräpositionen**, which take the accusative case when movement is implied, and the dative case when the emphasis is on location or position:

acc./dative: **an, auf, hinter, in, neben, über, unter, vor, zwischen**

Here are some examples:

Accusative (wohin?/*where to?*)	Dative (wo?/*where?*)
Gehen Sie **auf die** linke Seite.	Das Museum ist **auf der** linken Seite.
Wie komme ich **ins** Zentrum?	**Im** Zentrum kann man gut essen.
Stell dich **unter den** Baum.	Er steht **unter dem** Baum.

The verb used with the preposition can help you to determine whether to use the accusative or dative. Verbs indicating movement, such as **gehen**, **fahren**, **kommen**, **stellen**, **überqueren** require the accusative, while most other verbs including **sein**, **stehen**, **sich befinden**, **wohnen**, **essen** require the dative case.

 Practice 2

1 Akkusativ oder Dativ?

Identify (1) the preposition in the following sentences and (2) explain why the accusative or dative case is used.

Beispiel: Die Kneipe ist direkt neben dem Kino.

1 *The preposition is* neben. 2 *Because we're talking here about position (exemplified by* ist *is),* *not movement, the preposition requires the dative.*

- **a** Gehen Sie über die Kreuzung und dann immer geradeaus.
- **b** Wie komme ich am besten in die Stadt?
- **c** Die Touristeninformation befindet sich im Bahnhof.
- **d** Die Kneipe ist direkt neben der Kirche.
- **e** Stellen Sie Ihr Gepäck hier auf den Stuhl.

2 Welche Präposition passt nicht?
Decide which preposition is the odd one out.

- **a** aus, bei, mit, nach, gegen, seit
- **b** für, gegen, ohne, um, mit
- **c** an, auf, hinter, in, trotz, über
- **d** (an)statt, trotz, während, wegen, zwischen
- **e** für, seit, von, zu, gegenüber

3 Endungen nach Präpositionen.

Complete the article endings. The gender and number of the noun linked to the preposition is given in brackets (m: masculine, f: feminine, nt: neuter, pl: plural).

- **a** Du musst hier vorne durch d___ Tür gehen. (f)
- **b** Berlin bietet sehr viele Optionen für d___ Besucher. (pl)
- **c** Wegen d___ starken Sturmes war ein Großteil der Flugzeuge verspätet. (m)

d Ich war mit mein__ Hotelzimmer sehr zufrieden. (nt)

e Das neue Einkaufszentrum wurde schon vor ein__ Jahr eröffnet. (nt)

f Während d__ Ferien unternimmt er gerne Städtereisen. (pl)

g Gegenüber d__ Opernhaus gibt es ein schönes Lokal. (nt)

CULTURE TIP – BERLIN

Nach dem Fall der Mauer 1989 und der Wiedervereinigung Deutschlands 1990 wurde Berlin zur Hauptstadt der Bundesrepublik Deutschland gewählt. 1999 zog auch das deutsche Parlament, der Bundestag, wieder nach Berlin und hat seinen Sitz im alten Reichstag. Der britische Architekt Norman Foster hat dem Reichstag mit einer modernen Glaskuppel ein neues Design gegeben.

Berlin ist heute eine multikulturelle Metropole mit etwa 3,4 Millionen Einwohnern. Jährlich kommen mehr als 11 Millionen Besucher. Bekannte Sehenswürdigkeiten sind das Brandenburger Tor, der Fernsehturm, das Charlottenburger Schloss, das Holocaust-Mahnmal und die East Side Gallery, das größte offene Museum der Welt mit Überresten der Mauer.

Conversation 2

BERLIN IST EINE REISE WERT!

Frau Heine ist Touristenführerin in Berlin. In einem Radiointerview erzählt sie, wie sie nach Berlin kam, warum es ihr hier gefällt und welche Tipps sie Touristen geben würde.

 1 07.03 **Hören Sie, was sie erzählt und beantworten Sie die Fragen.**

    a Is she a 'real' Berliner?

    b What is a constant happening in the city?

    c What is available for those who simply want to go shopping?

die Eigenschaft (-en)	*characteristic, feature*
wirken	*to appear, to seem*
die Diktatur (-en)	*dictatorship*
der Krieg (-e)	*war*
die Möglichkeit (-en)	*possibility*
bieten	*to offer*
Es hängt davon ab ...	*It depends on ...*
edel	*noble*
die Szenekneipe (-n)	*trendy pub*

Journalist	Frau Heine, Sie arbeiten als Touristenführerin in Berlin. Sind Sie denn eigentlich auch eine richtige Berlinerin?
Frau Heine	Nein, ich bin in Nürnberg geboren, lebe aber schon seit über 20 Jahren in Berlin. Ich habe damals an der FU, an der Freien Universität, studiert und mir hat Berlin so gut gefallen, dass ich dann nach meinem Studium gleich hier geblieben bin.
Journalist	Was hat Ihnen denn so gut gefallen?
Frau Heine	Nun, zum einen die Berliner selber. Ich finde, die Leute haben Humor und sagen offen, was sie denken. Das ist eine Eigenschaft, die ich sehr mag. Gut, manchmal können sie auch etwas unfreundlich wirken, aber im Allgemeinen sind die Menschen humorvoll und auch tolerant.
Journalist	Hat sich denn Berlin in den Jahren stark verändert?
Frau Heine	Ja, das kann man wohl sagen. Aber das war schon immer typisch für diese Stadt. Sehen Sie, im 19. Jahrhundert war Berlin eigentlich nur ein großes Dorf. Erst nach dem 1. Weltkrieg – in den „Goldenen Zwanzigern"– wurde es zu einer wirklichen Weltstadt. Danach folgten 12 Jahre Diktatur der Nationalsozialisten. Und nach dem Krieg der Wiederaufbau, 1961 der Mauerbau und die Teilung. Seit dem Fall der Mauer 1989 ist Berlin aber wieder das wirkliche Zentrum von Deutschland.
Journalist	Was würden Sie denn einem Touristen empfehlen?
Frau Heine	Tja, es hängt davon ab, welche Interessen jemand hat. Wer sich für Kultur interessiert, für den bietet die Stadt natürlich fantastische Möglichkeiten: Museen, wie die Neue Nationalgalerie oder das Brücke-Museum, wo man expressionistische Kunst zeigt. Wer sich für Geschichte oder für Preußen interessiert, kann zum Beispiel das Deutsche Museum besuchen. Und wer nur zum Einkaufen kommt, dem bietet Berlin fast alles – von eleganten Kaufhäusern wie dem KaDeWe und edlen Boutiquen, bis zu alternativen Läden. Und die etwas jüngeren – die können nach Kreuzberg oder zum Prenzlauer Berg gehen, wo es viele Szenekneipen, Restaurants und Clubs gibt.

2 Beantworten Sie die Fragen.

a Seit wann lebt Frau Heine in Berlin?

b Was mag sie an den Berlinern?

c Wann wurde Berlin zu einer wirklichen Weltstadt?

d Was folgte nach den „Goldenen Zwanzigern"?

e Welche Kunst kann man im Brücke-Museum sehen?

f Was bietet Berlin jungen Leuten?

3 Wie heißt das? Finden Sie im Dialog die deutschen Wörter für:

a history

b village

c Prussia

d the Great War (WWI)

e expressionist art

f rebuilding

g the fall of the Wall

h shopping

tip Berlin

4 Was gehört wohin?

The following words and expressions relate to different aspects of Berlin. Put the items into the appropriate category to complete the table. Depending on your perception sometimes more than one category may be suitable.

~~3,4 Millionen Einwohner~~

ein großes Dorf im 19. Jahrhundert

Hauptstadt

das Brandenburger Tor

der Reichstag

können unfreundlich wirken

humorvoll und tolerant

das wirkliche Zentrum von Deutschland

Teilung von 1961 bis 1989

das KaDeWe

der Fernsehturm

das Holocaust-Mahnmal

der Mauerfall

multikulturelle Metropole

Berlin heute	Geschichte	Bewohner	Sehenswürdigkeiten
3,4 Millionen Einwohner			

5 Meine Stadt.

Now write a short description of your home town or a place you know well. Give some factual information; mention the most significant historical events; describe the inhabitants; and list places of interest for visitors.

Add any other information that you consider important.

For further writing models, look at **Exercise 2** in the **Test yourself** section or the text on Munich in **Unit 5**.

 Reading

1 **Read the following article about tourism in Berlin. Without looking at the vocabulary first, can you find out:**
   a the percentage increase in the number of tourists from the previous year?
   b which countries contribute the most foreign visitors (top four)?
   c the reason why Berlin is popular with British tourists, according to Mr Kieker?

Blog | Add post

Berlin – neuer Rekord bei Besucherzahlen

Die Hauptstadt meldet einen neuen Touristenrekord: Letztes Jahr kamen 11,3 Millionen Gäste nach Berlin. Die Übernachtungszahlen erreichten die 27-Millionen-Marke. Die meisten Touristen kamen aus Großbritannien.

Es werden immer mehr: Zum zehnten Mal in Folge meldet Berlin einen Rekord bei den Tourismuszahlen. Letztes Jahr wurden 11,3 Millionen Gäste in den Hotels und Herbergen der deutschen Hauptstadt gezählt – 4,4 Prozent mehr als noch im Jahr davor. Berlins oberster Tourismus-Chef, Burkhard Kieker, wirkte begeistert: „Das ist ein sensationelles Ergebnis." Im Laufe von zehn Jahren hat sich die Zahl der Übernachtungen mehr als verdoppelt.

„Berlin wirkt wie ein Magnet auf Menschen aus aller Welt", unterstrich Wirtschaftssenatorin Cornelia Yzer. Die Stadt hat sich fest unter den Top drei Reisezielen in Europa etabliert, nach London und Paris.

Mehr als die Hälfte der registrierten Berlin-Besucher kam aus Deutschland (57,1 Prozent). Knapp 43 Prozent (4,3 Millionen) reisten aus dem Ausland an. Das waren 5,1 Prozent mehr als im Jahr zuvor. Vor allem bei den Briten gilt Berlin offenbar tatsächlich als „the place to be", wie der Werbeslogan der deutschen Hauptstadt verspricht. Mit 450 600 stellten die Briten die größte ausländische Besuchergruppe, 10,9 Prozent mehr als im Vorjahr, und buchten 1 187 100 Übernachtungen (plus 18,4 Prozent). Außerordentlich beliebt war Berlin auch bei US-Amerikanern, Niederländern und Italienern.

Der Anteil an internationalen Übernachtungsgästen sei so hoch wie nie zuvor, sagte Kieker. Dennoch glaubt er, dass Berlin in diesem Bereich noch Nachholbedarf hat, vor allem bei Gästen aus dem außereuropäischen Ausland.

Doch um Ferntouristen zu gewinnen, brauche es gute Flugverbindungen, so Burkhard Kieker. Ein Grund, warum Berlin bei den Briten so beliebt ist, seien die vielen günstigen Direktflüge von Großbritannien nach Berlin.

Dass die Besucherzahlen ansonsten weiter steigen werden, bezweifelte Kieker nicht. „Im Ausland ist der Nimbus von Berlin sagenhaft", sagte er.

(Adapted from Berliner Zeitung)

	die Übernachtungszahlen (pl)	number of overnight stays
	zählen	to count
	der Werbeslogan (-s)	advertising slogan
	versprechen	to promise
	Nachholbedarf haben	to have a lot to catch up on
	außereuropäisch	non-European
	günstig	cheap, good value for money
	bezweifeln	to doubt
	der Nimbus (-se)	aura, halo
	sagenhaft	legendary, incredible

2 Richtig oder falsch? Korrigieren Sie die falschen Aussagen.

   a In den letzten 10 Jahren hat sich die Anzahl der Touristen in Berlin verdoppelt.

   b Berlin ist das Topreiseziel in Europa, vor London und Paris.

   c Es kamen mehr Touristen aus dem Ausland als aus Deutschland.

   d Die größte ausländische Besuchergruppe kam aus Großbritannien.

   e Es kamen 18,4 Prozent mehr Briten nach Berlin als im Jahr davor.

   f Kieker glaubt, dass Berlin noch viel mehr Gäste aus nicht-europäischen Ländern anlocken kann.

3 Sehenswürdigkeiten.

Here are some of Berlin's top attractions. Can you match them to their description?

a	**der Reichstag**	**1**	hat moderne Gebäude mit vielen Bars und Shops
b	**Prenzlauer Berg**	**2**	ist eines der größten Kaufhäuser in Europa
c	**das KaDeWe**	**3**	großes offenes Museum mit Resten der Mauer
d	**das Mauermuseum**	**4**	hat viele Szenekneipen
e	**das Deutsche Museum**	**5**	von hier hat man einen schönen Blick auf die Stadt
f	**das Holocost-Mahnmal**	**6**	zeigt die Teilung Berlins und die Geschichte der Mauer
g	**der Potsdamer Platz**	**7**	Sitz des Deutschen Parlaments, schöner Kuppelbau
h	**die East Side Gallery**	**8**	Gedenkstätte für die ermordete jüdische Bevölkerung
i	**der Fernsehturm**	**9**	erklärt die Geschichte Deutschlands

 4 Mein Wochenende in Berlin!

You have just returned from a weekend trip to Berlin and are keen to tell your German friend Kathrin all about it.

Pick your favourite attractions from **Exercise 3** and explain how you spent your Saturday and Sunday. Tell Kathrin how you travelled to Berlin. Then, give your impressions of the city in a detailed account. Was it crowded, easy to get around, polluted/clean, noisy/calm, were there good transport links, etc.?

Prepare your answers and then speak without interruption for three to four minutes, as if you were on the phone. (Yes, you can!)

At the end recommend at least two places Kathrin should not miss when she goes to Berlin. Use the expressions **Ich würde dir empfehlen, …** and **Du solltest auch unbedingt** …

Go further with grammar

1 INDIREKTE FRAGEN *INDIRECT QUESTIONS*

You've already seen in the **Language discovery 1** section how indirect questions can be used as a politer way of requesting information:

Könnten Sie mir sagen, wann der nächste Zug nach Berlin fährt?

Could you tell me when the next train leaves for Berlin?

You also saw that indirect questions are often used in reply to requests for information:

Es tut mir leid, aber ich weiß nicht, wann der nächste Zug nach Berlin fährt.

I'm sorry, but I don't know when the next train leaves for Berlin.

Here is a reminder of the main points:

Indirect questions are introduced either by a question word (**wann? warum? wie?**, etc.) or by **ob** *whether*. As with most subordinating clauses, the verb goes to the end of the clause. And don't forget to put a comma at the start of the indirect question.

2 KONJUNKTIV II *IMPERFECT SUBJUNCTIVE*

As mentioned in **Language discovery 1**, **Konjunktiv II** is most often used with the verbs **haben**, **sein** and **werden** and with the modal verbs.

Here are the forms for **haben**, **sein** and **werden**:

	would have	*would be*	*would*
ich, er/sie/es	hätte	wäre	würde
du	hättest	wärest	würdest
ihr	hättet	wäret	würdet
wir, Sie, sie	hätten	wären	würden

The forms for the modal verbs are as follows:

	might	*could*	*would like (to)*
ich, er/sie/es	dürfte	könnte	möchte
du	dürftest	könntest	möchtest
ihr	dürftet	könntet	möchtet
wir, Sie, sie	dürften	könnten	möchten

	would have to	*should*	*would want (to)*
ich, er/sie/es	müsste	sollte	wollte
du	müsstest	solltest	wolltest
ihr	müsstet	solltet	wolltet
wir, Sie, sie	müssten	sollten	wollten

You will recall that **Konjunktiv II** is used to say what might happen and also to add a degree of politeness:

a Dann **hätte** ich zu viel Arbeit.   *Then I'd have too much work.*

Das **wäre** nett von Ihnen.   *That would be nice of you.*

b **Dürfte** ich einen Bonbon haben?   *Might I have a sweet?*
Du **solltest** mehr Sport treiben.   *You should do more sport.*

You will soon return to **Konjunktiv II** and see how it is used in reported speech **(Unit 8)** and in conditional sentences **(Unit 9)**.

3 PRÄPOSITIONEN UND FÄLLE *PREPOSITIONS AND CASES*

It is important to know which cases prepositions require in German. Here is an overview:

Accusative	**bis**	*until*
	durch	*through*
	für	*for*
	gegen	*against, around*
	ohne	*without*
	um	*around, at*
Dative	**aus**	*from, out of*
	außer	*apart from*
	bei	*at, near*
	gegenüber	*opposite*
	mit	*with, by (for means of transport)*
	nach	*after, to*
	seit	*since, for*
	von	*from*
	zu	*to*
Accusative or dative	**an**	*at, on*
	auf	*on*
	hinter	*behind*
	in	*in, into*
	neben	*near, next to*
	über	*over, above, across*
	unter	*under, among*
	vor	*in front of, before*
	zwischen	*between*
Genitive	**(an)statt**	*despite, in spite of*
	trotz	*instead of*
	während	*during*
	wegen	*because of, due to*

❓ Test yourself

1 Was fehlt? Ergänzen Sie.

a Das Opernhaus liegt gegenüber d__ Humboldt-Universität.

b Gehen Sie über d__ Kreuzung bis z__ Goethe-Platz.

c Das Café Marina? Das liegt gleich hinter d__ Kirche.

d Z__ Museum für Deutsche Geschichte wollen Sie? Da fahren Sie am besten mit d__ U-Bahn.

e Gehen Sie hier um d__ Ecke. Da finden Sie auf d__ rechten Seite einen Supermarkt.

f Die Buchhandlung liegt zwischen d__ Bäckerei und d__ Secondhandshop.

g Wenn Sie hier durch d__ Tiergarten gehen, stehen Sie fast direkt vor d__ Reichstag.

2 07.04 Und jetzt Sie!

With the assistance of the English prompts and the map, play the role of the person giving directions.

Note that in German, street names ending in **-er** do not change their endings (**Konstanzer Straße**, **Düsseldorfer Straße**, etc.) but street names ending in **-isch** take the normal adjectival endings (e.g. Gehen Sie rechts in die **Bayerische Straße**; Wir stehen hier in der **Bayerischen Straße**).

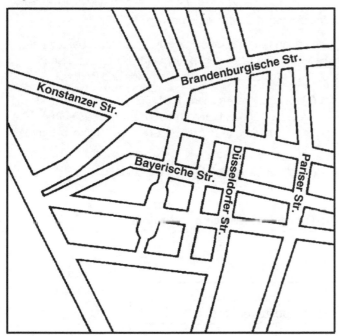

Tourist	Entschuldigen Sie, bitte. Wie komme ich zur Pariser Straße?
Sie	*Tell him that you're now in Brandenburgische Straße. Ask whether he can see the traffic lights at the next crossroads.*
Tourist	Ja, die sehe ich.
Sie	*Tell him to go right there into Düsseldorfer Straße. After about 300 metres he'll come to Konstanzer Straße. He should go over Konstanzer Straße, straight on for perhaps 300 metres till he gets to Bayerische Straße. Go left at this crossroads into Bayerische Straße.*
Tourist	Moment, bitte. Was sagten Sie? Hier rechts, dann geradeaus bis zur Düsseldorfer Straße, über die Düsseldorfer Straße und weiter geradeaus bis zur Bayerischen Straße. Dann rechts.
Sie	*Tell him, no, not right but left into Bayerische Straße. Then about one kilometre further on he'll come to Pariser Straße.*
Tourist	Vielen Dank.
Sie	*Tell him he's welcome.*

3 Berlin – früher und heute.

Hier ist eine kurze Geschichte von Berlin. Welches Wort fehlt? Setzen Sie ein.

> „Goldenen Zwanziger" Mauer Einwohnern ~~Stadt~~ Diktatur
> Nachtleben Nationalsozialisten Wiederaufbau Jahrhundert
> Magnet Weltkrieg Mauerbau Angebot Hauptstadt

Blog Add post

Berlin ist eine alte **(a)** *Stadt* und wurde 1337 gegründet. Zu einer wirklichen Weltstadt wurde Berlin aber erst nach dem Ersten **(b)** _____. Noch im 19. **(c)** _____ war es lange ein großes Dorf, bis nach 1870 die Industrialisierung in Deutschland begann.

Die Zwanzigerjahre des vorherigen Jahrhunderts werden oft als die **(d)** _____ bezeichnet. 1933 kamen die **(e)** _____ an die Macht und es folgten 12 Jahre **(f)** _____. Nach dem Ende des Zweiten Weltkrieges folgte der **(g)** _____ Deutschlands und Berlins.

Ein anderes wichtiges Ereignis war der **(h)** _____ im Jahre 1961. Für 28 Jahre war die Stadt getrennt. Seit dem Fall der **(i)** _____ 1989 ist Berlin wieder das wirkliche Zentrum von Deutschland und seit 1990 ist es auch die offizielle **(j)** _____ des wiedervereinigten Deutschlands.

Heute ist Berlin eine moderne, multikulturelle Metropole mit etwa 3,4 Millionen **(k)** _____. Es ist ein **(l)** _____ für Touristen aus dem In- und Ausland. Von einem erstklassigen kulturellem **(m)** _____ über hervorragende Einkaufsmöglichkeiten bis hin zu einem spektakulären **(n)** _____ bietet die Stadt für jeden Geschmack etwas.

SELF CHECK

	I CAN...
○	... make travel arrangements and polite requests.
○	... understand and give directions.
○	... talk about Berlin and its attractions.
○	... use prepositions with the appropriate cases.
○	... nuance my speech with indirect questions.
○	... write a detailed description of my home town.
○	... sustain a monologue about my visit to a foreign city.
○	... understand an article about tourism trends in Berlin.

8 Typisch deutsch?

In this unit you will learn how to:
▶ *discuss stereotypes and prejudices.*
▶ *make comparisons.*
▶ *report what others have said.*
▶ *recognize and use reported speech and* **Konjunktiv I.**
▶ *apply adjectival endings.*

CEFR: *Can understand complex factual texts, e.g. a magazine article about the image Germans have of themselves and the perception others have of them (C1); can synthesize and report information and arguments from a number of sources, e.g. write an opinion about national stereotypes (B2).*

Conversation 1

WIE SIND DIE DEUTSCHEN?

Darren aus Großbritannien und Martin aus Deutschland unterhalten sich über typisch deutsche Eigenschaften.

 1 08.01 **Study the vocabulary first. Then listen to the conversation in which Darren, an Englishman whose mother is German, shares his impressions of Germany with Martin from Frankfurt. Which four of these German characteristics does he mention?**

a	hard-working	**d**	tidiness
b	early risers	**e**	like celebrating Christmas
c	efficiency	**f**	punctuality

die Eigenschaft (-en)	*characteristic*
ordnungsliebend	*liking to see things neat and tidy*
fest/stellen	*to ascertain, to realize*
gepflegt	*well-kept*
übertreiben	*to exaggerate*
der Aufwand (-ˮe)	*expenditure (in time/money)*
Aufwand betreiben	*to make an effort*
der Anlass (-ˮe)	*occasion*
das Plätzchen (-)	*biscuit, cookie*

Martin	Ich habe gehört, deine Mutter ist Deutsche. Hast du denn schon früher mal in Deutschland gelebt?
Darren	Nein, ich bin zum ersten Mal hier in Deutschland. Meine Mutter hat aber meistens Deutsch mit mir gesprochen und mir auch viel über deutsche Geschichte, Kultur und das tägliche Leben erzählt, worüber ich natürlich sehr froh bin. Aber weißt du, besonders neugierig war ich darauf, diese sogenannten typisch deutschen Eigenschaften zu entdecken.
Martin	Welche Eigenschaften meinst du denn damit?
Darren	Naja, zum Beispiel hat meine Mutter immer gesagt, dass kein Volk so fleißig sei wie die Deutschen, das würde man ja schon daran sehen, dass sie so früh morgens aufstehen.
Martin	Das glaube ich dir gern. Ja, und hat dir deine Mutter auch erzählt, dass die Deutschen so ordnungsliebend und sauber sind?
Darren	Genau! Aber da muss ich dir sagen, das habe ich auch festgestellt. Ich finde, die Häuser und Straßen in Deutschland sehen viel sauberer und gepflegter aus als in England.
Martin	Ja, manchmal habe ich das Gefühl, dass wir es ein bisschen übertreiben. Hast du denn sonst noch Unterschiede bemerkt?
Darren	Mir ist besonders aufgefallen, dass man hier in Deutschland viel mehr Aufwand betreibt, wenn es um gewisse Anlässe geht, wie zum Beispiel Weihnachten, Ostern und so weiter. Die Leute hier machen sich so viel Arbeit mit den ganzen Vorbereitungen für das Fest, wie Dekoration, Essen kochen, Kuchen und Plätzchen backen. Und auch bei Geburtstagen wird viel mehr gefeiert, und die Leute schicken sich Karten, auch wenn sie nicht zusammen feiern. Das ist in England weniger der Fall.

2 Beantworten Sie die Fragen.

   a Wie oft war Darren schon in Deutschland?

   b Was wollte er entdecken?

   c Welches Beispiel gab Darrens Mutter für den Fleiß der Deutschen?

   d Wie ist Martins Meinung über deutsche Sauberkeit?

   e Was machen viele Leute, wenn sie ein Fest vorbereiten?

3 Wie heißt das im Text? Finden Sie ein passendes Adjektiv.

Beispiel: die Leute arbeiten viel → sie sind *fleißig*

   a eine Person ist glücklich → eine Person ist _____

   b jemand macht, was im Gesetz steht → jemand ist _____

   c es gibt keinen Dreck → es ist _____

   d man kümmert sich um den Garten → der Garten sieht _____ aus

4 Darrens Eindrücke von Deutschland. Was waren Darrens wichtigste Eindrücke von Deutschland? Lesen Sie den Text noch einmal und ergänzen Sie.

   a Kein Volk ist so ... .
   b Die Deutschen stehen ... .
   c Die ... und ... sehen gepflegt und sauber aus.
   d Bei gewissen Anlässen betreibt man ... .
   e Bei Geburtstagen schicken sich Leute Karten, ...

Language discovery 1

 You have already seen this language in action. Can you work out the rules?

1 **What do you add to the adjectives to make comparisons? Read the conversation again, if necessary.**

   a Ich finde, die Häuser und Straßen in Deutschland sehen viel sauber_____ und gepflegt_____ aus als in England.
   b Das ist in England wenig_____ der Fall.

2 **Look at these sentences. What endings do adjectives take when they follow a definite article in the nominative case (der, die, das)?**

   a Deutschland ist der bevölkerungsreichste Staat in der EU.
   b Die größte Stadt in Deutschland ist Berlin.
   c Das deutsche Parlament hat seinen Sitz ebenfalls in Berlin.
   d Die höchsten Berge Deutschlands befinden sich in den Alpen.

1 DER KOMPARATIV *THE COMPARATIVE*

Remember that the comparative in German is formed by adding **-er** to the adjective:
klein – Die Schweiz ist viel **kleiner** als Österreich.
hektisch – Das Leben in der Stadt ist **hektischer** als auf dem Land.

Many adjectives with only one syllable also need an umlaut in the comparative:
kalt → kält**er**, **dumm** → dümm**er**, **groß** → grö**ßer**

A few adjectives and adverbs are irregular:
gut → **besser**, **hoch** → **höher**, **gern** → **lieber**, **viel** → **mehr**

Another way of comparing is to use the expressions:

ähnlich ... wie ...	*similar ... to ...*
genauso ... wie ...	*just as ... as ...*
nicht so ... wie...	*not as ... as ...*
viel mehr ... (als ...)	*much more ... (than ...)*

Ist vieles in Deutschland nicht **ähnlich wie** in Großbritannien?

Das Wetter ist heute **genauso** schlecht **wie** gestern.

Berlin ist **nicht so** hektisch **wie** London.

Man betreibt hier **viel mehr** Aufwand **als** ich dachte.

Note that adjectives in the comparative or superlative follow the same pattern of endings as other adjectives when preceding a noun.

2 ADJEKTIVENDUNGEN (I) – NACH DEM BESTIMMTEN ARTIKEL *ADJECTIVAL ENDINGS (I) – AFTER THE DEFINITE ARTICLE*

Adjectival endings are often seen as a difficult area in German. The problem is that they might occur in four different ways in one sentence, each time needing slightly different endings. Note the four different categories:

a The adjective is not preceded by an article or possessive:
Trinkst du gern **deutsches** Bier?

b The adjective follows an indefinite article or a possessive:
Sie führt ein **interessantes** Leben.

c The adjective is preceded by a definite article:
Der **neue** Minister kommt aus Köln.

d The adjective stands on its own:
Die Leute sind sehr **freundlich**.

The last example is the easiest one, as no ending is needed. In the other three instances you have to consider the gender, case and which article is used – if any. But it is not as complicated as you might think, as the endings are quite often the same across categories and cases. With practice, you will eventually get a feel for what is correct.

Here you can see how the endings for the **definite articles** go:

	masculine	feminine	neuter	plural
nom.	der nett**e** Mann	die nett**e** Frau	das nett**e** Kind	die nett**en** Leute
acc.	den nett**en** Mann	die nett**e** Frau	das nett**e** Kind	die nett**en** Leute
dat.	dem nett**en** Mann(e)	der nett**en** Frau	dem nett**en** Kind	den nett**en** Leuten
gen.	des nett**en** Mannes	der nett**en** Frau	des nett**en** Kindes	der nett**en** Leute

Note that there are only two endings after the definite article, **-e** or **-en**:

▸ **-e** is used for all singular forms in the nominative and accusative case, with the exception of masculine nouns in the accusative.

▸ **-en** is used for all plural forms, all endings in the dative and genitive case, and for the masculine accusative forms.

For details on adjective endings with the indefinite article, see **Language discovery 2**.
For endings without articles, see the **Go further with grammar** section.

Practice 1

1 Adjektivendungen. Ergänzen Sie die Adjektivendungen nach dem bestimmten Artikel (-e oder -en).

   a Die deutsch_____ Wirtschaft kann nicht alle Akademiker beschäftigen.

   b Reisen ist einer der attraktivst_____ Aspekte bei meiner Arbeit.

   c Ich bin gern auf dem Laufenden, was die neuest_____ Filme angeht.

   d Das Theater finden Sie auf der link_____ Seite.

   e Als Radfahrer muss man die ganz_____ Abgase von den viel_____ Autos einatmen.

   f Berlin ist wieder das wirklich_____ Zentrum von Deutschland.

   g Für die jünger_____ Leute gibt es am Prenzlauer Berg oder in Berlin-Mitte viele Szenekneipen.

2 Als oder wie? Finden Sie das fehlende Wort.

   a Er macht alles genauso _____ sie.

   b Das kostet viel mehr _____ noch vor einem Jahr.

   c Das Bild sieht so ähnlich aus _____ ein Picasso.

   d Die Amerikaner sind nicht so _____ ich sie mir immer vorgestellt hatte.

   e Flächenmäßig ist Frankreich größer _____ Deutschland.

3 Stereotype.

Stereotype gibt es nicht nur zwischen verschiedenen Nationen, sondern auch in einem Land. Die folgenden Beispiele stammen aus Deutschland. Setzen Sie die Adjektive in den Komparativ.

Beispiel: Die Schwaben sind vielleicht *fleißiger* als die anderen Süddeutschen. (fleißig)

   a Leute aus Bayern gelten als _____ als die Norddeutschen, aber auch als _____. (gastfreundlich)/(konservativ)

   b Menschen aus Hamburg gelten als _____ als Ostdeutsche, sind vielleicht aber auch _____ kontaktfreudig. (tolerant)/(wenig)

   c Leute aus Ostdeutschland sind vielleicht _____ als Leute aus Berlin, aber vielleicht auch _____. (herzlich)/(intolerant)

   d Berliner sind vielleicht _____ als die Sachsen, aber gelten auch als _____. (weltoffen)/(arrogant)

   e Menschen aus Sachsen sind vielleicht _____ als Schwaben, aber die Schwaben gelten als _____. (humorvoll)/(sparsam)

> **LANGUAGE TIP**
> **Gelten als** bedeutet auf Englisch *to be regarded as/to be considered to be*:
> **Australier gelten als offen und unkompliziert.**   *Australians are considered to be open-minded and uncomplicated.*

4 Und in Ihrem Land?

Your German friend Lars is curious about the regional stereotypes in your country.

Tell him which region you come from and how the local people are perceived in the rest of the country. Say whether you think that's true or not.

Then talk about any of the stereotypes that relate to the people from other regions. Give your opinion on this.

Prepare your answers and then speak without interruption for three minutes. Use **gelten als** and the comparative form as often as you can.

Listen and understand

AUSBILDUNG IN DEUTSCHLAND UND GROSSBRITANNIEN – EIN VERGLEICH

Darren und Martin unterhalten sich weiter über Deutschland und Großbritannien. Diesmal geht es um das Ausbildungssystem in beiden Ländern.

 1 08.02 **In this part of their conversation, Darren and Martin compare aspects of the education system in both countries.**

    a What cliché does Darren think is true to a certain degree?

    b What does he say about foreign language learning?

    c And why is Martin sceptical about the typical German characteristics?

die Gründlichkeit	*thoroughness*
erläutern	*to explain, to exemplify*
gründlich	*thorough(ly)*
nimm doch nur mal ...	*just take ...*
regeln	*to regulate, settle*
fördern	*to promote, foster, encourage*
Wert legen auf (+ acc.)	*to attach importance to*
sich erstrecken auf (+ acc.)	*to stretch to*
ein Körnchen Wahrheit	*a grain of truth*

2 **Hören Sie den Dialog noch einmal und unterstreichen Sie die richtige Antwort.**

    a Darren meint, dass Deutsche und Engländer ähnlich/unterschiedlich/sehr verschieden sind.

    b Er sagt, die Ausbildung in Deutschland ist schnell/zu lang/gründlich.

    c Leute ohne Abitur bekommen einen guten/schlechten Start im Berufsleben.

    d In Großbritannien ist es genauso/ähnlich/weniger streng geregelt.

    e Als Verkäufer macht man eine einjährige/zweijährige/dreijährige Ausbildung.

    f Die Gründlichkeit erstreckt sich nicht nur auf die Arbeit/den Arbeitsbereich/den Beruf.

    g Da ist ein Körnchen Wahrheit drin/dran/drauf.

 3 08.03 **Sagen Sie's auf Deutsch!**

Die Sätze wurden im letzten Dialog benutzt. Überprüfen Sie Ihre Antworten und Aussprache auf der Audioaufnahme.

    a Just take training in Germany, ...

    b So much emphasis is put on qualifications.

c I think that the Germans in general tackle their leisure activities much more systematically.
   d There is certainly a grain of truth in that.
   e You don't strike me as the typical German.

📖 Reading

1 Read the following article on how Germany and Germans are perceived within and outside Europe. Without looking at the vocabulary first, can you find out:
   a What three German characteristics do Europeans think of first?
   b What Germans tend to do when looking at themselves?
   c How the image of Germany has changed historically?

Das Deutschlandbild in der Welt

Wenn man die Deutschen fragt, wie sich selber sehen, sagen sie, dass sie zuverlässig und fleißig seien, aber keinen Humor haben. Doch was denken Menschen aus anderen Ländern über die Bewohner der Bundesrepublik?

Die europäischen Nachbarn halten die Deutschen vor allem für gut organisiert, akkurat und leicht pedantisch. Das ergab eine aktuelle Studie, in der 12 000 Bürger in zehn europäischen Ländern befragt wurden.

Andere Eigenschaften, die oft in den Deutschen gesehen werden, sind Zuverlässigkeit und Umgänglichkeit. Beispielsweise beschreibt jeder fünfte Niederländer die Deutschen als nette und freundliche Menschen, und immerhin ein Fünftel der Franzosen betont die Partnerschaft mit den europäischen Nachbarn. In Russland geben acht Prozent der Menschen an, dass sie die Deutschen sympathisch finden. Allerdings: Fast jeder fünfte Tscheche hält die Deutschen für arrogant und acht Prozent der Österreicher geben zu, dass sie die Deutschen nicht mögen.

Es sind aber vor allem die Deutschen selbst, die dazu tendieren, die eigenen Schwächen zu stark zu betonen und sich zu viele Sorgen zu machen: So antworteten rund sieben Prozent der Bundesbürger auf die Frage „Was ist deutsch?", dass die Deutschen pessimistisch seien und zu viel jammern. Eine Einschätzung, die in den anderen Ländern Europas so gut wie überhaupt nicht geteilt wird.

Außerhalb Europas ist das Deutschlandbild oft ganz anders: Viele Amerikaner halten Deutsche für sehr freizügig, die Chinesen denken, dass die Deutschen langsam seien, und Menschen aus Costa Rica halten sie für eine offene und sehr zugängliche Nation. Zudem hat sich das Deutschlandbild historisch verändert. Assoziationen mit Hitler und den Nazis spielen heute kaum noch eine Rolle. Selbst Israel bezeichnet Deutschland als einen guten Freund und Verbündeten.

In den letzten Jahren kann man feststellen, dass es ein größeres Interesse an Deutschland und seinen Menschen gibt. Lange Zeit galt die Bundesrepublik – selbst nach der Wiedervereinigung – international als farblos und zurückhaltend. Spätestens seit der Eurokrise müssen deutsche Politiker klare Positionen beziehen und mehr Profil zeigen. Das hat nicht nur einige Länder verärgert – für viele hat es Deutschland und die Deutschen attraktiver gemacht.

(Adapted from Focus, Deutsche Welle)

V	zuverlässig	*reliable*
	die Zuverlässigkeit (-en)	*reliability*
	akkurat	*precise, meticulous*
	die Umgänglichkeit (no pl.)	*friendliness, sociability*
	betonen	*to emphasize, to stress*
	sich Sorgen machen	*to worry*
	jammern	*to moan, to whine*
	freizügig	*liberal, permissive*
	zugänglich	*(here) approachable*
	zurückhaltend	*restrained, reserved*
	beziehen	*(here) to take up, to adopt*

2 Richtig oder falsch? Korrigieren Sie die falschen Aussagen.

   a Deutsche glauben über sich, dass sie keinen Humor haben.

   b Die Mehrheit der Niederländer beschreibt die Deutschen als nette und freundliche Menschen.

   c Acht Prozent der Österreicher finden die Deutschen sympathisch.

   d Sieben Prozent der Bundesbürger sagen, dass die Deutschen sich zu sehr beklagen.

   e Deutschland wird immer noch viel mit dem Nationalsozialismus in Verbindung gebracht.

   f Das Interesse an Deutschland hat in den letzten Jahren abgenommen.

3 Gegenteile. Finden Sie das Adjektiv mit der gegenteiligen Bedeutung.

a	zuverlässig	**1**	faul
b	introvertiert	**2**	oberflächlich
c	fleißig	**3**	schmutzig
d	verschlossen	**4**	humorvoll
e	gründlich	**5**	progressiv
f	humorlos	**6**	unzuverlässig
g	sauber	**7**	verschwenderisch
h	konservativ	**8**	extrovertiert
i	sparsam	**9**	offen

4 Wer sagt was über die Deutschen?

Lesen Sie den Text noch einmal und finden Sie heraus, wer das Folgende sagt.

> Niederländer   Franzosen   Tschechen   Amerikaner
> Chinesen   Österreicher   Costa Ricaner

   a Amerikaner → Deutsche sind freizügig.

   b _____ → Deutsche sind langsam.

   c _____ → Deutsche sind offen und zugänglich.

   d _____ → mögen die Deutschen nicht.

   e _____ → betonen gute Partnerschaft.

   f _____ → Deutsche sind nett und freundlich.

   g _____ → Deutsche sind arrogant.

Language discovery 2

You have already seen this language in action. Can you work out the rules?

1 **In these examples of reported speech, what word is missing to complete the sentences?**

   a Die Deutschen sagen über sich, dass sie zuverlässig _____.

   b Die Chinesen denken, dass die Deutschen langsam _____.

2 **Can you supply the missing endings for these adjectives which follow an indefinite article in the accusative case? Compared to the endings for adjectives linked to a definite article (Language discovery 1): are they the same?**

   a Israel bezeichnet Deutschland als einen gut_____ Freund.

   b Sie halten sie für eine offen_____ und sehr zugänglich_____ Nation.

   c Es gibt ein größer_____ Interesse an Deutschland.

1 INDIREKTE REDE UND KONJUNKTIV I *REPORTED SPEECH AND PRESENT SUBJUNCTIVE*

If you want to report what someone said – for example, if Darren's mother said, 'No nation is as hard-working as the Germans.' – you use what is called reported speech: *She said that no nation is as hard-working as the Germans.*

German often uses a specific form of the verb for this purpose:

Sie hat immer gesagt, dass kein Volk so fleißig **sei** wie die Deutschen.	*She has always said that no nation is as hard-working as the Germans.*
Er meinte, er **komme** morgen.	*He said he would come tomorrow.*

This is a subjunctive form of the verb and is called **Konjunktiv I**. You form it by adding the appropriate endings to the stem of a verb, whether the verb is regular or irregular:

ich komm**e**	wir komm**en**
du komm**est**	ihr komm**et**
Sie komm**en**	Sie komm**en**
er/sie/es komm**e**	sie komm**en**

The only exception is the verb **sein**:

ich sei	**wir seien**
du seist	**ihr seiet**
er/sie/es sei	**Sie/sie seien**

If you use **dass** in reported speech, remember that the verb needs to go to the end:
Er meinte, dass er morgen **komme**.

For more information, see the **Go further with grammar** section in this unit.

2 ADJEKTIVENDUNGEN (II) – NACH DEM UNBESTIMMTEN ARTIKEL *ADJECTIVAL ENDINGS (II) – AFTER THE INDEFINITE ARTICLE*

Here you can see how the endings for the indefinite articles, the possessives (**mein**, **dein**, etc.) and the negative **kein**, go:

	masculine	feminine	neuter	plural
nom.	ein alt**er** Mann	eine alt**e** Stadt	ein schön**es** Land	meine schön**en** Bücher
acc.	einen alt**en** Mann	eine alt**e** Stadt	ein schön**es** Land	meine schön**en** Bücher
dat.	einem alt**en** Mann	einer alt**en** Stadt	einem schön**en** Land	meinen schön**en** Bücher**n**
gen.	eines alt**en** Mannes	einer alt**en** Stadt	eines schön**en** Landes	meiner schön**en** Bücher

Please note:

▶ in the genitive and dative case all singular and plural endings take **-en**, as does the singular masculine accusative

▶ all other singular endings take the ending associated with the (absent) definite article:

der Film → Oh, das war ein besonder**er** Film.

die Person → Sie ist eine weltoffen**e** Person.

das Buch → Das ist ein interessant**es** Buch.

Practice 2

1 Herbert Grönemeyer über sein Leben in London.

Hier ist ein kurzer Bericht über ein Interview mit Herbert Grönemeyer. Es gibt sechs Verben im Konjunktiv I. Können Sie sie finden?

In einem Interview sagte Herbert Grönemeyer, dass er sehr gerne in London lebe. Besonders gefalle ihm die Anonymität, die er hier haben würde. Daneben genieße er die Kreativität der Musikszene in London. Er habe manchmal Probleme mit dem Chaos, das es oft in London gebe und mit einer gewissen Unhöflichkeit. Aber London sei trotzdem zu einer zweiten Heimat geworden.

2 Was haben die Personen gesagt?

Setzen Sie die folgenden Sätze in die indirekte Rede und benutzen Sie dass + Konjunktiv I. Alle Formen von sein finden Sie in der Tabelle oben.

Beispiel: Frau Knoob findet: „Hamburg ist eine wirklich tolle Stadt." → *Frau Knoob findet, dass Hamburg eine wirklich tolle Stadt sei.*

    a Iain meint: „Die Schotten sind wirklich gastfreundlich. "

    b Kathrin sagt: „New York ist zu hektisch."

    c Clara und Jan erklärten: „Die Restaurants in Berlin sind wirklich gut."

    d Maike fügte hinzu: „Die Musikszene in Berlin ist nach London die beste in Europa."

3 Adjektivendungen. Ergänzen Sie die richtigen Adjektivendungen nach dem unbestimmten Artikel oder den Possessivpronomen (mein, dein, etc.)

    a Für mich ist es ein sehr interessant___, aber auch schwierig___ Buch.

    b Die Stadt ist durch ihren alt___ Dom und ihre neu___ Hightech-Industrie weltbekannt.

    c Was? Er ist wirklich ohne sein neu___ Smartphone in die Stadt gegangen?

d Von ihrer englisch___ Ausstauschschülerin hat sie lange nichts mehr gehört.

e Sie warf einen kritisch___ Blick auf die Leute.

f Er bekommt dort sicherlich eine sehr gründlich___ Ausbildung.

g Einen stark___ Kaffee und einen grün___ Tee, bitte.

h Für mich ein groß___, kalt___ Bier!

Conversation 2

VORURTEILE – UND DIE REALITÄT

Helga war im Urlaub in Großbritannien. Sie erzählt über die Klischees, die Deutsche gegenüber den Engländern haben und was sie wirklich erlebt hat.

1 08.04 **Hören Sie, was sie erzählt und beantworten Sie die Fragen.**

a What places did Helga visit?

b What did she think of English people before she travelled?

c Where did her view of the English come from?

die Landschaft (-en)	scenery, landscape
was ... anbelangt	as far as ... is concerned
verregnet	rainy, rain-swept
auf/schnappen	to pick up
das Vorurteil (-e)	prejudice
der Badeurlaub (-e)	seaside holiday

Karin	Und wie hat es dir in England gefallen?
Helga	Also, ich muss dir sagen, es war einfach super. Ich war erst eine Woche in London und bin dann für eine Woche nach Cornwall gefahren. London ist natürlich eine tolle Stadt und in Cornwall ist die Landschaft einfach fantastisch. Ich werde auf jeden Fall in meinem nächsten Urlaub wieder nach England fahren!
Karin	Ach, ich kann mich aber erinnern, dass du zu Anfang recht kritisch warst, was England und die Engländer anbelangt. Erst hast du doch gemeint, dass England ein so kaltes und verregnetes Land sei, und dass man dort nichts außer Steak and Kidney Pie und Fish and Chips zu essen bekäme. Und von den Engländern hast du gesagt, sie seien so kühl und reserviert, dass man nie mit ihnen in Kontakt käme, erst recht nicht, wenn man ihre Art von Humor nicht versteht!
Helga	Naja, das waren halt so die typischen Vorurteile, die man irgendwann mal aufgeschnappt hat. Ehrlich gesagt, ich habe so viele nette Leute kennen gelernt, mit denen ich mich großartig verstanden habe. Ein paar mal war ich zum Essen eingeladen und es war ausgezeichnet. Was das Wetter anbelangt, so ist es eigentlich fast so wie in Deutschland – natürlich kann man nicht gerade einen Badeurlaub dort verbringen ...
Karin	Und hast du auch irgendwelche Vorurteile gegenüber den Deutschen bemerkt?
Helga	Im Großen und Ganzen nicht.

2 Beantworten Sie die Fragen.

   a Wie war ihr Eindruck von London?

   b Was hat Helga in Cornwall gefallen?

   c Was dachte sie über das Wetter in England?

   d Wie fand sie die Leute?

   e Hat sie Vorurteile gegenüber Deutschen bemerkt?

   f Wohin will sie in ihrem nächsten Urlaub fahren?

3 Indirekte Rede. Welches Wort fehlt? Setzen Sie das fehlende Wort ein.

> käme   sei   bekäme   seien

   a Erst hast du gemeint, dass England ein so kaltes und verregnetes Land _____ und dass man dort nichts außer Steak and Kidney Pie und Fish and Chips zu essen

   _____ .

   b Und von den Engländern hast du gesagt, sie _____ so kühl und reserviert und dass man nie mit ihnen in Kontakt _____ .

> **LANGUAGE TIP**
>
> Haben Sie gemerkt: **sein** und **seien** sind **Konjunktiv-I**-Formen und **bekäme** und **käme** stehen im **Konjunktiv II**. Bei indirekter Rede benutzt man oft beide Konjunktiv-Formen im Deutschen. Mehr in **Go further with grammar**.

4 Vorher, nachher. Wie war Helgas Bild von England vor ihrer Reise und wie hat es sich verändert? Ergänzen Sie und fassen Sie die wichtigsten Punkte zusammen.

Vor ihrer Reise:	Nach ihrer Reise:
Wetter	**Wetter**
Sie meinte, dass England *ein kaltes und verregnetes Land sei.*	Es ist fast so … Man kann nicht …
Essen	**Essen**
Helga meinte, man könne in England …	Sie war ein paar mal …
Leute	**Leute**
Helga dachte, dass die Engländer …	Sie hat viele nette Leute kennen gelernt, mit denen …

 5 Das Deutschlandbild in meinem Land.

In the article *Das Deutschlandbild in der Welt*, you read that the typical German self-view is that 'we are reliable and hard-working, but we have no sense of humour'. Does this reflect your impressions of the Germans you've met? How has the image of Germans and Germany evolved since you were a child? Why do you think that is?

Write an email response to the magazine editor, Tina Götze, stating your views. Use these prompts to help you.

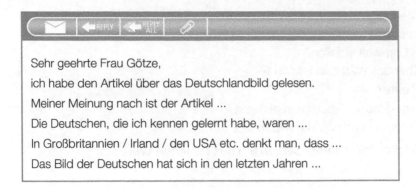

Sehr geehrte Frau Götze,

ich habe den Artikel über das Deutschlandbild gelesen.

Meiner Meinung nach ist der Artikel ...

Die Deutschen, die ich kennen gelernt habe, waren ...

In Großbritannien / Irland / den USA etc. denkt man, dass ...

Das Bild der Deutschen hat sich in den letzten Jahren ...

Go further with grammar

1 ADJEKTIVENDUNGEN *ADJECTIVAL ENDINGS*

As mentioned in **Language discovery 1** there are four categories of adjectival endings. You already know that adjectives standing on their own don't need any endings and you have practised adjectival endings after the definite article and the indefinite article.

Here is the remaining category:

Adjektivendungen (III) – Adjective not preceded by an article or a possessive

	masculine	feminine	neuter	plural
nom.	deutsch**er** Wein	englisch**e** Musik	kalt**es** Wetter	gut**e** Ideen
acc.	deutsch**en** Wein	englisch**e** Musik	kalt**es** Wetter	gut**e** Ideen
dat.	deutsch**em** Wein	englisch**er** Musik	kalt**em** Wetter	gut**en** Ideen
gen.	deutsch**en** Weines	englisch**er** Musik	kalt**en** Wetters	gut**en** Ideen

Note that in this category, in the absence of an article or possessive, the adjective takes the endings associated with the definite article:

Der Wein ist gut. → Deutsch**er** Wein ist gut.

Das Wetter ist schlecht. → Seit Tagen herrscht schlecht**es** Wetter.

Bei **dem** Wetter bleibe ich zu Hause. → Bei kalt**em** Wetter bleibe ich zu Hause.

For a reminder of the endings on adjectives after the definite and indefinite article, see **Language discovery 1** and **2**.

Don't forget that adjectives in the **comparative or superlative** – when in front of a noun – follow the pattern of the three categories described:

Die Schweizer haben den höchst**en** Lebensstandard in Europa.

Humorvoller**e** Leute wirst du kaum finden.

Bayern ist ein reicher**es** Bundesland als Bremen.

Try not to feel overwhelmed by adjectival endings in German. There are certain patterns and only a few endings you need to apply. With practice you will become increasingly confident when dealing with adjectives in German.

2 INDIREKTE REDE *REPORTED SPEECH*

In **Language discovery 2** you saw that in reporting what someone said you use what is called reported speech. Here are several different examples of reported speech:

a Christiane hat gesagt, Florian Wörle **ist** mit Birgit Klarmann **verheiratet**.
b Christiane hat gesagt, **dass** Florian Wörle mit Birgit Klarmann **verheiratet ist**.
c Christiane hat gesagt, Florian Wörle **sei** mit Birgit Klarmann **verheiratet**.
d Christiane hat gesagt, **dass** Florian Wörle mit Birgit Klarmann **verheiratet sei**.

There is no difference in meaning between these four sentences, however, the use of **Konjunktiv I** is perceived as much more formal. As you can see, in two of the sentences **dass** introduces the second clause and the verb therefore goes to the end. In two cases the verb is the one you would normally expect (**ist**) and in two other cases it is **sei**, the **Konjunktiv I** form mentioned in **Language discovery 2**.

While you may not choose to use the **Konjunktiv I** forms yourself very often, you do need to be able to recognize them when they occur.

In the **Konjunktiv I** the irregular and mixed verbs do not undergo vowel changes. You just take the stem of the infinitive and add the appropriate endings as indicated below. Bear in mind that **sein** is an exception:

	spiel-en	woll-en	werd-en	hab-en	sein
ich	spiel-**e**	woll-**e**	werd-**e**	hab-**e**	sei
du	spiel-**est**	woll-**est**	werd-**est**	hab-**est**	sei(e)st
er/sie/es	spiel-**e**	woll-**e**	werd-**e**	hab-**e**	sei
wir	spiel-**en**	woll-**en**	werd-**en**	hab-**en**	seien
ihr	spiel-**et**	woll-**et**	werd-**et**	hab-**et**	seiet
sie/Sie	spiel-**en**	woll-**en**	werd-**en**	hab-**en**	seien

Note that the other form of the subjunctive, **Konjunktiv II**, can also be used in reported speech, particularly in the case of **haben** and **sein**:

Konjunktiv I   Petra hat gesagt, dass Köln sehr schön **sei**.
Konjunktiv II   Petra hat gesagt, dass Köln sehr schön **wäre**.
Konjunktiv I   Anna und Frank haben gesagt, dass sie bald Urlaub **haben**.
Konjunktiv II   Anna und Frank haben gesagt, dass sie bald Urlaub **hätten**.

In the second example, **Konjunktiv II** would be preferred, because the **Konjunktiv I** form happens to be the same as the normal form of the verb.

You will find an overview of **Konjunktiv II** in **Unit 9**.

Test yourself

1 Helgas Eindrücke von England.

Here are some of Helga's impressions of England. Rewrite them by using reported speech and **Konjunktiv I + dass**, as in the example, to quote what she said.

Beispiel: Helga meinte: „London ist eine tolle Stadt." → *Helga meinte, dass London eine tolle Stadt sei.*

    a Helga sagte: „In Cornwall kann man sehr gut wandern."

    b Außerdem meinte sie: „Ich habe viele nette Leute kennen gelernt."

    c Sie betonte: „England ist eine sehr multikulturelle Gesellschaft."

    d Sie erklärte: „Die meisten Menschen sind sehr tolerant."

    e Helga sagte: „Ich will nächstes Jahr wieder nach England fahren."

2 Wie heißen die Endungen?

Supply the appropriate endings for adjectives which are preceded by an article or possessive:

    a Ich mag klassisch _____ und modern _____ Musik.

    b Wichtig _____ Feste feiert man mit groß _____ Aufwand.

    c Was hältst du denn von deutsch _____ Wein?

    d Von elegant _____ Boutiquen bis zu alternativ _____ Läden findet man hier alles.

    e Aufgrund von privat _____ Stress fehlt manchmal der Ausgleich.

    f Gut _____ Tag. Gut _____ Nacht. Schön _____ Feierabend.

3 Mehr Adjektivendungen.

Practise more adjectival endings.

    a Herr Smith, sind Sie ein richtig_____ Londoner?

    b Vor allem sind ihm die sauber_____ Straßen aufgefallen.

    c Wegen des schlecht_____ Wetters konnte die geplant_____ Veranstaltung nicht stattfinden.

    d Sie fand die Leute dort sehr offen_____ und gastfreundlich_____.

    e Ein stressfrei_____ Arbeitsplatz ist eine Utopie – und auch kein erstrebenswert_____ Ziel.

    f Ist das der schnellst_____ Weg?

 4 08.05 Und jetzt Sie!

Holger und Stefanie sind zwei Deutsche, die schon lange in England leben. Oftmals begegnen sie Vorurteilen oder Klischees bezüglich Deutschlands und der Deutschen. Gerade sprechen sie über ihre Erfahrungen.

Übernehmen Sie die folgende Rolle und sprechen Sie mit Hilfe der englischen Hinweise. Die Übersetzung für *They are more the exception than the rule* ist: Sie sind mehr die Ausnahme als die Regel.

Holger	Sag mal, Stefanie, fühlst du dich eigentlich mehr als Engländerin oder als Deutsche?
Stefanie	*Tell him that you have largely adapted to the English way of life, although you have made an effort not to forget your German culture and language.*
Holger	Und wirst du von den Engländern akzeptiert oder hast du auch gegen Vorurteile und Klischees anzukämpfen?
Stefanie	*Tell him that you know they exist, but that luckily you find that they are more the exception than the rule. Tell him that sometimes people ask you about the typical German characteristics such as German thoroughness, or whether the Germans really get up so early in the morning and work so hard.*
Holger	Und was antwortest du auf solche Fragen?
Stefanie	*Tell him that mostly you laugh and say that you are very skeptical as far as these typical German characteristics are concerned, and that you think that one can find them in people of other nationalities as well.*

SELF CHECK

I CAN. . .

- ... discuss stereotypes and prejudices in relation to Germany.
- ... make comparisons.
- ... report what others have said.
- ... recognize the correct forms of **Konjunktiv I** in reported speech.
- ... use adjectival endings correctly.
- ... write a personal opinion about national stereotypes.

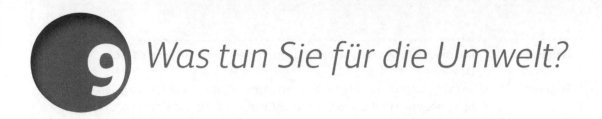

Was tun Sie für die Umwelt?

In this unit you will learn how to:
▶ *discuss environmental issues.*
▶ *talk about hypothetical situations.*
▶ *use* **Konjunktiv II** *and the conditional.*
▶ *form and use the passive.*

CEFR: *Can understand specialized articles with the help of a dictionary to check terminology, e.g. a magazine article about Germany's energy policy; can write different kinds of texts in a style appropriate for the reader, e.g. an overview of recycling practices (B2).*

Conversation 1

TUN WIR GENUG FÜR DIE UMWELT?

Zwei Abiturienten, Sascha und Ela, unterhalten sich mit ihrem Lehrer darüber, ob wir genug für die Umwelt tun und wie man Energie sparen kann.

1 09.01 **Listen to the conversation in which a teacher talks to two of his A-level students, Sascha and Ela, about the environment and how we can save energy.**

   a What would Sascha like to have more information about?
   b What alternatives to conventional energy does Ela mention?
   c How does Sascha conserve energy at home?

der Umweltschutz	*environmental protection*
das Energiesparen (no plural)	*saving of energy*
die Erforschung (-en)	*research*
die Nutzung (-en)	*usage, use*
die Energiequelle (-n)	*source of energy*
der Strom	*(here) electricity*
die Atomkraft	*atomic energy*
weg/kommen von	*to get away from*
die Biomasse (-n)	*biomass*
erneuerbar	*renewable*
die Sonnenenergie/die Solarenergie	*solar energy*
der Zähler (-)	*meter*

Lehrer	Glaubt ihr, dass Umweltschutz und Energiesparen Sache der Regierung ist, oder dass die Bürger auch etwas dafür tun müssen?
Sascha	Es langt nicht, wenn ich allein etwas tue, auch die Politiker und die Industrie müssten mehr unternehmen. Man sollte mehr Geld für die Erforschung und Nutzung alternativer Energiequellen ausgeben. Außerdem wünsche ich mir mehr Informationen, wo und an welcher Stelle ich Energie noch aktiver einsparen könnte.
Lehrer	Was könnte man denn zum Beispiel tun, um mehr Strom zu sparen?
Ela	Das mit dem Strom ist so eine Sache. Von Atomkraft sollte man auf Dauer ganz wegkommen. Biomasse könnte doch mehr genutzt werden. Erneuerbare Energien sind meiner Meinung nach langfristig sowieso viel sinnvoller. Abgesehen davon müsste die Sonnenenergie stärker genutzt werden – das wäre vielleicht auch eine ganz gute Alternative.
Lehrer	Wie spart ihr denn zu Hause Energie?
Sascha	Wenn ich aus meinem Zimmer gehe, mache ich den Computer und das Licht aus. Das Radio machen wir auch immmer aus, wenn wir es nicht mehr brauchen.
Ela	Wir haben einen speziellen Zähler an der Heizung, der uns anzeigt, wie viel Energie wir verbrauchen. Außerdem haben wir Solarzellen auf dem Dach und Energiesparlampen im Haus. Ich glaube aber, dass allgemein noch zu wenig getan wird.
Lehrer	Und was haltet ihr davon, auf das Autofahren zu verzichten, um Energie zu sparen?
Sascha	Ich finde, man kann einiges an Energie sparen, wenn man mit dem Bus fährt, anstatt jeder für sich mit dem eigenen Auto.

2 Richtig oder falsch? Korrigieren Sie die falschen Aussagen.

   a Sascha denkt, dass Politiker und Industrie genug für den Umweltschutz tun.

   b Er fordert mehr Geld für die Erforschung alternativer Energien.

   c Ela ist der Meinung, dass wir von Atomkraft nicht wegkommen werden.

   d Zuhause benutzt Elas Familie Solarzellen.

   e Sascha meint, es wäre sinnvoll, wenn Leute mehr den Bus benutzen würden.

LANGUAGE TIP – VOKABELN UND UMWELT:

Wie Sie bestimmt gemerkt haben, gibt es sehr viele neue Wörter, die mit dem Thema „Umwelt" zu tun haben. So kann man ihre Bedeutung leichter verstehen:

1 Viele Wörter sind sehr ähnlich oder identisch mit den englischen Wörtern, zum Beispiel: Solar *solar*, das Atom *atom*, die Energie *energy*.

2 Viele Wörter sind Kombinationen aus Wörtern, die Sie wahrscheinlich schon kennen, zum Beispiel: die Solarenergie, die Sonnenenergie, die Biomasse.

3 Was man für die Umwelt tun kann …

Lesen den Text noch einmal ergänzen Sie die wichtigsten Punkte von Conversation 1.

Zu Hause	Allgemein
Den Computer und das Licht ausmachen, wenn man *aus dem Zimmer geht.*	Mehr Geld für …
Das Radio …	Mehr Biomasse und Sonnenenergie …
Es gibt einen speziellen Zähler, der …	Erneuerbare Energien sind langfristig …
Auf dem Dach …	Wenn man mit dem Bus fährt, kann …

Haben Sie noch andere Ideen? Schreiben Sie sie auf.

Language discovery 1

 You have already seen this language in action. Can you work out the rules?

1 Here are two examples of the Konjunktiv II form *könnte* (from können *can*).

   a Was **könnte** man denn zum Beispiel tun, um mehr Strom zu sparen?

   b Biomasse **könnte** doch mehr genutzt werden.

Can you find in Conversation 1 more examples of this structure with müssen, sollen and sein?

2 Look at the compound nouns (two nouns strung together). What do you observe about the spelling when the first noun ends in -schaft, -tät or -ung?

Energiequelle, Landschaftsgärtner, Sonnenenergie, Universitätspark, Regenwald, Atomkraft, Heizungsanlage, Windenergie

1 KONJUNKTIV II (TEIL 2) *IMPERFECT SUBJUNCTIVE (PART 2)*

In Units 7 and 8 you learned about two situations in which the subjunctive form of a verb (e.g. **wäre**, **hätte**) is used in German: to add a tone of politeness, and in reported speech when a person is being quoted.

Another function of **Konjunktiv II** is to express ideas and situations which are not real but just imagined, often indicating wishful thinking:

Dann hätte ich mehr Zeit. *Then I would have more time.*

Man könnte mehr Energie sparen. *One could save more energy.*

As you probably expect, in addition to the verbs **haben** and **sein**, modal verbs are used frequently in the subjunctive.

The subjunctive is also used in conditional sentences to express situations in which people imagine events which are fairly hypothetical:

Wenn ich viel Geld hätte, würde ich *If I had a lot of money, I would fly*
morgen auf die Bahamas fliegen. *to the Bahamas tomorrow.*

Wenn ich Bundeskanzler wäre, *If I were Chancellor, I would*
würde ich mehr für die Umwelt tun. *do more for the environment.*

In these structures **würde** + Infinitive is normally used for all verbs (apart from **haben**, **sein** and the modals) instead of the **Konjunktiv II** form, which would sound too unnatural.

For more details, including how to form **Konjunktiv II** for regular and irregular verbs, see the **Go further with grammar** section.

2 ZUSAMMENGESETZTE NOMEN *COMPOUND NOUNS*

Compound nouns are a key feature in German. These are words that consist of two or more nouns strung together and written as one long word.

When joining nouns, an extra **-s** is normally added when the first words end in **-heit**, **-ing**, **-ion**, **-keit**, **-ling**, **-schaft**, **-tät** or **-ung**:

der Liebling + die Gruppe → die Lieblings**s**gruppe

die Mannschaft + der Sport → der Mannschaft**s**sport

die Gesundheit + das System → das Gesundheit**s**system

Remember that the noun that comes at the end determines the gender.

Practice 1

1 Was gehört zusammen?

Form compound nouns connected to environmental issues. Don't forget to put the additional -s where required and make sure you know what all the words mean. Sometimes there could be more than one possibility.

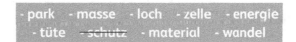

- park   - masse   - loch   - zelle   - energie
- tüte   - schutz   - material   - wandel

   a der Umwelt*schutz* (*protection of the environment*)

   b die Bio_____

   c das Ozon_____

   d die Sonnen_____

   e der Landschaft_____

   f die Solar_____

   g der Klima_____

   h die Plastik_____

   i das Verpackung_____

2 Was wäre wenn ... ?

Write down what Elena Paul would do under the following circumstances.

Beispiel: mehr Zeit hätte? (mehr im Garten arbeiten) → *Wenn Elena Paul mehr Zeit hätte, würde sie mehr im Garten arbeiten.*

   a in der Stadt ihrer Wahl leben könnte? (in Mailand)

   b im Lotto gewinnen würde? (eine Weltreise machen)

   c in der Vergangenheit leben könnte? (in der Antike oder im 19. Jahrhundert)

   d eine bekannte Person interviewen könnte? (am liebsten Angelina Jolie)

   e in einem Film mitspielen könnte? (im neuen James Bond-Film)

   f für einen Tag Bundeskanzlerin wäre? (mehr Feiertage einführen)

3 Und Sie? Was würden Sie machen, wenn …?

Now go through the questions from **Exercise 2** again, this time answering them for yourself. Try to come up with at least three sentences per question. Use the **Konjunktiv II** forms for **haben**, **sein** and the modal verbs and **würde** + infinitive for all other verbs. Make some notes, then practise the questions and answers out loud.

> Beispiel: Wenn ich mehr Zeit hätte, würde ich mehr meinen Hobbys nachgehen. Ich würde öfters ins Fitnessstudio gehen. Außerdem würde ich ein Instrument lernen. Dann könnte ich einige meiner Lieblingsstücke selber spielen.

Listen and understand

ROLAND – DER UMWELTFLEGEL

Roland, ein junger Mann, hat im Park eine Dose auf die Wiese geworfen. Eine ältere Frau, die sehr umweltbewusst ist, konfrontiert ihn.

1 09.02 Roland, a young man has just thrown away his empty drink container. He is confronted by an elderly woman. What reasons does he give for not bothering about dropping litter?

der Flegel (-)	*lout*
umweltbewusst	*environmentally conscious*
die Auffassung (-en)	*(here) attitude*
ersticken	*to suffocate*
die Müllhalde (-n)	*rubbish tip*
schwafeln	*to waffle*
die Nase voll haben	*to have had enough*
jemanden auf den Arm nehmen	*to pull someone's leg*
entsorgen	*to dispose of*
jemanden bekehren	*to convert someone*
sich täuschen	*to be wrong about something*
die Moralpredigt (-en)	*(moralizing) lecture*

2 Hören Sie den Dialog noch einmal und unterstreichen Sie die richtige Antwort.

   a Roland hat eine Coladose/Wasserdose/Bierdose auf die Wiese geworfen.

   b Außerdem hat er den Mund/den Hals/die Nase voll von all dem Recycling.

   c Die Frau antwortet, Recycling ist eine sinnvolle/wichtige/gute Sache.

   d Roland soll zum Kiosk/zum Container/Mülleimer rennen.

   e Er könnte die Dose in die Tasche/Jacke/Hose packen.

   f Roland sagt, dazu sei das Leben zu schön/amüsant/kurz.

3 Was passt zusammen? Verbinden Sie die passenden Satzteile.

a Wenn jeder so denken würde wie Sie,   **1** wie sieht das Leben für unsere Kinder aus?

b Sind Sie auch so eine,   **2** habe ich keine Zeit.

c Davon habe ich die Nase   **3** in Ruhe!

d Wenn wir jetzt nichts tun,   **4** dann würden wir bald im Müll ersticken.

e Für Ihre Moralpredigten   **5** die dauernd von Recycling schwafelt?

f Und jetzt lassen Sie mich   **6** schon lange voll.

 4 09.03 **Sagen Sie's auf Deutsch!**

Die Sätze wurden im letzten Dialog benutzt. Überprüfen Sie Ihre Antworten und Aussprache auf der Audioaufnahme.

a What business is that of yours?

b It's all too late anyway.

c Are you pulling my leg?

d All that nonsense ...

e Leave me alone now!

┌─────────────────────────────────────┐
CULTURE TIP – UMWELTSCHUTZ

In Deutschland spielt der Umweltschutz eine große Rolle. So ist es kein Zufall, dass die Partei Bündnis 90/ Die Grünen eine der größten und wichtigsten Umweltparteien der Welt ist.

Gegründet wurde die Partei 1979. Mittlerweile ist sie die drittgrößte Partei in Deutschland. Sie ist im Bundestag und im Europaparlament vertreten.

Mehr Informationen: www.gruene.de
└─────────────────────────────────────┘

 Reading

1 Read the following article about energy policy in Germany. Without looking at the vocabulary first, can you find out:

a what the government plans to do by 2022?

b what other measurable change is planned by 2050?

c what critics say about the policy?

V die Energiewende	*Germany's official energy policy; lit: energy transition*
die Öffentlichkeit (-en)	*public*
ab/schalten	*to switch off, to turn off*
vom Netz nehmen	*to decommission*
fossile Energieträger (plural)	*fossil fuels*
verzichten auf (+ acc)	*to abandon, to do without*
entfallen auf (+ acc.)	*to be allotted to, to be apportioned to*
nahezu	*nearly*
der Ausstieg (-e)	*withdrawal, pull-out*
weltführend	*world-leading*
der Aufbau (no plural)	*set-up, construction*

Deutschlands Energiewende

Die Energiewende ist zurzeit eines der wichtigsten Themen in Deutschland. Ausgelöst wurde sie zum großen Teil durch die Katastrophe in Fukushima im März 2011. Unter dem Druck der Öffentlichkeit beschloss die Regierung im Juni desselben Jahres, dass alle Kernkraftwerke in Deutschland bis zum Jahr 2022 abgeschaltet werden sollen. Bereits im Frühjahr 2011 wurden acht Atomkraftwerke endgültig vom Netz genommen.

Ein weiteres Ziel der Energiewende ist es, den Anteil erneuerbarer Energien an der Stromversorgung bis zum Jahr 2050 auf mindestens 80% zu steigern. Das bedeutet, dass man auf fossile Energieträger wie Kohle, Öl und Gas weitgehend verzichten will. Stattdessen soll der Strom aus regenerativen Quellen, vor allem aus der Wind- und Solarenergie, kommen.

Der Erfolg der Energiewende hängt stark davon ab, dass die Energieeffizienz weiter gesteigert wird. Derzeit entfallen 40 % der insgesamt verbrauchten Energie auf das Heizen von Häusern. Nach Plänen der Regierung sollen bis 2050 alle Wohnhäuser nahezu klimaneutral werden und so gut wie ohne Heizöl und Erdgas auskommen.

Es ist klar, dass die Energiewende hohe Kosten mit sich bringt. Kritiker befürchten, dass die Strompreise stark ansteigen könnten. Außerdem betonen sie, dass Deutschland zu lange von russischem Erdgas abhängig sei. Befürworter sehen eine große Chance für die deutschen Unternehmen, im Umweltbereich weltführend zu werden.

Auch andere Länder planen Veränderungen in ihrer Energiepolitik. Die Schweiz möchte einen Ausstieg aus der Atomkraft bis 2050 erreichen. Frankreich will den Anteil der Atomenergie bis 2025 auf 50 % senken und plant den Aufbau einer Windkraftindustrie. Die USA setzen weiterhin auf die Atomkraft als „saubere" Energie und planen das Fracking zur Energiegewinnung ein. Immerhin ist ein Ziel der US-Regierung die Energieeffizienz zu steigern und den Energieverbrauch bis 2020 um 15 % zu reduzieren.

(Adapted from Reset, Bundesregierung)

Die Energiewende ist Deutschlands offizielle Energiepolitik. Sie wurde von der Bundesregierung zuerst im September 2010 beschlossen und dann im Sommer 2011 erweitert und legt die Energiepolitik für die nächsten 40 Jahre fest. Für die Energiewende müssen über 8000 km lange Stromleitungen neu gebaut werden. Diese Maßnahme stößt in einigen Regionen Deutschlands auf starke Kritik.

2 Richtig oder falsch? Korrigieren Sie die falschen Aussagen.

  a Die Bundesregierung beschloss bis 2020 acht Atomkraftwerke abzuschalten.

  b 2050 sollen fossile Energien keine große Rolle mehr spielen.

  c Wohnhäuser werden aber noch viel Heizöl und Erdgas brauchen.

  d Die Energiewende kann auch positiv für deutsche Unternehmen sein.

  e Die Schweiz will bis 2050 alle Atomkraftwerke abschalten.

3 Wie heißt das im Text? Erklären Sie, was die folgenden Prozentzahlen bedeuten:

  a 80%

  b 40%

  c 50%

  d 15%

4 Sind Sie ein Umweltexperte? Ergänzen Sie.

  a Die Umweltpolitik der Bundesregierung heißt die ...

  b Fossile Energien sind zum Beispiel ...

  c Erneuerbare Energien sind ...

  d Die zwei Hauptenergiequellen der USA für die Zukunft sind ...

Language discovery 2

You have already seen this language in action. Can you work out the rules?

1 Look at these sentences showing 'active' then 'passive' constructions. What is the shift in perspective between the two sentences in each pair? How does the sentence structure change from active to passive?

  a Die Mechaniker reparieren das Auto. (active)

  b Das Auto wird repariert. (passive)

  c Die Bundesregierung schaltete bereits 2011 acht Atomkraftwerke ab. (active)

  d 2011 wurden bereits acht Atomkraftwerke abgeschaltet. (passive)

2 The following sentences show how *werden* can be used for different purposes. In which of the sentences does it: 1) refer to a future event, 2) form a passive structure, and 3) mean *to become* or *to get*?

  a Erst Mitte des 19. Jahrhunderts wurde Berlin eine wirkliche Weltstadt.

  b Sie werden am Wochenende einen Ausflug an die Ostsee machen.

  c Er wurde gestern zum Präsidenten gewählt.

1 WIE MAN DAS PASSIV BILDET *FORMING THE PASSIVE*

When talking about environmental issues or recycling you will often come across the passive. You may already be aware that the passive is usually formed with the verb **werden** + a past participle, and that it is mostly used in the present or simple past tense:

Der Müll **wird** alle zwei Wochen **abgeholt**.   *The rubbish is collected every two weeks.*

Sein altes Auto **wurde recycelt**.   *His old car was recycled.*

Here is an example of a sentence containing more than one verb in the passive voice:

In Deutschland wird jetzt alles getrennt gesammelt und dann wiederverwertet oder umweltfreundlich entsorgt.

In Germany everything is now separated before collection and then recycled or disposed of in an environmentally friendly manner.

For more information, see the **Go further with grammar** section.

2 DAS VERB WERDEN *USING WERDEN*

The verb **werden** can take on various functions in German:

a When it stands on its own it means *to become, to get*:

    Sie wurde Architektin.   *She became an architect.*

    Es wird heller.   *It's getting lighter.*

b It is used to form the future tense:

    Sie werden am Wochenende einen   *At the weekend, they will do a*

      Ausflug an die Ostsee machen.   *trip to the Baltic Sea.*

c It is used in most passive constructions:

    Er wurde gestern zum Präsidenten   *Yesterday, he was elected president.*

      gewählt.

d Its **Konjunktiv II** forms translate to the English *would*:

    Wenn ich du wäre, würde ich   *If I were you I would sleep more.*

      mehr schlafen.

Practice 2

1 Wie heißt das auf Deutsch? Übersetzen Sie die folgenden Sätze ins Deutsche.

Beispiel: I would do this differently. → *Ich würde das anders machen.*

    a It's getting dark.

    b If I were her I wouldn't smoke so much.

    c Next summer we'll fly to Greece.

    d That will cost a lot.

    e He became a politician.

    f All houses should become more energy efficient.

2 Wie heißt es richtig?

Setzen Sie die richtige Form von *werden* ein. Alle Sätze sind in der Gegenwart.

   a In Deutschland _____ jetzt etwa 80% des Altpapiers recycelt.

   b Der Müll _____ jetzt jede Woche abgeholt.

   c Zeitungen _____ heutzutage zu einem hohen Anteil aus Recyclingpapier hergestellt.

   d Was _____ mit seinem alten Auto gemacht?

   e Die neuen Elektroautos _____ jetzt in China produziert.

3 Eine kurze Geschichte von Berlin.

Bilden Sie das Passiv. Beginnen Sie die Sätze mit der Jahreszahl.

Beispiel: 1237 – Gründung von Berlin → *1237 wurde Berlin gegründet.*

   a 1871 – Wahl zur Hauptstadt des Deutschen Reiches

   b 1945 – Zerstörung

   c 1945–9 – Wiederaufbau

   d 1961 – Bau der Mauer

   e 1989 – Wiedervereinigung der Stadt

   f 2012 – Feier – 775. Stadtjubiläum

Conversation 2

ANDERE LÄNDER – ANDERE SITTEN

Frau Müller hat einen neuen Untermieter, Herrn Schmitt, der seit längerer Zeit nicht mehr in Deutschland war und daher mit dem neuen Prinzip der Müllentsorgung noch nicht vertraut ist.

1 09.04 **Frau Müller has a new tenant, Herr Schmitt, who hasn't lived in Germany for many years, and who is not familiar with the recycling procedures.**

   a Why aren't there any recycling schemes where he lives?

   b How does he react when Frau Müller shows him the different bins?

   c How should materials like paint be disposed of?

andere Länder, andere Sitten	*when in Rome, do as the Romans do (lit. other countries, other customs)*
die Müllentsorgung (-en)	*waste disposal*
die Mülltrennung (-en)	*separation of waste*
die Müllsortierung (-en)	*sorting of waste*
die Tonne (-n)	*(here) rubbish bin*
wiederverwerten	*to recycle*
entsorgen	*to dispose of*
eine schöne Stange Geld	*a small fortune*
die Sammelstelle (-n)	*collection point, recycling centre*
das kann ja heiter werden	*(ironical) that will be fun*

Frau Müller	Und mit der Müllsortierung wissen Sie ja Bescheid, Herr Schmitt, oder?
Herr Schmitt	Ich habe schon darüber gelesen – es hört sich aber komisch an. Vielleicht habe ich es ja auch falsch verstanden? Wie Sie sich vorstellen können, hat man in Südamerika andere Sorgen, als sich um den Müll zu kümmern.
Frau Müller	Ja, also hier sieht das ganz anders aus. Kommen Sie mal mit! (Führt ihn zur Garage, wo drei verschiedene Tonnen stehen.)
Herr Schmitt	Machen Sie Witze? Wozu braucht man denn drei Tonnen? Das erscheint mir aber alles sehr merkwürdig.
Frau Müller	Gar nicht! In Deutschland wird jetzt alles getrennt gesammelt und dann wiederverwertet oder umweltfreundlich entsorgt.
Herr Schmitt	Das kann ich mir aber überhaupt nicht vorstellen. Wie soll denn das funktionieren?
Frau Müller	Ganz einfach, Herr Schmitt. Die blaue Tonne hier ist für Papier. Die braune Tonne ist für Biomüll und der Sack ist für alle Verpackungen, die den Grünen Punkt aufweisen. Alles wird im Wechsel vierzehntägig abgeholt.
Herr Schmitt	Ist das denn nicht ungeheuer zeitaufwendig?
Frau Müller	Eigentlich nicht. Sie werden sich schon schnell daran gewöhnen. Auf jeden Fall kann jetzt jeder 'was für die Umwelt tun – auch Sie!
Herr Schmitt	Aber wäre es denn nicht besser, Müll erst gar nicht zu produzieren, als ihn dann hinterher zu sammeln und nicht zu wissen, wohin damit?
Frau Müller	Naja, natürlich. Aber mit diesem System ist zumindest mal ein Anfang gemacht. Und mitmachen müssen Sie auf jeden Fall – es kostet nämlich eine schöne Stange Geld, wenn man den Müll nicht sortiert!
Herr Schmitt	Und was ist denn eigentlich das da drüben?
Frau Müller	Ach ja, das sind die Container für Glas und Altbatterien. Wenn Sie außerdem Sondermüll wie Farben oder Lacke haben, müssen Sie zur Sammelstelle fahren.
Herr Schmitt	Na, das kann ja heiter werden!

2 Beantworten Sie die Fragen.

a Hat Herr Schmitt schon etwas von der Müllsortierung gewusst?

b Wie viele Tonnen hat Frau Müller in ihrer Garage stehen?

c In welche Tonne kommt das Altpapier?

d Was – sagt Frau Müller – kann jetzt jeder machen?

e Was passiert, wenn man bei der Mülltrennung nicht mitmacht?

f Wohin kommen Glas und alte Flaschen?

3 Wie heißt das? Finden Sie im Text die deutschen Wörter für:

a organic waste
b packaging
c fortnightly
d time-consuming
e hazardous waste
f used batteries

4 Welcher Müll kommt wohin? Ordnen Sie zu.

| Altpapier | Batterien | Blechdosen | Biomüll | Karottenschalen | Lacke |
| Konservendosen | Plastiktüten | Zeitungen | Farben | Glasflaschen | |

blaue Tonne	braune Tonne	gelber Sack	Container	Sammelstelle
_____	_____	_____	_____	_____
_____	_____	_____	_____	_____
	_____	_____		

5 Recycling und Müllentsorgung in meiner Stadt.

Tina, an Austrian friend of yours, is enquiring about the recycling and environmental initiatives where you live. Respond to her email and include information about:

▶ any recycling schemes in your town

▶ waste separation: what you throw away, what you recycle

▶ the frequency of rubbish collections

▶ anything you might do at home to go 'above and beyond'

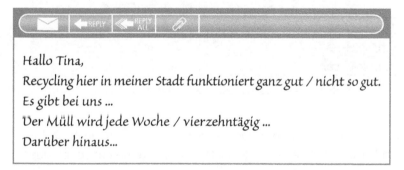

Hallo Tina,
Recycling hier in meiner Stadt funktioniert ganz gut / nicht so gut.
Es gibt bei uns ...
Der Müll wird jede Woche / vierzehntägig ...
Darüber hinaus...

Go further with grammar

1 KONJUNKTIV II – ÜBERSICHT *IMPERFECT SUBJUNCTIVE – SUMMARY*

In the last few units you have come across various situations in which the **Konjunktiv II** is used in German. Here is a short overview.

It is used:

1 to add a degree of politeness
2 in reported speech
3 to express hypothetical situations and ideas
4 in connection with **wenn** in conditional sentences

Remember that it is mostly **haben** and **sein** and the modal verbs that appear in the subjunctive. You can find a list of their forms in the **Go further with grammar** section in **Unit 7**.

For most other verbs – especially in spoken German, **würde(n)**, the **Konjunktiv II** form of **werden**, is used together with the infinitive:
Wenn ich im Lotto **gewinnen würde, ...**
Wenn du weniger **rauchen würdest, ...**
Wenn wir weniger Müll **produzieren würden, ...**

You will encounter more verbs in the subjunctive form, especially in written texts, such as news articles or novels. To help you recognize them, here are some tips on how these verbs form the **Konjunktiv II**:

Regular verbs

The **Konjunktiv II** form of regular verbs is constructed by adding the following endings to the stem:

ich spiel-**te**	wir spiel-**ten**
du spiel-**test**	ihr spiel-**tet**
Sie spiel-**ten**	Sie spiel-**ten**
er/sie spiel-**te**	sie spiel-**ten**

Irregular verbs

The **Konjunktiv II** form of most irregular verbs is formed from their past simple tense, by adding the appropriate endings, as indicated as follows. Note also that an umlaut is added whenever possible:

Infinitive Präteritum/ Simple past	fahren fuhren	kommen kamen	gehen gingen	wissen wussten
ich	führ-**e**	käm-**e**	ging-**e**	wüsst-**e**
du	führ-**est**	käm-**est**	ging-**est**	wüsst-**est**
er/sie/es	führ-**e**	käm-**e**	ging-**e**	wüsst-**e**
wir	führ-**en**	käm-**en**	ging-**en**	wüsst-**en**
ihr	führ-**et**	käm-**et**	ging-**et**	wüsst-**et**
sie/Sie	führ-**en**	käm-**en**	ging-**en**	wüsst-**en**

Here is an example of **wissen** in the subjunctive:

Ich wüsste gern, wann der   *I would like to know when*
  nächste Zug nach Berlin fährt.   *the next train goes to Berlin.*

Note also that the **Konjunktiv II** is used in some expressions like:

Wenn ich du wäre, würde ich ...   *If I were you, I would ...*
An deiner Stelle würde ich ...   *In your position, I would ...*

2 DAS PASSIV *THE PASSIVE*

One area that needs frequent revision is the passive. As you saw in **Language discovery 2**, the passive is formed with the verb **werden** in the appropriate tense together with the past participle of the main verb:

Present:	Das Essen **wird** gerade **gekocht**.	*The meal is just being cooked.*
Simple past:	Das Buch **wurde** von Heinrich Heine **geschrieben**.	*The book was written by Heinrich Heine.*
Present perfect:	Die Rechnung **ist bezahlt worden**.	*The bill has been/was paid.*
Future:	Das Gebäude **wird** bald **renoviert werden**.	*The building will soon be renovated.*

Note that in the present perfect passive the past participle of **werden** is simply **worden** and has no **ge-** prefix. The present perfect form of the passive can also be used for events that happened in the distant past:

Dieses Haus ist 1666 gebaut worden.   *This house was built in 1666.*

You may remember that in the passive, the person who carries out the action is introduced by **von**:

Dieses Stück wurde **von** Haydn komponiert.   *This piece was composed by Haydn.*

When the action is not carried out by a person, **durch** should be used:

Die Fabrik wurde **durch** ein Feuer zerstört.   *The factory was destroyed by a fire.*

To indicate the instrument or implement which with something is done, **mit** is required:

Er wurde **mit** einem Messer getötet.   *He was killed with a knife.*

Here is some more information that you might find useful when dealing with the passive.

Passive of dative verbs

Verbs which in German are followed by the dative case, such as **helfen**, **raten**, **gratulieren** and **folgen**, cannot be made passive in the usual way. It is, however, possible to produce a kind of passive if the dative object is retained:

Mir wurde von einem Freund geholfen.   *I was helped by a friend.*
Ihr wurde geraten, gesünder zu leben.   *She was advised to live more healthily.*
Ihnen wurde zu ihrer Hochzeit gratuliert.   *They were congratulated on their wedding.*

Use of man

The pronoun **man** is often used in German where a passive would be more common in English:

Hier spricht man Deutsch. *German spoken here.*

Man glaubt, dass ... *It is thought that ...*

So etwas macht man eben nicht. *That sort of thing is just not done.*

Test yourself

1 Was könnten wir noch für die Umwelt tun?

Setzen Sie die Verben in den **Konjunktiv II**.

Beispiel: Wir _____ mehr mit öffentlichen Verkehrsmitteln fahren. (sollen) → *Wir sollten mehr mit öffentlichen Verkehrsmitteln fahren.*

    a Die Industrie _____ weniger Schadstoffe produzieren. (müssen)

    b Man _____ die Häuser viel besser isolieren. (sollen)

    c Es _____ gut für die Umwelt, wenn es mehr Elektroautos _____. (sein/geben)

    d Es _____ der Umwelt helfen, wenn wir mehr recyceln _____. (werden/werden)

    e Außerdem _____ man viel Strom im Haushalt sparen. (können)

    f Auf jeden Fall _____ die Regierungen besser zusammenarbeiten. (müssen)

2 Wie heißt es richtig?

Setzen Sie die fehlenden Präpositionen ein: **durch**, **mit** oder **von**?

    a Der Brief wurde _____ der Hand geschrieben.

    b _____ wem wurde die Nachricht getextet?

    c Das Haus ist _____ den Sturm nahezu zerstört worden.

    d Der Strom hier wird _____ Windenergie erzeugt.

    e Das Auto wird _____ einem Mechaniker repariert.

    f Das Konzept ist _____ unserem Team entwickelt worden.

3 09.05 Und jetzt Sie!

John, ein britischer Student, der gerade in Deutschland angekommen ist, redet mit Volker, einem deutschen Studenten, über die Müllsortierung. Spielen Sie mit Hilfe der englischen Anregungen die Rolle von Volker.

John	Du, wie funktioniert eigentlich diese Müllsortierung?
Sie	*Tell him that there is a brown bin for organic waste, a blue one for paper, and a plastic bag for all packages which bear the 'Green Dot', and that everything gets collected fortnightly on a rota system.*
John	Funktioniert das denn?
Sie	*Tell him yes, most people do join in. If you don't join in, you pay heavy fines. Ask him if there are actually many differences between Germany and England.*
John	Oh ja, in England wird zwar auch etwas für die Umwelt getan, aber nicht so viel wie hier. Aber hat das alles denn überhaupt einen Sinn, oder ist es nicht schon zu spät für die Erde?
Sie	*Tell him that you believe recycling is a very useful measure because if nothing is done for the environment now, what will the earth be like for children of the future?*
John	Aber ist es denn nicht besser, Müll zu vermeiden, anstatt ihn hinterher zu entsorgen?
Sie	*You say yes of course, but at least it's a start.*

SELF CHECK

I CAN. . .

○	... discuss environmental issues.
○	... talk about hypothetical situations, such as what I would do if I won the lottery.
○	... use the **Konjunktiv II** and form conditional sentences.
○	... form and use the passive.
○	... write an overview of recycling practices where I live.
○	... understand a text about Germany's energy policy.

10 Deutschland heute

In this unit you will learn how to:

▶ *talk about newspapers and magazines.*
▶ *answer a quiz about Germany's political structure.*
▶ *understand facts and opinions about economic and political issues.*
▶ *form relative clauses.*
▶ *identify adjectival and weak nouns.*

CEFR: *Can read articles and reports concerned with contemporary problems, e.g. texts about Germany's political institutions and the national economy; can pass on information and give reasons to support an opinion, e.g. write a summary of national views about the European Union (B2).*

Conversation 1

ZEITUNGEN UND MAGAZINE IN DEUTSCHLAND

Matthias Hinschken arbeitet als Journalist in Hamburg. Im folgenden Interview spricht er über die wichtigsten Zeitungen und Zeitschriften in der Bundesrepublik Deutschland.

 1 10.01 **Matthias Hinschken, a journalist from Hamburg, talks about the German newspaper industry.**

    a What sort of newspapers dominate the market?
    b What does Matthias say about the *Bild* newspaper?
    c What is different about Sunday papers in Germany and Great Britain?

die tageszeitung

Mindener Tageblatt

V	ausführlich	detailed
	entsprechend	corresponding
	überregional	national, nationwide
	eher	(here) rather
	das Blatt (-¨er)	(here) paper
	das Qualitätsblatt (-¨er)	quality paper, broadsheet
	die Boulevardzeitung (-en)	tabloid
	die Redaktion (-en)	editorial staff, editorial board
	erscheinen	(here) to be published
	die Zeitschrift (-en)	magazine, journal

Der deutschsprachige Zeitungsmarkt ist einer der größten der Welt. Anders als zum Beispiel in Großbritannien dominieren Lokal- und Regionalzeitungen den Markt. Diese Zeitungen berichten ausführlich über Ereignisse in der entsprechenden Region, haben aber auch Welt- und Wirtschaftsnachrichten.

Wer sich noch weiter informieren möchte, wird dann vielleicht noch eine der überregionalen Zeitungen lesen, die man in ganz Deutschland bekommen kann: *die Süddeutsche Zeitung, die Frankfurter Rundschau, die Frankfurter Allgemeine Zeitung* oder *Die Welt*. Die letzten beiden gelten als konservativ, während die *Süddeutsche Zeitung* und die *Frankfurter Rundschau* eher linksliberal sind.

All diese Zeitungen könnte man als Qualitätsblätter bezeichnen. Daneben gibt es dann die sogenannten Boulevardzeitungen. Am bekanntesten ist dabei die *Bild*-Zeitung.

Außer Tageszeitungen gibt es auch noch Sonntags- und Wochenzeitungen. Sonntagszeitungen spielen eine weit geringere Rolle als in Großbritannien, da die meisten Redaktionen einen Ruhetag haben und viele Zeitungen sonntags nicht erscheinen.

Neben Zeitungen gibt es natürlich auch einen riesigen Zeitschriftenmarkt. Gewinner der letzten Jahre waren vor allem Computerzeitschriften, Magazine für Essen und Trinken und Zeitschriften über Motorsport. Bekannt sind aber auch Nachrichtenmagazine, wie *Focus* oder *Der Spiegel*, der schon seit 1947 auf dem Markt ist.

2 Beantworten Sie die Fragen.

a Was ist typisch für Lokal- und Regionalzeitungen?

b Welche bekannten überregionalen Zeitungen gibt es?

c Wo steht die *Frankfurter Allgemeine Zeitung* politisch?

d Was für Zeitschriften haben in den letzten Jahren viele neue Leser gewonnen?

e Seit wann gibt es das Nachrichtenmagazin *Der Spiegel*?

3 Was passt am besten?

Lesen Sie das Interview noch einmal und finden Sie ein Wort, das passt.

a Der deutschsprachige _____ ist einer der größten der Welt.

b Ein Beispiel für ein _____ ist die *Süddeutsche Zeitung*.

c Politisch ist die *Süddeutsche Zeitung* eher _____.

d Bild ist die bekannteste _____.

e Sonntags _____ viele Zeitungen nicht.

f *Focus* und *Der Spiegel* sind bekannte _____.

Language discovery 1

 You have already seen this language in action. Can you work out the rules?

1 **Look at Conversation 1 again and complete the compound words. Can you figure out what the hyphen is used for?**

   a Lokal- und _____zeitungen

   b Welt- und Wirtschafts_____

   c Sonntags- und Wochen_____

2 **Here are three examples of relative clauses (in italics). What would be the English equivalents of *der*, *dem* and *dessen*?**

   a Bekannt ist auch Der Spiegel, *der schon seit 1974 auf dem Markt ist.*

   b Da drüben ist Carsten, *dem ich 100 Euro gegeben habe.*

   c Das ist Rudi Bergmann, *dessen Frau Journalistin ist.*

1 ZUSAMMENGESETZTE WÖRTER *COMPOUND WORDS*

To avoid repetition, it's customary in spoken and written German to leave out the common part of two words when it appears twice in rapid succession. This is often the case with the final noun in compound words:

Welt**nachrichten** und Wirtschafts**nachrichten** → Welt- und Wirtschafts**nachrichten**

Sonntags**zeitungen** und Wochen**zeitungen** → Sonntags- und Wochen**zeitungen**

Winter**semester** und Sommer**semester** → Winter- und Sommer**semester**

Titel**seite** und Rück**seite** → Titel- und Rück**seite**

In writing, the part of the word which is omitted is replaced with a hyphen. Note how this feature also occurs with combinations of verbs, adverbs and adjectives:

ein**steigen** und aus**steigen** → ein- und aus**steigen**

an**machen** und aus**machen** → an- und aus**machen**

vor**wärts** und rück**wärts** → vor- und rück**wärts**

ein**mal** oder zwei**mal** → ein- oder zwei**mal**

2 RELATIVSÄTZE *RELATIVE CLAUSES*

A relative clause is a type of subordinate clause which gives more information about a specific item in the main clause:

Bekannt ist auch *Der Spiegel*, **der seit 1947 auf dem Markt ist.**

Viel gelesen wird die *Bild*, **die eine Auflage von etwa 2,9 Millionen hat.**

Die *Tagesschau* ist ein Nachrichtenprogramm, **das um 20.00 Uhr gesendet wird.**

Die Welt und *Bild* sind Zeitungen, **die auch sonntags erscheinen.**

In these examples, the second clause is subordinate. It provides more details about the subject of the main clause: for example, about *Der Spiegel*, which has been on the market since 1947 or about *Bild*, which has a circulation of about 2.9 million.

A relative clause is usually introduced by a relative pronoun (equivalent to *who(m)*, *that*, *which*, *whose*). In the nominative case – as shown in the previous examples – the pronouns are quite straightforward: **der** for masculine, **das** for neuter and **die** for feminine and plural nouns.

You probably won't be surprised to find that in a relative clause – as with most subordinate clauses – the verb goes to the end.

For more information about relative clauses, including the relative pronouns for the other cases, see the **Go further with grammar** section.

Practice 1

1 Sagen Sie es kürzer!

Leave out the common element in these sentences.

Beispiel: Ich möchte ein Ticket mit Hinfahrt und Rückfahrt, bitte. → *Ich möchte ein Ticket mit Hin- und Rückfahrt, bitte.*

    a Der Vorschlag hat viele Vorteile und Nachteile.

    b Die Universität bietet sowohl Bachelorkurse wie auch Masterkurse an.

    c Die Großschreibung und Kleinschreibung verursacht vielen Leuten Probleme.

    d Es hängt davon ab, ob ich Frühschicht oder Spätschicht habe.

    e Probier es einmal oder zweimal aus.

    f Sie müssen hier einsteigen und dort aussteigen.

2 Verbinden Sie!

a Überregionale Zeitungen sind Zeitungen, 1 die einmal pro Woche erscheinen.

b Lokalzeitungen sind Blätter, 2 die oft viel Sex and Crime haben.

c Die *Süddeutsche* ist eine Zeitung, 3 das es seit 1947 gibt.

d Wochenzeitungen sind Zeitungen, 4 die man in ganz Deutschland kaufen kann.

e Boulevardblätter sind Zeitungen, 5 die aus München kommt.

f *Der Spiegel* ist ein Nachrichtenmagazin, 6 die viel über die eigene Region berichten.

3 Formen Sie Relativsätze.

Combine these sentences using the appropriate nominative relative pronoun.

Beispiel: Das Smartphone hat ein neues Display. Es ist sehr gut designed. → *Das Smartphone hat ein neues Display, das sehr gut designed ist.*

a Die Telekom hat einen Handytarif im Angebot. Er ist sehr günstig.

b Das Sportmagazin *Kicker* hat eine neue Internetseite. Sie sieht sehr gut aus.

c Hier ist das Tablet von Timo. Es hat nur 99 Euro gekostet.

d Das ist die neue App. Sie wurde von einer Firma in Berlin entwickelt.

 4 Soziale Netzwerke und ich.

Your German friend Nadia would like to know about newspapers in your country and the way you access media. Tell her about the most well-known newspapers and provide some details about them. Then, tell her what paper(s) and/or magazine(s) you read, how much time you spend online, what your favourite social network is and why.

Jot down some notes to prepare your answers, then try to speak for a full three minutes. Remember to incorporate some relative clauses in your talk.

Listen and understand

DEUTSCHLAND-QUIZ

Was wissen Sie über Deutschland? Lesen Sie zunächst die sechs Quizfragen und entscheiden Sie dann jeweils, welche Antwort stimmt. Hören Sie sich dann die Audioaufnahme an und überprüfen Sie, ob Sie recht hatten.

1 10.02 **Answer the quiz to test your knowledge about Germany. Then listen to the radio programme and check your answers.**

Some of the details provided on the audio might of course change; for example, the number of MPs in the Bundestag varies from election to election. For up-to-date information on various aspects of Germany, see http://www.deutschland.de or http://www.bundestag.de

a Flächenmäßig ist Deutschland

   1 größer als Frankreich

   2 etwa so groß wie Frankreich

   3 deutlich kleiner als Frankreich.

b Bundesländer gibt es

   1 12

   2 14

   3 16.

c Deutschland hat eine Grenze mit

   1 8 Ländern

   2 9 Ländern

   3 10 Ländern.

d Das Parlament heißt

   1 Bundesrat

   2 Bundestag

   3 Reichstag.

e Abgeordnete gibt es

   1 498

   2 556

   3 656.

f Die meiste politische Macht hat

   1 der Bundespräsident

   2 der Bundeskanzler

   3 der Bundestagspräsident.

g Die politische Struktur ist

   1 föderalistisch

   2 zentralistisch

   3 anti-föderalistisch.

bevölkerungsreich	*densely populated*
flächenmäßig	*in area*
die Bevölkerungsdichte (-n)	*population density*
zusammengedrängt	*(here) crowded together*
verzählen	*to miscount*
einzigartig	*unique*
der/die Abgeordnete	*Member of Parliament*
benennen	*to appoint, to designate*
das Grundgesetz (-e)	*Basic Law/the German constitution*
der Grundpfeiler (-)	*cornerstone*

2 Beantworten Sie die folgenden Fragen.

   a Wie werden Hamburg, Bremen und Berlin auch genannt?

   b Welches ist das größte Bundesland?

   c Was ist besonders an der geografischen Lage von Deutschland?

   d Was für Aufgaben hat der Bundespräsident?

   e Was ist ein Grundpfeiler der politischen Struktur Deutschlands?

> **CULTURE TIP – INFORMATIONEN ÜBER ÖSTERREICH UND DIE SCHWEIZ**
>
> Auf der letzten Audioaufnahme haben Sie einige wichtige Fakten über Deutschland erfahren. Wenn Sie Ähnliches über Österreich oder die Schweiz wissen wollen, besuchen Sie bitte die folgenden Webseiten: www.austria.info/at/oesterreich-fakten/ oder www.swissworld.org/de/
>
> Dort finden Sie Informationen über die Geschichte, die Bevölkerung, das politische System, den Umweltschutz, Kunst und Kultur, sowie viele andere Themen.

3 10.03 **Sagen Sie's auf Deutsch!**

a Our first topic today is Germany.

b Now, just imagine a map of Europe ...

c As you know, Germany consists of 16 Länder.

d Altogether there are nine countries ...

e But how many members does the Bundestag actually have?

f More about this in the next week.

Reading

1 **Read the following article on the views Germans have about Europe. Without looking at the vocabulary first, can you find out:**

a What the general attitude of Germans towards Europe is?

b What they think about the Euro?

c What many young people wish for?

Deutsche glauben weiter an Europa

Während in vielen Mitgliedsstaaten das Vertrauen in die EU und ihre Institutionen schwindet, ist in Deutschland der Glaube an eine gemeinsame Zukunft auf dem europäischen Kontinent immer noch groß.

Laut einer Umfrage des US-Meinungsinstituts Pew unterstützen 60% der Bundesbürger die Übertragung von mehr Kompetenzen an Brüssel, um die aktuelle Krise zu bewältigen. Und im Vergleich zu anderen Ländern sehen die Deutschen die wirtschaftliche Entwicklung optimistischer: Immerhin glauben 27% von ihnen an einen Aufschwung in den nächsten Monaten, während nur 15% der übrigen Europäer eine Verbesserung erwartet.

Als zwei der wichtigsten Errungenschaften der EU nennen die Deutschen, dass sie innerhalb Europas ohne Grenzen reisen können und die Möglichkeit haben, in allen Mitgliedsstaaten zu arbeiten. Einen weiteren großen Vorteil sehen sie auch im Frieden, den die EU-Zusammenarbeit in Europa gebracht hat. Daneben glauben 80%, dass die EU ein Vorbild für andere Regionen der Welt sein könnte.

Auf der anderen Seite hat sich die Skepsis gegenüber dem Euro in den letzten Jahren deutlich verstärkt. Mittlerweile sind nur noch etwa 35% der Deutschen besonders stolz auf die gemeinsame europäische Währung und etwa ein Drittel glaubt, dass es ihnen persönlich besser ginge, wenn es anstelle des Euro noch die D-Mark gäbe. Besonders stark ist die Euroskepsis bei älteren Leuten sowie bei Leuten mit geringerem Einkommen. Auch meint mehr als ein Drittel, dass die EU zu bürokratisch sei und dass ihre Institutionen zu weit von den Bürgern entfernt seien.

Wenn es um die Zukunft der EU geht, wünschen sich viele Deutsche eine bessere Sozialpolitik und die Schaffung eines europäischen Mindestlohns, der in Deutschland nur unter großem Widerstand vieler Arbeitgeber eingeführt wurde. 41% wollen eine effektivere Umweltpolitik, die mehr für die Umwelt erreicht. Fast die Hälfte der 18- bis 24-Jährigen wünscht sich, dass die Berufs- und Studienabschlüsse in ganz Europa anerkannt werden. Das könnte darauf hindeuten, dass viele junge Leute im Ausland arbeiten oder studieren möchten.

(Adapted from Pew, Die Zeit)

V das Vertrauen		*(no plural) trust*
schwinden		*to shrink, to fade*
die Übertragung (-en)		*(here) transfer*
bewältigen		*(here) to overcome, to manage*
der Aufschwung (-ˋe)		*upswing, recovery*
die Errungenschaft (-en)		*achievement*
das Vorbild (-er)		*role model, example*
der Mindestlohn (-ˋe)		*minimum wage*
der Widerstand (-ˋe)		*resistance, opposition*
an/erkennen		*to recognize*

2 Wie heißt das im Text?

Finden Sie im Text die Ausdrücke, die eine ähnliche Bedeutung haben.

Beispiel: In vielen Staaten, die zur EU gehören ... → *In vielen Mitgliedsstaaten ...*

a Das Vertrauen wird weniger ...

b Als zwei der wichtigsten Erfolge ...

c Die Skepsis hat sich stark erhöht ...

d Im Moment sind nur etwa 35% vollkommen begeistert von ...

e Leute, die nicht so viel verdienen.

f ... unter großer Opposition ...

3 Richtig oder falsch? Korrigieren Sie die falschen Aussagen.

a 60% der Deutschen wollen, dass Deutschland wieder mehr Kompetenzen von Brüssel erhält.

b Die Deutschen sehen die wirtschaftliche Entwicklung optimistischer als die anderen Europäer.

c Die Möglichkeit in Europa ohne Grenzen zu reisen, sehen die Deutschen als nicht besonders wichtig an.

d Vor allem jüngere Leute sind skeptisch gegenüber dem Euro.

e Viele Deutsche unterstützen die Einführung eines europäischen Mindestlohns.

f Über 40% der Deutschen wünschen sich eine bessere EU-Umweltpolitik.

4 Vor- und Nachteile der EU.

Lesen Sie den Text noch einmal und ergänzen Sie die Argumente pro und contra Europa.

Pro EU	Contra EU
Man kann ohne Grenzen ...	Es gibt Skepsis gegenüber ...
Es gibt die Möglichkeit, ...	Viele denken, ...
Die EU-Zusammenarbeit ...	Die EU ist ...
Die EU kann ...	Die Institutionen ...

Language discovery 2

You have already seen this language in action. Can you work out the rules?

1 **Look at these sentences. What spelling change do you notice in the word Journalist when it is used in different structures?**

nom: Ein Journalist sollte eigentlich die Wahrheit schreiben.

acc: Kennst du den Journalisten?

dat: Mit diesem Journalisten möchte niemand zusammenarbeiten.

gen: Hier ist das neue Buch des Journalisten.

2 **Can you spot which adjective is 'hidden' in each of these six nouns?**

a ein Kranker

b ein Reicher

c ein Verwandter

d ein Deutscher

e ein Fremder

f ein Verlobter

1 SCHWACHE NOMEN *WEAK NOUNS*

In this unit you came across the words **der Journalist** and **der Präsident**. These belong to a group of masculine nouns called **weak nouns**, usually referring to job titles, people or animals (the males of the species).

Weak nouns take **-(e)n** in all cases except the nominative singular:

	singular	plural
nom.	ein/der Junge	die Jungen
acc.	einen/den Jungen	die Jungen
dat.	einem/dem Jungen	den Jungen
gen.	eines/des Jungen	der Jungen

Other frequently used nouns in this group include:

der Architekt, der Assistent, der Fotograf, der Herr, der Kandidat, der Kollege, der Kunde, der Mensch, der Nachbar, der Soldat, der Student, der Tourist, der Affe, der Bär, der Löwe.

Note that **Herr** adds **-n** in the singular, but **-en** in the plural:
Kennst du Herr**n** Schröder?   Guten Tag, meine Damen und Herr**en**!

2 ADJECTIVAL NOUNS

Adjectival nouns are derived from adjectives:

krank → **ein Kranker, eine Kranke** *a sick person, patient*

reich → **ein Reicher, eine Reiche** *a rich person*

verwandt → **ein Verwandter, eine Verwandte** *a relative*

Adjectives used as nouns follow the pattern of adjectival endings. As you can see, male and female forms sometimes have different endings.

This overview may help to remind you of the endings needed:

	masculine	feminine	plural
nom.	der Verwandt**e** / mein Verwandt**er**	die/meine Verwandt**e**	die/meine Verwandt**en**
acc.	den/meinen Verwandt**en**	die/meine Verwandt**e**	die/meine Verwandt**en**
dat.	dem/meinem Verwandt**en**	der/meiner Verwandt**en**	den/meinen Verwandt**en**
gen.	des/meines Verwandt**en**	der/meiner Verwandt**en**	der/meiner Verwandt**en**

Note that the indefinite articles follow the pattern of the possessives.

In the nominative and accusative plural, the adjectival noun only adds an **-e** when it is not preceded by an article or a possessive:

Rita und Marga sind Deutsch**e**.

Das Parlament hat über 600 Abgeordnet**e**.

Such nouns include **Deutscher** *German*, **Fremder** *stranger*, **Verlobter** *fiancé*, **Abgeordneter** *Member of Parliament*, **Arbeitsloser** *unemployed person*, **Erwachsener** *adult*

For more information, including endings after a definite article, see the **Go further with grammar** section.

Practice 2

1 **Schwache Nomen. Brauchen die Wörter eine Endung oder nicht?**

   a Hast du noch einmal mit dem Fotograf___ geredet?

   b Mario ist Student___ an der Humbold-Universität in Berlin.

   c Sie haben den neuen Kollege___ zum Abendessen eingeladen.

   d Der Kunde___ wollte unbedingt ein neues Gerät.

   e Bruno hat immer noch Ärger mit seinem Nachbar___.

   f Kennst du Herr___ Weidfeld, der zum neuen Präsident___ gewählt worden ist?

   g Meine Damen und Herr___!

2 **Seien Sie kreativ! Benutzen Sie die Adjektive und bilden Sie Nomen. Was bedeuten die neuen Wörter auf Englisch?**

Beispiel: angestellt → *ein Angestellter, eine Angestellte (an employee)*

   a selbstständig → ein _____, eine _____

   b heilig → ein _____, eine _____

   c arm → ein _____, eine _____

   d verrückt → ein _____, eine _____

   e bekannt → ein _____, eine _____

   f jugendlich → ein _____, eine _____

3 Wie heißt es richtig? Ergänzen Sie die fehlenden Endungen.

a Rosanna wohnt mit einem Deutsch_____ zusammen.

b Sie ist eine gute Bekannt_____.

c Wie geht es deiner Verlobt_____?

d Er ist ein Verrückt_____

e Ein Verwandt_____ von mir wohnt in London.

f Der Abgeordnet_____ ist nicht wiedergewählt worden.

g Die Jugendlich_____ haben noch lange gefeiert.

Conversation 2

DIE DEUTSCHE WIRTSCHAFT

Im folgenden Interview spricht Frau Matthiesen von der Industrie- und Handelskammer (Chamber of Commerce) über die wirtschaftliche Situation in Deutschland.

1 10.04 **Hören Sie sich die Höraufnahme an und entscheiden Sie, ob die folgenden Aussagen richtig oder falsch sind:**

a The manufacturing industry is the driving force of the German economy.

b Every fifth job in Germany is linked to exports.

c The most important trading partners are, in ranking order, Europe, the USA and Asia.

die Industrienation (-en)	*industrialized nation*
sozusagen	*so to speak*
der Betrieb (-e)	*business, factory*
aus/führen	*to export*
gesättigt	*(here) saturated*
annähernd	*almost*
entstehen	*to create*
vorsichtig	*(here) cautiously*
die Arbeitslosenzahl (-en)	*unemployment figures*
an/halten	*(here) to continue*

Journalist	Frau Matthiesen, die Bundesrepublik gehört zu den international führenden Industrienationen. In welchen Bereichen ist die deutsche Wirtschaft denn besonders stark?
Eva Matthiesen	Nun, traditionell im produzierenden Gewerbe. Das ist sozusagen das Herz und der Motor der deutschen Wirtschaft. Dazu gehört der Maschinenbau oder auch die chemische Industrie. Dann muss man natürlich auch die Autoindustrie nennen, mit Betrieben wie Volkswagen, BMW oder Mercedes. Diese Marken sind alle weltweit bekannt.
Journalist	Wie wichtig ist denn der Export für die deutsche Industrie?
Eva Matthiesen	Extrem wichtig. Jeder vierte Arbeitsplatz in Deutschland ist vom Export abhängig. Nehmen Sie zum Beispiel die Autoindustrie, die mittlerweile mehr als 80% ihrer Produkte ausführt, weil der Markt in Deutschland doch relativ gesättigt ist. Hier geht der Trend im Moment weg vom eigenen Auto und hin zu Carsharing oder öffentlichen Verkehrsmitteln. In Berlin zum Beispiel hat nur noch jeder zweite Haushalt ein Auto.
Journalist	Und welches sind die wichtigsten Handelspartner Deutschlands?
Eva Matthiesen	Am wichtigsten sind immer noch die Länder der EU, in die annähernd 60% der Exporte gehen. In den letzten Jahren ist aber der asiatische Raum, besonders China, immer wichtiger geworden. Wir exportieren mittlerweile doppelt so viel Waren nach Asien als wie in die USA.
Journalist	Und wie sehen Sie die Zukunft für die deutsche Wirtschaft?
Eva Matthiesen	Da bin ich vorsichtig optimistisch. Die Wirtschaft in Europa wird sich bald wieder erholen und das wäre natürlich auch für uns in Deutschland gut. Es sind bei uns in den letzten Jahren viele neue Arbeitsplätze entstanden und die Arbeitslosenzahlen sind deutlich gesunken. Ich hoffe, dass diese Entwicklung anhält.

2 Wie heißt das? Finden Sie die deutschen Wörter für:

a manufacturing industry

b area

c engine, driving force

d mechanical engineering

e chemical industry

f household

g trading partners

h development

3 Beantworten Sie die Fragen.

a Was sind – neben der Autobranche - die zwei wichtigsten Industrien Deutschlands?

b Wie viel Prozent der produzierten Autos werden exportiert?

c Was sagt Frau Matthiesen über den Automarkt in Deutschland?

d Wohin hat Deutschland in den letzten Jahren immer mehr Waren exportiert?

e Was denkt Frau Matthiesen über die Zukunft der Wirtschaft in Europa?

Im Vergleich zu Großbritannien ist das produzierende Gewerbe (*manufacturing industry*) in Deutschland immer noch sehr wichtig. Jeder 7. Arbeitsplatz in Deutschland steht mit der Autoindustrie in Verbindung. Aber auch andere Sektoren wie der Gesundheitsbereich (*health care*) oder das Erziehungswesen (*education*) spielen eine wichtige Rolle. In den letzten Jahren sind zudem im Dienstleistungsbereich (*service sector*) und bei den neuen Technologien viele neue Arbeitsplätze entstanden.

4 Relativsätze. Ergänzen Sie die Relativsätze mit Informationen aus Conversation 2.

  a Volkswagen, BMW und Mercedes sind Marken, die weltweit ...

  b Der Export ist ein wichtiger Bereich, von dem jeder vierte Arbeitsplatz ...

  c Berlin ist ein Beispiel für eine Stadt, in der nur noch jeder zweite ...

  d Asien ist ein Gebiet, das für die deutsche Wirtschaft in den letzten Jahren ...

5 Was denken Sie über Europa?

In a recent opinion survey by the European Commission, Germans ranked the most positive aspects of belonging to the EU like this:

> 1 Frieden in Europa   76%
>
> 2 Die Möglichkeiten, in Europa reisen und arbeiten zu können   65%
>
> 3 Die Schaffung einer gemeinsamen Währung   42%

Write a paragraph in which you will explain:

▶ if you agree with these points

▶ if any of the reasons listed are seen as negatives in your country

▶ what the EU should do to make improvements.

You can use some of these expressions to structure your writing:

> Ich stimme mit den drei Punkten überein/nicht überein.
> Eine der wichtigsten Errungenschaften der EU ist für mich ...
> Auch finde ich es positiv, dass ...
> Auf der anderen Seite ...
> Die gemeinsame Währung ...
> In meinem Land gibt es eine große Skepsis gegenüber ...
> Die EU sollte/müsste meiner Meinung nach ...

Look back to the reading passage **Deutsche glauben weiter an Europa** to find advantages and disadvantages of the EU.

Go further with grammar

RELATIVSÄTZE *RELATIVE CLAUSES*

As you learned in **Language discovery 1**, relative clauses provide more information about an item in the main clause. They are usually introduced by a relative pronoun.

In German, the relative pronoun agrees in gender (masculine, feminine, neuter) and number (singular, plural) with the noun that it stands for.

Note that the relative pronoun's case depends on its function within the clause that is introduced by it. For instance, if it is the **subject** of the relative clause, it takes the appropriate **nominative** form:

Sie sahen einen Film, **der** (subject, nominative) in den 90er Jahren gedreht wurde.
They watched a film which was made in the 1990s.

The function of the relative pronoun within the relative clause becomes clear when you convert it into a statement:

Der Film (subject, nominative) wurde in den 90er Jahren gedreht.

Likewise, if the relative pronoun refers to the direct object, it takes the appropriate **accusative** form:

Ist das der Laptop, **den** du gestern gekauft hast?
Is this the laptop you bought yesterday?

Du hast den Laptop (direct object, accusative) **gestern gekauft.**

Relative clauses can be nominative, accusative, dative or genitive. Let's look at them all in detail.

As you already know by now, in the nominative case the pronouns are: **der**, **die**, **das**, and **die** in the plural.

In the accusative case there is a change for masculine nouns only:
m: Das ist Peter, **den** ich noch aus der Schule kenne.

In the dative case the pronouns are: **dem** for masculine and neuter, **der** for feminine and **denen** for the plural:
m: Das ist Herr Kaiser, **dem** ich 100 Euro geliehen habe.
f: Das ist Petra, **der** ich das Buch über New York gegeben habe.
n: Das ist das Kind, **dem** ich geholfen habe.
pl: Das sind die Leute, **denen** wir gestern begegnet sind.

In the genitive case, the case of possession, the German words meaning *whose* are:
m: Das ist Marcus, **dessen** Tochter Journalistin ist.
f: Ist das nicht Helga, **deren** Tochter in den USA lebt?
n: Das ist das Kind, **dessen** Eltern aus Bern kommen.
pl: Das sind die Studenten, **deren** Tests sehr gut waren.

Here is an overview of all relative pronouns:

	masc.	fem.	neuter	plural
nom.	der	die	das	die
acc.	den	die	das	die
dat.	dem	der	dem	denen
gen.	dessen	deren	dessen	deren

As in English, relative pronouns are often used together with prepositions:

Das ist die Firma, **bei der** ich ein Praktikum gemacht habe.

Das sind Ulrike und Edda, **von denen** ich dir schon viel erzählt habe.

Don't forget that in a relative clause the verbs go to the end. Remember also that the relative clause is separated from the main clause with commas. Always put a comma at the beginning, and one at the end if the relative clause appears – as it often does – in the middle of the main clause:

Meine Freundin, **die in Berlin wohnt**, kommt morgen nach Hannover.

Nehmen Sie zum Beispiel die Autoindustrie, **die mittlerweile mehr als 80% ihrer Produkte ausführt,** weil der Markt in Deutschland gesättigt ist.

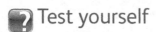 Test yourself

1 Üben Sie Relativsätze.

Bilden Sie Relativsätze wie in dem folgenden Beispiel. Beginnen Sie alle Sätze mit: Das ist Herr Franke, ...

Beispiel: Er kommt aus Stuttgart. → *Das ist Herr Franke, der aus Stuttgart kommt.*
  a Er arbeitet als Journalist.
  b Seine Frau ist auch Journalistin.
  c Sein Sohn studiert in den USA.
  d Er fährt einen roten Ferrari.
  e Er trägt meistens italienische Anzüge.
  f Man sieht ihn auf vielen Partys.
  g Von ihm bekomme ich noch €400.

2 Welches Wort passt am besten?

gewählt Handelspartner Macht Demokratie Export
Bundeskanzler ~~Europas~~ Bundestag Branchen
Aufgaben Einwohner Abgeordnete Bundespräsident

Deutschland liegt im Zentrum **(a)** *Europas* und hat mehr als 81,5 Millionen **(b)** _____. Es ist eine parlamentarische **(c)** _____. Das Parlament heißt der **(d)** _____, in dem mehr als 600 **(e)** _____ sitzen. Es wird alle vier Jahre **(f)** _____. Die größte politische **(g)** _____ hat der Chef der Regierung, der **(h)** _____. Das Staatsoberhaupt, der **(i)** _____, erfüllt dagegen nur repräsentative **(j)** _____.
Wirtschaftlich hängt Deutschland stark vom **(k)** _____ ab. Bedeutende **(l)** _____ sind die Automobilindustrie und die chemische Industrie. Die wichtigsten **(m)** _____ sind die Länder der EU.

 3 10.05 Und jetzt Sie! Spielen Sie die Rolle eines deutschen Journalisten, der über verschiedene Aspekte der deutschen Wirtschaft befragt wird.

Reporter	Die Bundesrepublik Deutschland ist eine der führenden Industrienationen der Welt. In welchen Bereichen ist die deutsche Wirtschaft denn besonders stark?
Sie	*Say that the manufacturing industry is very important. Say it's the driving force of German industry.*
Reporter	Gibt es noch andere bedeutende Wirtschaftszweige?
Sie	*Say that the chemical industry and mechanical engineering are also quite important.*
Reporter	Kann man sagen, dass viele Bereiche primär exportorientiert sind?
Sie	*Say yes. Explain that the car industry for instance exports 80% of its products. Say that one quarter of all jobs depend on exports.*
Reporter	Und was sind die wichtigsten Handelspartner?
Sie	*Say that the most important trading partners are the countries of the EU. Then come Asia and the USA. Say that China has become increasingly important in recent years.*
Reporter	Und was denken Sie über die weitere wirtschaftliche Entwicklung?
Sie	*Say you think that the economy in Europe will recover soon. Explain that in the last years many new jobs have been created in Germany. Say that overall you are quite optimistic.*

SELF CHECK

I CAN. . .

○	... talk about newspapers and magazines.
○	... answer a quiz about Germany's political structure.
○	... read about Germany's political institutions and the national economy.
○	... understand facts and opinions about economic and political issues.
○	... form relative clauses.
○	... identify adjectival and weak nouns.

Key to the exercises

UNIT 1

Conversation 1

1 She is interested in languages and works as a multilingual secretary for an insurance company.

2 a Ulrike lives in Cologne. **b** She works as a multilingual secretary. **c** She speaks French and English fluently; she also gets by in Spanish and Italian. **d** She is married with two children. **e** Languages is her hobby, she takes an advanced English course once a week.

3 a F. Die Arbeit macht ihr viel Spaß. **b** R. **c** F. Sie ist seit fast zehn Jahren verheiratet. **d** F. Er ist selbstständig (und hat ein kleines Architektenbüro in Köln). **e** F. Sie geht zu einem Englischkurs für Fortgeschrittene.

4 a halbtags **b** Spaß **c** verheiratet **d** selbstständig **e** fließend **f** interessiert

Language discovery 1

1 a and **c** are yes/no questions; **b** and **d** are open-ended. Yes/no questions start with a verb, whereas open-ended questions begin with a question word (welche, was).

2 a in **b** bei **c** an **d** seit, mit **e** zu

Practice 1

1 a in **b** aus **c** aus **d** an **e** als **f** in **g** seit **h** aus **i** in **j** als **k** bei

2 a Wie **b** Woher **c** Wie **d** Wo **e** Welche **f** wann **g** was **h** Was

3 a-4 **b**-8 **c**-5 **d**-1 **e**-7 **f**-2 **g**-3 **h**-6

4 Answers will vary.

Listen and understand

1

Name	Alter	Familienstand	Wohnort	Beruf	Hobbys
Martin	32	geschieden	Apolda, in Thüringen	Krankenpfleger	Kino, Skifahren
Petra	44	verheiratet	Salzburg, in Österreich	Hotelfachfrau	Geschichte, Lesen
Max	22	ledig/single	Lübeck, in Nord-deutschland	Student der Mathematik	Bungeespringen, Surfen

2 a-1 **b**-1 **c**-2 **d**-1 **e**-2

3 a Können Sie sich bitte kurz vorstellen? **b** Was sind Sie von Beruf? **c** Was machen Sie in Ihrer Freizeit? **d** Was für Hobbys haben Sie? **e** Ich gehe gern ins Kino. **f** In den Ferien gehe ich surfen.

Conversation 2

1 Susanne wants to see an old friend from school. She wanted to visit Berlin for a while but never had the time. Marcus complains about the high cost of travelling as he goes to Berlin almost every other weekend.

2 a Ja, sie fährt das erste Mal nach Berlin. **b** Seine Freundin wohnt in Berlin. **c** Sie studiert Film (an der Hochschule der Künste). **d** Sie möchte ihr das Berliner Nachtleben zeigen. **e** Er findet, dass die meisten Leute sehr offen sind./Er findet die meisten Leute sehr offen.

3 a ... schon seit langem besuchen. **b** ... aus Hannover. **c** ... ganz schön kostspielig. **d** ... sie einen Studienplatz an der HdK bekommen hat. **e** ... alte Schulfreundin von ihr. **f** ... Menschen aus der ganzen Welt treffen. **g** ... sehr lebendig.

Language discovery 2

1 a feminine **b** masculine **c** neuter. There are certain endings which can help you identifying a noun's gender. Typical feminine endings are: -tät, -e, - heit, -ion; typical masculine endings are: -or, -ismus, -ig; typical neuter endings are: -o, -ment, ing.

2 Söhne, Gäste, Kurse; Sprachen, Personen, Informationen; Konzerte, Feste, Kinder. Typical plural endings are: masculine nouns: -e plus umlaut and -e without umlaut; feminine nouns: -n and -en; neuter nouns: -e and -er.

Practice 2

1 a die **b** die **c** die **d** das **e** der **f** der **g** das **h** das **i** die **j** die **k** die **l** der **m** das

2 a Berufe **b** Kurse **c** Gäste **d** Züge **e** Kneipen **f** Zeitungen **g** Städte **h** Häuser **i** Restaurants **j** Büros

Reading

1 His hobbies are computer games, surfing the internet, chatting and model building. He is happy that he has his own car, a Mazda 3, 1.4, and he wants to drive it to Italy on his holiday.

2 a Er macht dieses Jahr sein Abitur. **b** Er hat ihn seit zwei Monaten. **c** Ja, seine Hobbys sind Computerspiele, Internetsurfen, Chatten. **d** Er hat es seit einer Woche. **e** Das Auto (die Kiste) frisst (braucht) sehr viel Benzin. **f** Später möchte er gern als Programmierer (vielleicht bei Siemens) arbeiten.

3 Model answer: Mein Name ist Susanne Pechstein. Ich bin in Wien geboren und bin dort auch aufgewachsen. Ich lebe jetzt seit fünf Jahren in München und arbeite als Verkäuferin in einer Boutique. Die Arbeit macht mir sehr viel Spaß. Ich bin nicht verheiratet, aber habe seit zwei Jahren einen Freund. Mein Freund arbeitet als Fitnesstrainer in einem Sportstudio. Meine Hobbys sind Musik und Tanzen und ich reise auch sehr gern. Ich spreche fließend Englisch und Spanisch und ein bisschen Chinesisch. In den Ferien möchte ich mit meinem Freund nach China fahren. Ich lebe sehr gern in München. Die Stadt ist sehr grün und die Menschen sind offen und freundlich. Aber leider ist München auch sehr teuer.

Test yourself

1 a halbtags **b** selbstständig **c** berufstätig **d** verheiratet **e** getrennt **f** Anfängerkurs **g** Fremdsprache **h** Führerschein **i** Abitur **j** kostspielig **k** offen

2 a Kommen Sie aus Berlin? **b** Wo sind Sie aufgewachsen? **c** Welche Sprachen sprechen Sie? **d** Was sind Sie von Beruf? **e** Sind Sie verheiratet? **f** Haben Sie Kinder? **g** Was sind Ihre Hobbys?

3

der	die	das
Dezember, Audi	Landschaft, Fußballmannschaft	Gold
Mittwoch, Ferrari	Natur, Pension	Gymnasium
Schnaps	Passion, Nationalität	Mädchen
Sommer	Region, Freundschaft	Märchen
Sonntag	Rose, Identität	Schwimmen
Wein	Temperatur, Intelligenz	Silber
Winter	Woche, Sprache	Tanzen

4 Ja, natürlich. Mein Name ist Matthias Brandt und ich bin in Hannover geboren, aber seit 20 Jahren wohne ich in Berlin. / Ja, ich bin selbstständig. Ich bin Architekt. / Ja, und ich habe eine Tochter, Steffi. Sie ist Studentin und studiert an der Universität Heidelberg. / Ich gehe gern ins Kino und ich lese gern. Ich interessiere mich auch für Sprachen. / Ja, die Menschen in Berlin sind sehr freundlich und die Stadt ist wirklich interessant.

UNIT 2

Conversation 1

1 In the morning Lorenz prepares his seminar or reads at his desk at home. He says that he doesn't have a hobby as such because his work has become his hobby. He likes literature and is a writer himself.

2 a For breakfast he normally has rolls with jam or with Nutella and drinks a cup of Turkish coffee. **b** He eats at the university canteen. **c** He goes home in the early afternoon, does the shopping or does whatever needs to be done. **d** He visits friends or his parents-in-law.

3 a F. Er steht gegen halb acht auf. **b** R. **c** F. Er fährt meistens mit dem Bus, manchmal läuft er auch in die Stadt. **d** F. Es sind nur zehn Minuten zu Fuß. **e** F. Abends bleibt er meistens zu Hause. / Abends liest er die Zeitung, schaut Nachrichten im Fernsehen, manchmal noch einen Film. Gewöhnlich liest er oder hört Radio. **f** R.

4 a beginnen **b** aufstehen **c** frühstücken **d** stattfinden **e** laufen **f** einkaufen, gehen **g** besuchen

Language discovery 1

1 In all four sentences the subject appears after the verb: **a** esse ich...; **b** gehe ich... ; **c** habe ich... ; **d** besuchen wir... This is because if you start a German a sentence with, for instance, an expression of time or frequency, the subject–verb inversion is needed to keep the verb in the second position.

2 anschließend (4) zuerst (1) danach (3) dann (2) zum Schluss (5)

Practice 1

1 a Zuerst mache ich 15 Minuten Yoga. **b** Zum Frühstück trinke ich Orangensaft und esse ein Croissant mit Marmelade. **c** Normalerweise gehe ich gegen acht Uhr aus dem Haus.

d Meistens arbeiten wir bis 18.00 Uhr. **e** Am Wochenende besuche ich öfters Freunde oder gehe essen. **f** In den Ferien fahren mein Freund und ich zum Windsurfen an den Starnberger See.

2 a immer **b** selten **c** Gewöhnlich **d** nie

3 a Zuerst steht Herr Müller um halb acht auf. **b** Dann frühstückt er. **c** Danach arbeitet er zu Hause am Schreibtisch. **d** Anschließend fährt oder geht er zur Arbeit. **e** Als Nächstes isst er in der Mensa. **f** Später gibt er Seminare an der Universität. **g** Zuletzt liest er oder hört er Musik.

4 Answers will vary.

Listen and understand

1 Corinna is keen to brush up her English because many foreign visitors come to the restaurant where she works.

2 a For two years. **b** She has a shower and goes to bed immediately. **c** At 4 p.m. **d** She can have her meals for free.

3 a bis um Mitternacht **b** gegen eins, halb zwei **c** eine Scheibe Toast **d** ab und zu auf **e** ins Kino **f** höchstens viermal im Jahr

4 a Es kommt darauf an … **b** gegen eins. **c** Ich stelle mich schnell unter die Dusche. **d** eine Scheibe Toast. **e** ab und zu. **f** höchstens viermal im Jahr. **g** zu Weihnachten. **h** bei Geburtstagen.

Reading

1 About 60% go by car, 13% by public transport and about 8% take the bike.

2 a The percentage of Germans who can start the day free of stress. **b** Some just find it more convenient, others live so far out of town that there is no other possibility for them than using their own car. **c** A good feeling that they are doing something for the environment. **d** More people need to travel longer distances. The number of people who travel 10 km or less to work has in decreased from 52% to 45% in the last ten years. **e** They need to travel more than 25 km to work.

3 a-4 **b**-5 **c**-2 **d**-3 **e**-1

Language discovery 2

1 The first part of these verbs is called a prefix. Prefixes are highlighted: **auf**stehen, **auf**räumen, **auf**frischen, **aus**sehen, **ein**kaufen, **mit**machen, **statt**finden, **vor**bereiten.

2	ich	du	Sie	er/sie/es
essen	esse	isst	essen	isst
fahren	fahre	fährst	fahren	fährt
laufen	laute	läufst	laufen	läuft

Apart from the endings the stem vowel also changes in the du and er/sie/es form.

Practice 2

1 a liest **b** fährt **c** nimmt **d** spricht **e** hilft **f** trifft **g** läuft

2 Here are 10 possible combinations: anfangen, abwaschen, abräumen, stattfinden, mitgehen, abholen, zumachen, einladen, ausmachen, einkaufen. (If you found more, please check your answers in the glossary or in a dictionary.)

3 a fangen ... an/finden ... statt. **b** bereitet ... vor. **c** waschen ... ab. **d** räumt ... ab. **e** findet ... statt.
f sehen ... fern. **g** lädt ... ein. **h** auffrischen.

Conversation 2

1 During the day she likes to visit one of her friends, or they take a stroll in the main park (Stadtpark). Occasionally, she has lunch in a restaurant. She says that she doesn't mind going to bed late because at her age one doesn't need much sleep.

2 a Zum Frühstück isst sie ein paar Brötchen und trinkt Kaffee. **b** Nach dem Frühstück liest sie die Zeitung. **c** Mit ihren Freundinnen geht sie im Stadtpark spazieren. **d** Er besucht sie fast jedes Wochenende. / Er kommt fast jedes Wochenende. **e** Ihr Hobby ist Stricken. **f** Im März war sie eine Woche bei ihrer Enkelin (in Osnabrück) zu Besuch. **g** Sie sieht gern Nachrichtensendungen, Podiumsdiskussionen und Dokumentarfilme.

3 a ... langweilig? **b** ... um 7 Uhr auf. **c** ... auf meinem Balkon. **d** ... für Politik. **e** ... zu Mittag.
f ... in die Umgebung. **g** ... zu stricken. **h** ... gar kein Interesse.

4 Model answer: Freitagabend bleibe ich oft zu Hause und sehe fern. Am Samstag stehe ich normalerweise um acht Uhr auf. Zuerst dusche ich und frühstücke. Danach räume ich mein Zimmer auf und mache die Wohnung sauber. Anschließend kaufe ich oft ein. Am Samstagnachmittag treffe ich meistens Freunde und wir gehen zusammen ins Fitnesscenter. Anschließend gehen wir oft zusammen essen oder ins Kino. Manchmal gehen wir auch tanzen.

Am Sonntag schlafe ich normalerweise bis 10 Uhr. Dann hole ich Brötchen, koche Kaffee und frühstücke gemächlich. Anschließend besuche ich oft Freunde oder lade Gäste ein. Ich koche sehr gern, am liebsten chinesisch. Manchmal mache ich auch Ausflüge in die Umgebung. Sonntagabend verbringe ich meistens mit meiner Playstation und spiele die neuesten Games.

Test yourself

1 b stellen **c** abwaschen **d** laufen **e** anschauen **f** vorbereiten **g** aufräumen **h** stricken
i erledigen **j** übersetzen **k** machen **l** auffrischen

2 The separable verbs are: auffrischen, aufräumen, anschauen, abwaschen, vorbereiten. The verbs with inseparable prefixes are: besuchen, erledigen. The verb with a separable / inseparable prefix is: übersetzen.

3 a Claudia fährt im Winter mit der U-Bahn zur Universität. **b** Kommst du heute Abend mit ins Kino? **c** Theo und Anke gehen in der Mittagspause zu Fuß ins Restaurant. **d** Manfred fährt nachmittags mit seinem Auto zu seinem Freund ins Krankenhaus. **e** Hans Martinek geht oft nach der Arbeit ins Fitnesscenter. **f** Frau Tiedke kauft abends noch schnell im Supermarkt ein. **g** Die Fuhrmanns wollen nächstes Wochenende eine Radtour an die Ostsee machen.

4 f, b, h, g, j, a, c, e, i, d

5 Während der Woche stehe ich gewöhnlich gegen sieben Uhr auf, am Wochenende meistens gegen halb zehn. / Normalerweise hole ich Brötchen von der Bäckerei. Dann koche ich Kaffee und esse Brötchen mit Marmelade und Butter und trinke ein Glas Saft. Gewöhnlich lese ich auch die Zeitung. / Meistens fahre ich mit dem Auto und nur selten mit dem Bus. / Gewöhnlich habe ich zwischen 12.30 Uhr und 13.15 Uhr Mittagspause.

Meistens esse ich in meiner Firma und nur gelegentlich esse ich in einem Restaurant zu Mittag. / Gewöhnlich schaue ich Nachrichten im Fernsehen, lese ein Buch oder höre Radio. / Manchmal besuche ich Freunde oder meine Eltern, gehe gelegentlich spazieren oder mache die Arbeit, die während der Woche liegen geblieben ist. Sonntags mache ich manchmal Tagesausflüge in die Umgebung.

UNIT 3

Conversation 1
1 Birgit thinks that there are too many university graduates in Germany.
2 a The Deutsche Bank. **b** It is difficult to find work and she did not want to be unemployed. **c** Because she is going to work in the bank's Florence branch for a year. **d** She is very satisfied with her profession.
3 a bestehen **b** Stellung **c** überfüllt **d** aufnehmen **e** mache Gebrauch von (meinen Englischkenntnissen) **f** zufrieden.
4 a F. Für Akademiker in Deutschland bestehen Schwierigkeiten, Arbeit zu finden. **b** F. Birgit kennt sehr viele Leute, die studiert haben und jetzt arbeitslos sind. **c** R. **d** R. **e** F. Birgit macht in ihrem Beruf jeden Tag von ihren Englischkenntnissen Gebrauch.

Language discovery 1
1 a beworben **b** gefunden **c** gemacht **d** studiert; **a** and **b** are irregular – they both have a vowel change: bewerben → beworben, finden → gefunden; **c** and **d** are regular verbs.
2 a Ich hatte … **b** Ich wollte … **c** Ich war … The tense is called das Präteritum, the simple past. It is normally used in writing.

Practice 1
1 a wurde **b** ging **c** machte **d** wusste **e** sollte **f** war **g** bewarb **h** bekam **i** begann **j** arbeitete **k** lernte … kennen **l** fand
2 a gearbeitet **b** studiert **c** beworben **d** passiert **e** verbracht **f** gegangen **g** geworden **h** gefahren **i** besucht **j** beendet. Verbs which take sein are: **d** passieren **f** gehen **g** werden **h** fahren.
3 a Dort habe ich auch die Schule besucht. **b** Mit 17 Jahren habe ich meinen Schulabschluss gemacht. **c** Dann habe ich ein Jahr für ein soziales Projekt mit Kindern gearbeitet. **d** Anschließend habe ich mich um eine Lehre als Hotelfachmann beworben. **e** Es gab viele Bewerber, aber ich hatte Glück. **f** Ich durfte auch drei Monate in Berlin arbeiten. **g** Das war eine wichtige Erfahrung für mich und ich habe auch viele neue Sachen gelernt. **h** Vor einem halben Jahr habe ich meine Lehre beendet.
4 Answers will vary.

Reading
1 a They go to school at the age of six. **b** 12 years **c** 9 semester or 4.5 years.
2 a Normally three: die Hauptschule, die Realschule, das Gymnasium; **b** They often pursue a career in middle-management, in business or in the public sector. **c** They follow an academic curriculum. **d** The three different types of schools (Hauptschule, Realschule, Gymnasium) are combined under one roof. It's similar to a comprehensive school. **e** They have to attend a vocational school, called die Berufsschule.

3 a Kindergarten **b** Grundschule **c** Hauptschule **d** Realschule **e** Gymnasium **f** Berufsschule
g das Abitur **h** Staatsexamen.

4 a in die Schule / in die Grundschule. **b** drei verschiedene Schultypen: die Hauptschule, die
Realschule und das Gymnasium. **c** 12 Jahre zur Schule gehen. **d** das Abitur. **e** zwei Semester:
das Wintersemester und das Sommersemester. **f** drei Jahre für ein Bachelorstudium und ein
oder zwei Jahre für ein Masterstudium / zwischen drei und fünf Jahren.

5 Answers will vary.

Conversation 2

1 She wants to work for the Ministry of the Environment. She is worried that there is stiff
competition for any position.

2 a F. Vera studiert Anglistik im vierten Semester. **b** R. **c** F. Ilona will Ende nächsten Semesters
das Staatsexamen ablegen. **d** F. Sie wird sich beim Umweltministerium bewerben. **e** R. **f** R.

3 a Ist hier noch frei? **b** Ich studiere Anglistik im dritten Semester. **c** Du hast aber Glück!
d Ende nächsten Semesters will ich das Staatsexamen ablegen. **e** Und was möchtest du
(dann) werden? **f** Und was hast du vor? **g** Ich möchte Gymnasiallehrerin für Englisch werden.
h Es hat viel Spaß gemacht.

Language discovery 2

1 The verb is **werden**: **a** ich werde ... **b** ... wird hoffentlich wieder Nachfrage nach Lehrern
bestehen.

2 a Bald **b** Ende nächsten Semesters

Practice 2

1 a Peter wird nächsten Sommer in die Schule kommen. **b** Das Seminar wird um 16.00 Uhr
anfangen. **c** Frau Dr. Martini wird die Vorlesung halten. **d** Susanne wird ihre Lehre bei der
Telekom machen. **e** Lisa und Annette werden ihren Sprachkurs in Madrid machen. **f** Thomas
wird seinen neuen Job in zwei Wochen anfangen.

2 a übermorgen **b** November **c** kommenden **d** Wochen **e** bald **f** Sommer **g** Wochenende

3 a Morgen besuchen wir unsere Eltern. **b** Am Dienstag arbeite ich im Garten. **c** Demnächst
lassen wir das Haus renovieren. **d** Ich fange bald mit meinem Englischkurs an. **e** Im Oktober
fahren wir nach England. **f** Im September kommt Martin in die Schule. **g** In zwei Wochen fange
ich meinen Job als Bedienung an. **h** Übermorgen gehe ich zum Friseur. **i** Am Wochenende
gehen wir zum Windsurfen. **j** Übrigens, das Abendessen ist gleich fertig!

4 Answers will vary.

Test yourself

1 a machen **b** bewerben **c** studieren **d** durchführen **e** treffen **f** beenden **g** besuchen
h bestehen **i** diskutieren **j** schreiben **k** ablegen **l** kennen lernen.

2 a wird **b** Werdet **c** wird **d** werden **e** wird **f** werde **g** Wirst

3 a Mit 16 Jahren machte er seinen Schulabschluss. **b** Als Teenager interessierte er sich schon
für Elektronik. **c** Nach der Schule fing er eine Ausbildung als Elektroniker an. **d** Die Ausbildung
dauerte dreieinhalb Jahre. **e** Nach der Ausbildung bewarb er sich bei Siemens und arbeitete
zunächst im IT-Bereich. **f** Nach ein paar Jahren wechselte er in den Energiebereich.
g Bald wurde er Abteilungsleiter und leitete ein Team von 25 Leuten.

4 Ich habe mich um einen Studienplatz für Biologie an der Universität Heidelberg beworben. / Das Bachelorstudium dauert normalerweise drei Jahre. Danach kann man noch einen Masters machen. Das dauert ein oder zwei Jahre. / Ich bin noch nicht sicher. Vielleicht kann ich für das Umweltminsterium arbeiten oder für eine große, internationale Firma. Aber ich möchte kein Lehrer werden. / Sie hat vor zwei Jahren eine Banklehre angefangen. Sie ist sehr zufrieden mit ihrer Stellung. Letztes Jahr hat sie für drei Monate in London gearbeitet. Es hat ihr viel Spaß gemacht.

UNIT 4

Conversation 1

1 They like that they can go on business trips.

2 a R **b** F **c** F **d** R

3 a Sie geht dort zu einem Ingenieurkongress. **b** Er arbeitet seit sieben Jahren bei seiner Firma. **c** Die Firma stellt Werkzeugmaschinen her. **d** Er fliegt nach Budapest, um dort Verhandlungen mit einer ungarischen Firma zu führen. **e** Er möchte mehr Zeit für seine Frau und Kinder haben. **f** Sie nehmen viel Zeit in Anspruch.

4 a Männerberuf **b** bilden **c** herstellen **d** führen **e** beschäftigt **f** im Allgemeinen **g** Zeitmangel

Language discovery 1

1 a aber **b** und – these words are used to link, or coordinate, two phrases into a single sentence.

2 The verbs take the last position in the clause. When there are two verbs, the <u>main verb</u> precedes the *modal verb*: **a** ..., wenn ich <u>fragen</u> *darf*. **b** ... , dass die meisten Leute sehr offen sind. **c** ... , weil meine Seminare erst später stattfinden. **d** obwohl sie eigentlich <u>studieren</u> *wollte*.

Practice 1

1 a Monika Kubig kommt aus Stuttgart und sie ist Bauingenieurin. **b** Sie fährt nach Wien, denn sie möchte einen Kongress besuchen. **c** Vlado Krause ist kein Ingenieur, sondern er ist leitender Angestellter. **d** Seine Arbeit gefällt ihm, denn er lernt viele neue Dinge. **e** Er reist viel und Geschäftsreisen nehmen viel Zeit in Anspruch. **f** Machen Sie jetzt die nächste Übung oder möchten Sie eine Pause machen?

2 a 2 **b** 5 **c** 6 **d** 3 **e** 4 **f** 1

3 a ..., weil er geschäftlich oft in München ist. **b** ..., weil er Verhandlungen auf Deutsch führen muss. **c** ..., weil er sich für die deutsche Kultur interessiert. **d** ..., weil er gern deutsches Bier trinkt. **e** ..., weil seine Freundin aus Berlin kommt. **f** ..., weil er vielleicht einmal in Deutschland oder Österreich leben möchte.

4 Answers will vary.

Listen and understand

1 Heiko says that his students are motivated and hard-working because they need to learn German as fast as possible. Gerd finds it tiring that he often has to work at night or on the weekends.

2 a Deutsch als Fremdsprache **b** sehr gut **c** die Bezahlung **d** Gymnasiallehrer **e** Sozialpädagoge **f** Kinder **g** zwölf Monate.

3 a-1 **b**-2 **c**-3 **d**-2

4 a Lange nicht gesehen. **b** Und was machst du jetzt für eine Arbeit? **c** im Allgemeinen **d** Sie haben es nötig ... **e** wenn das so ist ... **f** Wie du weißt **g** Es gefällt mir sehr gut.

Reading

1 personal data, work experience, internships/work placement, (higher) education, (special) skills), IT skills

2 a Sie ist Personalleiterin bei Hapag-Lloyd. **b** Sie arbeitete vier Jahre bei Unilever in Hamburg (zunächst als Personalberaterin, dann als stellvertretende Personalleiterin). **c** Sie studierte Psychologie von Oktober 2004 bis Juni 2009. **d** Ihre Gesamtnote war eine 1 (sehr gut). / Sie erhielt eine 1 (sehr gut). **e** Ihre Kindheit verbrachte Maria in München. **f** Sie hat Anfängerkenntnisse in Japanisch.

3 a geboren **b** Grundschule / Schule **c** Abitur **d** Studium **e** Psychologie **f** Schwerpunkt **g** Freizeit **h** Arbeitsplatz **i** Praktika **j** Personalberaterin **k** stellvertretende **l** Personalleiterin **m** Freizeit **n** fahre

Conversation 2

1 a She works in public relations. **b** She now works full-time.

2 a Normalerweise arbeitet sie von neun Uhr morgens bis halb fünf oder fünf Uhr abends. **b** Die Arbeitsatmosphäre ist sehr gut. Mit ihren Kollegen arbeitet sie gut im Team zusammen. Außerdem ist ihr Job eigentlich nie langweilig oder Routine, da sie immer an neuen Projekten arbeiten. **c** Ihr gefällt es, dass ihr Job sehr kreativ ist und ihr gefällt die Arbeit im Team. **d** Ihr gefällt nicht, dass sie oft unter Termindruck arbeiten muss. **e** Sie verdient etwa 3000,- Euro brutto. **f** In ein paar Jahren möchte sie sich selbstständig machen.

3 a Teilzeitkraft **b** Vollzeitkraft **c** Urlaubsgeld **d** Weihnachtsgeld **e** Rentenversicherung **f** selbstständig **g** eine Herausforderung

4 a einer PR-Firma. **b** für Humor. **c** langweilig. **d** zufrieden. **e** Termindruck arbeiten muss. **f** Kranken und Rentenversicherung. **g** selbstständig machen. **h** richtige Herausforderung.

Language discovery 2

1 a Wenn wir wichtige Aufträge haben, ...; **b** Wenn wir wichtige Deadlines haben, ..; **c** Bevor ich hier in der Firma angefangen habe, ...

2 a no comma, **b** comma before **dass**.

Practice 2

1 a Yes, before **wenn**. Und was sind Sie von Beruf, **wenn** ich fragen darf? **b** No. **c** Yes, before **aber**. Die Konkurrenz ist stark, **aber** vielleicht schaffe ich es ja trotzdem. **d** Yes, before **dass**. Diese Leute haben das schöne Gefühl, **dass** sie etwas für die Umwelt tun. **e** Yes, before **da**. Hobbys habe ich insofern keine, **da** mein Beruf mein Hobby geworden ist. **f** No.

2 a Herr Krause fliegt oft nach Budapest, weil er dort geschäftlich zu tun hat. **b** Claudia gefällt ihr Beruf, obwohl sie oft unter Termindruck arbeiten muss. **c** Sie arbeitet gern im Team, weil ihre Kollegen alle Sinn für Humor haben. **d** In der Zukunft möchte sie sich selbstständig machen, obwohl das mehr Stress bedeutet. **e** Claudia möchte eine eigene Firma gründen, weil dies eine Herausforderung ist.

3 a Weil er dort geschäftlich zu tun hat, fliegt Vlado Krause oft nach Budapest. **b** Obwohl sie unter Termindruck arbeiten muss, gefällt Claudia ihr Beruf. **c** Weil ihre Kollegen alle Sinn für Humor haben, arbeitet sie gern im Team. **d** Obwohl das mehr Stress bedeutet, möchte sie sich später selbstständig machen. **e** Weil dies eine Herausforderung ist, möchte Claudia eine eigene Firma gründen.

4 Answers will vary.

Test yourself

1 a Aktienhändler *stock broker, equity trader*; Apotheker *pharmacist*; Architekt *architect*; Arzt *doctor*; Bauarbeiter *builder*; Bauingenieur *civil engineer*; Beamter *civil servant*; Büroangestellter *office worker*; Dolmetscher *interpreter*; Elektriker *electrician*; Friseur *hairdresser*; Informatiker *IT-specialist*; Journalist *journalist*; Juwelier *jeweller*; Klempner *plumber*; Kellner *waiter*; Koch *chef*; Krankenpfleger *(male) nurse*; Künstler *artist*; Landwirt *farmer*; Lehrer *teacher*; Makler *estate agent, broker*; Metzger *butcher*; Modedesigner *fashion designer*; Personalberater *HR consultant*; Rechtsanwalt *solicitor*; Reiseleiter *tour guide*; Schauspieler *actor*; Schriftsteller *writer*; Sozialarbeiter *social worker*; Tierarzt *vet;* Übersetzer *translator*; Verkäufer *sales assistant*; Werbetexter *copywriter*; Wirt *landlord (pub, restaurant);* Zahnarzt *dentist*

b 1 Arzt › Ärztin, Koch › Köchin, Rechtsanwalt › Rechtsanwältin, Tierarzt › Tierärztin, Zahnarzt › Zahnärztin **2** Krankenpfleger › Krankenschwester (although die Krankenpflegerin is increasingly being used nowadays) Beamter › Beamtin, Büroangestellter › Büroangestellte.

2 a Friseurin **b** Ärztin **c** Klempner **d** Lehrerin **e** Kellner **f** Apothekerin **g** Übersetzer **h** Landwirt **i** Psychologin **j** Aktienhändlerin **k** Architektin.

3 a Zeitmangel ist oft ein Problem, wenn man berufstätig ist. **b** Carsten hört gern klassische Musik, während er seine E-Mails checkt. **c** Pia und Tim sind gestresst, da sie viele Deadlines haben. **d** Er hat einen befristeten Vertrag, obwohl er lange bei der Firma arbeitet.
e Sie wissen noch nicht, ob sie den Auftrag bekommen. **f** Sie ist zufriedener, seitdem sie regelmäßig Yoga und Pilates macht.

4 Ich bin Bauingenieurin und bin im Allgemeinen sehr zufrieden mit meinem Beruf. Mir gefällt besonders, dass ich soviel reisen kann. Aber natürlich ist Zeitmangel eines meiner größten Probleme. Und was machst du jetzt? / Das stelle ich mir aber sehr schwierig vor. Was willst du jetzt machen? / Das ist eine gute Idee! Zurzeit werden ja viele Stellen angeboten, die auf diesem Gebiet Kenntnisse verlangen. Ich wünsche dir viel Glück dabei.

UNIT 5

Conversation 1

1 ballet (**c**) and poetry (**f**) are not mentioned.

2 a She says it's nice of her to ask but she is not particularly interested in the opera.
b She likes to keep informed about the latest films, theatre productions and so on.
c Because she can brush up her language skills. **d** She saw an exhibition on Impressionism.

3 a R. **b** F. Sie findet Sport langeilig. **c** F. Sie sagt, dass es in München sehr viele Möglichkeiten gibt. **d** R. **e** F. Sie fand die Ausstellung fantastisch. **f** F.

4 a Ich interessiere mich eben für alles, was ... **b** Was ich ganz toll finde, ist ... **c** Ich schätze die Klassiker... **d** Im Allgemeinen ziehe ich ... vor. **e** Das interessiert mich nicht. **f** Sport hat mich schon immer gelangweilt.

Language discovery 1
1 In English you use **about** in expressions such as: to think, to talk, to write, to tell about something.
2 a Ich interessiere mich für alles, was mit Kultur zu tun hat. **b** Ich habe mich deshalb um eine Banklehre beworben. Although the usage of prepositions with verbs is sometimes similar in English and German (as in the case of about/über), there is often no direct correlation: sich interessieren für – to be interested in and sich bewerben um – to apply for.
3 a-3, **b**-4, **c**-2, **d**-1; du → dich, er/sie/es → sich, wir → uns

Practice 1
1 a euch **b** sich **c** uns **d** sich **e** dich
2 a-6 **b**-7 **c**-2 **d**-5 **e**-4 **f**-1 **g**-8 **h**-3
3 b an **c** an/über **d** um **e** mit/über **f** mit **g** mit/über **h** von **i** auf
4 a Ärgern Sie sich über das Wetter? **b** Verstehen Sie sich gut mit Ihren Kollegen? **c** Glauben Sie an Ufos? **d** Interessieren Sie sich für Kunst? **e** Können Sie sich für Techno-Musik begeistern? **f** Freuen Sie sich auf die Ferien?

Listen and understand
1 Sebastian wants to get his driving licence and is taking driving lessons. Jochen wants to attend a dancing class.
2 a 20 **b** dritten **c** Turnieren **d** schwimmt **e** Leute **f** eingebunden **g** flexibel
3 a-2 **b**-3 **c**-1 **d**-2
4 a machen **b** interessieren **c** durchfallen **d** eintreten **e** treiben **f** aufpolieren **g** besuchen **h** gehen **i** halten

Reading
1 a House and rent prices **b** Munich is the biggest publishing centre in Europe. **c** the Marienkirche
2 a R. **b** F. Sie ist die drittgrößte Stadt Deutschlands. **c** R. **d** F. München hat 102 Millionen Tagesbesucher und über 12 Millionen Übernachtungen pro Jahr. **e** R. **f** F. Es findet meistens von Mitte September bis Anfang Oktober statt.
3 a Rent prices in Munich, in Euros per square metre. **b** Number of museums. **c** Number of theatres. **d** Number of daily commuters. **e** Number of inhabitants of Munich. **f** Overnight stays per year. **g** Day-trippers to Munich.

Conversation 2
1 a Helga and Peter cannot attend Birgit's party because they will be on a trip to England with their bowling club. **b** Devoting all her free time to a club would not be to Birgit's taste. **c** Peter likes the many interesting activities organized by the club, particularly the city trips they did. He also likes that it's possible to keep bowling into old age.

2 a F. Sie geben nächstes Wochenende eine große Party. **b** F. Sie fahren mit ihrem Kegelclub nach England. **c** R. **d** F. Ihr gefällt es, dass man öfters neue Leute trifft. **e** R. **f** F. Sie haben schon Städtereisen mit dem Club gemacht.

3 Positiv: a ...viele Vorteile. **b** mag ganz besonders **c** lustig. **d** ... uns beiden doch viel Spaß machen. **Negativ: a** ... längst genug. **b** ... uns beiden nicht so gefällt. **c** ... meinem Geschmack. **d** ... mir überhaupt nicht gefallen.

4 a Habt ihr nächste Woche schon was vor? **b** Toll, da kommen wir gern. **c** Könnt ihr das nicht mal ausfallen lassen? **d** So ein Pech. **e** Das sagt uns auch nicht immer zu. **f** Also, ich hätte schon längst genug. **g** Das wäre ganz und gar nicht nach meinem Geschmack.

Language discovery 2

1 Wo is added in front of the prepositions: Wofür, Wovon; in the case of Worüber there is an additional 'r': Worüber.

2 The missing word is zu.

Practice 2

1 a Worauf freust du dich? **b** Woran glaubst du? **c** Worüber denkst du nach? **d** Woran erinnerst du dich? **e** Worauf wartest du? **f** Wonach suchst du? **g** Worüber unterhältst du dich?

2 a-7 **b**-5 **c**-8 **d**-2 **e**-4 **f**-3 **g**-6 **h**-1

3 a ... tanzen zu gehen. **b** ... bald meinen Führerschein zu machen. **c** ... ein Bier zu trinken. **d** ... nachher ins Restaurant zu gehen. **e** ... noch Karten für das Konzert zu bekommen. **f** ... meine Freizeit selbst zu gestalten.

4 Answers will vary.

Test yourself

1 a Ja, darauf freue ich mich sehr. **b** Nein, daran erinnere ich mich leider nicht. **c** Ja, darum bewerbe ich mich bestimmt. **d** Nein, darüber ärgere ich mich überhaupt nicht. **e** Ja, dafür interessiere ich mich ungeheuer. **f** Nein, darüber habe ich mich ganz und gar nicht gefreut.

2 a-4 **b**-6 **c**-5 **d**-1 **e**-7 **f**-2 **g**-3

3 Ich schwimme seit acht Jahren für einen Club und bin auch Mitglied in einem Kegelclub. / Manchmal denke ich ja auch, dass es ein bisschen zu viel ist. Aber es hat auch eine Menge Vorteile. / Man trifft viele Leute, Man hält sich auch fit und sieht viele neue Orte, wenn man mit den Clubs auf Turniere geht. / Doch, ich interessiere mich für Kultur, aber ich mag Sport lieber. / Ehrlich gesagt ziehe ich moderne Musik vor und ich gehe auch gerne ins Kino.

UNIT 6

Conversation 1

1 He is against a ban.

2 a R. **b** F. Er sagt, die Antiraucherfanatiker sind schon viel zu weit gegangen. **c** F. Er ist Raucher. **d** F. Er sagt, sie verpesten die Luft. **e** R. **f** F. Er macht sich keine Sorgen.

3 a Ganz und gar nicht! **b** Das ist ja ein Witz! **c** Da ist bestimmt 'was dran. **d** Das ist mir egal. **e** Mir macht das Rauchen unheimlich viel Spaß.

Language discovery 1

1 a-4 **b**-3 **c**-1 **b**-2. Questions **b** and **d** are more formal than questions **a** and **c**.

2 a The unabridged word is etwas. **b** **Nein** is the standard German word.

Practice 1

1 a Mach's nochmal. **b** Gib's her! **c** Habt ihr 'was Schönes unternommen? **d** Jetzt wird's ernst. **e** Hast du's verstanden? **f** Morgen wird's regnen. **g** Das war's.

2 Possible answers: **a** Da bin ich ganz deiner Meinung. Da stimme ich mit dir überein. **b** Da bin ich Ihrer Meinung. **c** Da bin ich anderer Meinung./Da muss ich widersprechen. **d** Nein. Da bin ich (ganz) anderer Meinung. **e** Da bin ich deiner Ansicht. Da stimme ich mit dir überein. **f** Da bin ich ganz deiner Meinung./Da stimme ich mit dir überein.

3 a Wie **b** Was denkst du über die Politik ... **c** von der **d** Sind (Sie) der ... **e** darin überein **f** Wie ist deine/Ihre Ansicht ...

4 Answers will vary.

Reading

1 a It's work. **b** A third of all people who are in employment. **c** Back pain and fatigue.

2 a F. Most Germans (more than 50%) feel more stressed today. **b** F. The group most affected are people between 35 and 45. (Apart from looking after their children and their career, they often need to take care of their parents). **c** R. **d** F. It's important to find the resources to fight off stress. For one out of two employees, stress is a motivation; and one out of five says they work best under stress. **e** R. **f** F. It has become more difficult. **g** F. One third of all people find it difficult to disconnect from work. 40% (every 4th person) say that they are 'always on'.

3 a Dauerdruck **b** eine Frage der inneren Einstellung **c** Ansprüche **d** eine Utopie **e** Ressourcen **f** der Ausgleich **g** richtig abzuschalten **h** stets

4 a-4 **b**-5 **c**-6 **d**-1 **e**-9 **f**-8 **g**-2 **h**-3 **i**-7

Listen and understand

1 b alcoholism

2 a In Berlin. **b** Er warnte vor den Gefahren des zunehmenden Alkoholismus. **c** Es gibt etwa zehnmal so viel Alkoholtote wie Drogentote. **d** Es gibt anderthalb bis zwei Millionen Alkoholiker. **e** Krankheiten wie Leberzirrhose, Hirnabbau und verschiedene Krebserkrankungen.

3 a, **c**, **d** and **g** indicate an increase; **b**, **e** and **f** indicate a decrease

4 a Kongress **b** Ärztekammer **c** Alkoholismus **d** unbemerkt **e** Öffentlichkeit **f** Zahl **g** hoch **h** Insgesamt **i** Alkoholmissbrauchs **j** Leber **k** Hirn **l** Krebs **m** Einschätzung **n** verkannt

Language discovery 2

1 masculine: des, feminine: der, neuter: des, plural: der. Masculine and neuter nouns add an -s or -es. An -s is normally added to longer words (des Alkoholmissbrauchs) and -es for shorter words (des Geldes)

2 c

Practice 2

1 a des Rauchens **b** meines Bruders **c** der Fußballmannschaft **d** ihres Mannes **e** deiner Meinung **f** Meines Erachtens **g** meiner beiden Brüder

2 a Die Lehrerin des Kurses hat lange in Kalifornien gelehrt. **b** Die Ansprüche der Menschen an sich selber sind manchmal sehr hoch. **c** Die Unternehmungen unseres Vereins machen uns viel Spaß. **d** Geschäftsreisen sind ein angenehmer Aspekt ihres Berufs. **e** Das kulturelle Angebot Münchens ist wirklich aufregend. **f** Baden-Baden ist der bekannteste Kurort Deutschlands. Note that there is no apostrophe in **Münchens** and **Deutschlands**.

3 a Darf **b** Könnt **c** kann **d** soll **e** will **f** Kannst **g** könnt, wollt, müsst

Conversation 2

1 a She was five years old when she started swimming. **b** She says firstly it's fun because you train with other swimmers. Secondly, she likes the various competitions because you know what you train for, even if you don't win all the time. **c** It's a good regime for keeping fit and in good health.

2 a Ihre Lehrerin hat Susanne geraten, in einen Schwimmclub einzutreten. **b** Seit zehn Jahren. **c** Am Anfang hat sie zweimal eineinhalb Stunden, also drei Stunden trainiert.
d Nein, sie trainieren mit anderen zusammen. **e** Im Moment trainiert sie fünfmal pro Woche.
f Es ist eine gute Methode, sich gesundheitlich fit zu halten. **g** Beim Schwimmen trainiert man alle Muskeln des Körpers.

3 a der Schwimmclub **b** der Wettkampf (competition) **c** die Trainingszeiten (practice time)
d die Kreislaufstörungen (problems with circulatory system, lit.: circulatory disturbances)
e das Trainingsprogramm (training programme) **f** die Rückenschmerzen (back pain)
g der Drogenmissbrauch (drug misuse) **h** die Gesundheitsversorgung (health care)
i der Schwimmunterricht (swimming lessons).

4 Soziale Aspekte: Man trainiert mit anderen Schwimmern zusammen. Man hat viel Spaß. Dann kommen noch die verschiedenen Wettkämpfe dazu. Da weiß man, wofür man trainiert hat. Gesundheitliche Aspekte: Es ist eine gute Methode, sich gesundheitlich fit zu halten. Es bringt den Kreislauf in Schwung. Beim Schwimmen belastet man die Gelenke am wenigsten. Außerdem trainiert man alle Muskeln des Körpers.

5 Answers will vary.

Test yourself

1 a Wie ist Ihre Meinung/Ansicht über ....? **b** Wie finden Sie ...?/Was halten Sie von ...?/Was denken Sie über ...? **c** Glauben Sie, dass ...? **d** Ich bin der Meinung/Ansicht, dass ...
e Ich stimme mit Ihnen überein. **f** Da muss ich Ihnen widersprechen. **g** Das ist ja ein Witz.
h Sicher, aber ...

2 a durfte/konnte **b** muss **c** können **d** durfte/konnte **e** mochte/mag **f** musste **g** kann

3 a-6; 6 is less formal. **b**-3; 3 is less formal; **c**-4; c is less formal; **d**-2; d is less formal;
e-7; e is less formal. **f**-8; 8 is less formal. **g**-5; 5 is less formal. **h**-1; 1 is less formal.

4 Ich habe mir Sorgen um meine Gesundheit gemacht. Außerdem ist mein Mann allergisch gegen Rauch. / Ja, sehr sogar. Ich bin der Meinung, dass das Rauchen in der Öffentlichkeit verboten werden sollte. / Oh, ja. Hast du eigentlich deinen Alkoholkonsum gedrosselt? / War das, weil du dir Sorgen um die Folgeschäden des Alkoholmissbrauchs gemacht hast?

UNIT 7

Conversation 1
1 Silke wants to fly out Friday evening and return Sunday night or Monday morning. The Monday morning flight gets in at 8 a.m. which is cutting it close to report to the office for 9 a.m., but she'll speak with her supervisor.
2 a Um 14.20 Uhr. **b** Um 19.00 Uhr. **c** Um 20.25 Uhr. **d** Sie möchte am Sonntagabend oder Montagmorgen zurückfliegen. **e** Sie muss noch mit ihrer Chefin sprechen.
3 a wenn es geht **b** die Maschine **c** es sind noch Plätze frei **d** startet der letzte Flug **e** das wäre nicht so schlimm **f** Was kostet ...

Language discovery 1
1 a Ich hätte gern gewusst, ... **b** Dann müsste ich auch noch wissen, ...
2 b and **d**

Practice 1
1 a hätte **b** hätten **c** könntest **d** müsstest **e** dürften **f** möchtet, könnten **g** wäre, würde
2 a Wäre es möglich, die Spätmaschine zu nehmen? **b** Ich müsste noch mal mit dem Reisebüro sprechen. **c** Hättest du Lust, mit ins Kino zu kommen? **d** Wissen Sie, wie teuer es wäre, mit dem Taxi zu fahren? **e** Dürfte ich Ihr Handy benutzen? **f** Könnten Sie mir sagen, wo man in Berlin gut ausgehen kann?
3 Entschuldigung, könnten Sie mir sagen, ... / Entschuldigung, wissen Sie, ... **a** ... wie weit es bis in die Stadtmitte ist? **b** ... was eine Tageskarte für die U-Bahn kostet? **c** ... wie ich am schnellsten nach Charlottenburg komme? **d** ... wo es hier in der Nähe eine Touristeninformation gibt? **e** ... ob das hier vorne eigentlich die Gedächtniskirche ist? **f** ... wo sich die nächste öffentliche Toilette befindet? **g** ... wo man hier in der Nähe gut essen gehen kann?
4 Model answer: Ich hätte gern gewusst, ob morgen früh gegen neun Uhr ein Zug nach Berlin fährt. / Und wissen Sie, wann der Zug in Berlin ankommt? / Könnten Sie mir noch sagen, was die Fahrt kostet? / Dann würde ich noch gern wissen, ob ich umsteigen muss. / Und könnten Sie mir sagen, ob der Zug einen Speisewagen und WLAN-Zugang hat?

Listen and understand
1 It's the cheapest way to go into town, it's 10 times cheaper than going by taxi. She can buy a ticket from the driver on the bus.
2 a Mit der Linie 109. **b** Wenn man viel Gepäck hat. **c** Mit der U-Bahn. **d** Es sind nur drei Stationen. **e** Durch den Ausgang, dann nach links und circa 50 Meter geradeaus.
3 a hätte **b** ungefähr **c** vielleicht **d** Güntzelstraße **e** rechten
4 a der Bahnhof *train station* **b** der Taxistand *taxi rank* **c** die Bushaltestelle *bus stop* **d** U-Bahnstation *underground station* **e** das Tagesticket *day ticket* **f** die öffentlichen Verkehrsmittel *public transport* **g** der Flughafen *airport* **h** die Flugverbindung *flight connection* **i** der Fahrkartenautomat *ticket machine*

Language discovery 2

1 a nach **b** Vom, zum **c** in **d** auf

2 a für (acc.) **b** wegen (gen.) **c** mit (dat.) **d** durch (acc.) **e** von (dat.)

Practice 2

1 a 1 über **2** because of 'gehen' it takes the accusative **b 1** in **2** because of 'kommen' it takes the accusative **c 1** in **2** it takes the dative because 'befinden' puts the emphasis on location **d 1** neben **2** it requires the dative because of 'sein' i.e. location **e 1** auf **2** the verb 'stellen' indicates movement so it's the accusative

2 a gegen **b** mit **c** trotz **d** zwischen **e** für

3 a die **b** die **c** des **d** meinem **e** einem **f** der **g** dem

Conversation 2

1 a No, she was born in Nuremberg, but studied in Berlin and has lived there for over 20 years. **b** Change; Berlin is a city of perpetual change. **c** There is a great range of shopping on offer, from elegant department stores such as the KaDeWe, to classy boutiques and alternative shops.

2 a Sie lebt seit über 20 Jahren in Berlin. **b** Sie sagt, dass die Berliner Humor haben und sagen, was sie denken. **c** Nach dem 1. Weltkrieg. **d** Es folgten 12 Jahre Diktatur. **e** Im Brücke-Museum wird expressionistische Kunst gezeigt. **f** Sie können nach Kreuzberg oder zum Prenzlauer Berg gehen, wo es viele Szenekneipen, Restaurants und Clubs gibt.

3 a Geschichte **b** Dorf **c** Preußen **d** der 1. Weltkrieg **e** expressionistische Kunst **f** Wiederaufbau **g** der Fall der Mauer / der Mauerfall **h** Einkaufen

4 Depending on your perception you may have put some of the items from the last category under *Geschichte*.

Berlin heute	Geschichte	Bewohner	Sehenswürdigkeiten
3,4 Millionen Einwohner Hauptstadt das wirkliche Zentrum von Deutschland multikulturelle Metropole	ein großes Dorf im 19. Jahrhundert Teilung von 1961 bis 1989 der Mauerfall	können unfreundlich wirken humorvoll und tolerant	das Brandenburger Tor der Reichstag das KaDeWe der Fernsehturm das Holocaust-Mahnmal

5 Answers will vary.

Reading

1 a It increased by 4.4 %. **b** Great Britain, USA, the Netherlands and Italy. **c** Because there are many cheap and direct flights to Berlin.

2 a R. **b** F. Berlin ist die Nummer 3, nach London und Paris. **c** F. Die meisten (57,1 Prozent) kamen aus Deutschland. **d** R. **e** F. Es kamen 10,9 Prozent mehr als im Vorjahr. Die Briten buchten 18,4 Prozent mehr Übernachtungen. **f** R.

3 a-7 **b**-4 **c**-2 **d**-6 **e**-9 **f**-8 **g**-1 **h**-3 **i**-5

4 Answers will vary.

Test yourself

1 a der **b** die, zum **c** der **d** Zum, der **e** die, der **f** der, dem **g** den, dem

2 Wir sind hier in der Brandenburgischen Straße. Sehen Sie die Ampel an der nächsten Kreuzung? / Dort biegen Sie rechts in die Düsseldorfer Straße. Nach ungefähr 300 Metern kommen Sie zur Konstanzer Straße. Gehen Sie über die Konstanzer Straße, ungefähr 300 Meter geradeaus, bis Sie zur Bayerischen Straße kommen. Biegen Sie an dieser Kreuzung links in die Bayerische Straße. / Nein, nicht rechts, sondern links in die Bayerische Straße. Dann ungefähr einen Kilometer weiter kommen Sie zur Pariser Straße. / Bitte schön.

3 a Stadt **b** Weltkrieg **c** Jahrhundert **d** „Goldenen Zwanziger' **e** Nationalsozialisten **f** Diktatur **g** Wiederaufbau **h** Mauerbau **i** Mauer **j** Hauptstadt **k** Einwohnern **l** Magnet **m** Angebot **n** Nachtleben.

UNIT 8

Conversation 1

1 a hard-working **b** early risers **d** tidiness **e** like celebrating Christmas

2 a Er ist zum ersten Mal in Deutschland. **b** Die sogenannten typisch deutschen Eigenschaften. **c** Sie sagte ihm, dass die Deutschen sehr früh aufstehen. **d** Er findet, dass die Deutschen manchmal ein bisschen übertreiben. **e** Sie kochen zum Beispiel Essen und backen Plätzchen und Kuchen.

3 a froh **b** ordnungsliebend **c** sauber **d** gepflegt

4 a ... fleißig wie die Deutschen. **b** ... morgens früh auf. **c** ... Häuser und Straßen ... **d** ... viel Aufwand. **e** ... auch wenn sie nicht zusammen feiern.

Language discovery 1

1 -er is added: **a** Ich finde, die Häuser und Straßen in Deutschland sehen viel sauberer und gepflegter aus als in England. **b** Das ist in England weniger der Fall.

2 In the singular all adjectives add -e regardless of whether they precede a masculine, feminine or neuter noun; in the plural -en is added.

Practice 1

1 a -e **b** -en **c** -en **d** -en **e** -en, -en **f** -e **g** -en

2 a wie **b** als **c** wie **d** wie **e** als

3 a gastfreundlicher / konservativer **b** toleranter / weniger **c** herzlicher / intoleranter **d** weltoffener / arroganter **e** humorvoller / sparsamer

4 Answers will vary.

Listen and understand

1 a The cliché about German thoroughness (Gründlichkeit). **b** He says that studying foreign languages is encouraged much more in Germany. **c** Martin thinks that there may be a grain of truth in it, but that you can find all these characteristics in people from other countries as well.

2 a unterschiedlich **b** gründlich **c** guten **d** weniger **e** dreijährige **f** den Arbeitsbereich **g** dran

3 a Nimm doch nur mal die Ausbildung in Deutschland ... **b** So viel Wert wird auf Qualifikationen gelegt. **c** Ich glaube, dass die Deutschen im Allgemeinen ihre Freizeitaktivitäten viel systematischer angehen. **d** Da ist sicher ein Körnchen Wahrheit dran. **e** Du erscheinst mir nicht wie der typische Deutsche.

Reading

1 a They think that the Germans are well organized, precise/meticulous and a bit pendantic. **b** They tend to exaggerate their own weaknesses and worry too much. **c** Germany is no longer associated with its Nazi past; that is no longer seen as relevant.

2 a R. **b** F. Jeder fünfte Niederländer beschreibt die Deutschen als nette und freundliche Menschen. **c** F. Acht Prozent der Österreicher mögen die Deutschen nicht. **d** R. **e** F. Assoziationen mit Hitler und den Nazis spielen heute kaum noch eine Rolle. **f** F. Das Interesse an Deutschland und den Deutschen hat in den letzten Jahren zugenommen.

3 a-6 **b**-8 **c**-1 **d**-9 **e**-2 **f**-4 **g**-3 **h**-5 **i**-7

4 a Amerikaner **b** Chinesen **c** Costa Ricaner **d** Österreicher **e** Franzosen **f** Niederländer **g** Tschechen

Language discovery 2

1 a Israel bezeichnet Deutschland als einen guten Freund. **b** Sie halten sie für eine offene und sehr zugängliche Nation. **c** Es gibt ein größeres Interesse an Deutschland.

The endings for masculine and feminine nouns are the same (-en, -e), but the endings preceding a neuter noun are different: with the definite articles they take −e in the accusative, with the indefinite article it's -es.

2 seien (a subjunctive form of sein; it's explained in the next grammar entry in this unit.)

Practice 2

1 In einem Interview sagte Herbert Grönemeyer, dass er sehr gerne in London **lebe**. Besonders **gefalle** ihm die Anonymität, die er hier haben würde. Daneben **genieße** er die Kreativität der Musikszene in London. Er **habe** manchmal Probleme mit dem Chaos, das es oft in London **gebe** und mit einer gewissen Unhöflichkeit. Aber London **sei** trotzdem zu einer zweiten Heimat geworden.

2 a Iain meint, dass die Schotten wirklich gastfreundlich seien. **b** Kathrin sagt, dass New York zu hektisch sei. **c** Clara und Jan erklärten, dass die Restaurants in Berlin wirklich gut seien. **d** Maike fügte hinzu, dass die Musikszene nach London die beste in Europa sei.

3 a -es, -es **b** -en, -e **c** -es **d** -en **e** -en **f** -e **g** -en, -en **h** -es, -es

Conversation 2

1 a First she spent a week in London and then went to Cornwall for another week. **b** She thought the English were cold and reserved and that she would never be able to make contact with them, especially with their different sense of humour. **c** She said she picked up stereotypes from somewhere at some point.

2 a Sie sagt, London sei eine tolle Stadt. **b** Sie fand die Landschaft einfach fantastisch. **c** Sie dachte, dass es ein kaltes und verregnetes Land sei. **d** Sie hat viele nette Leute kennen gelernt, mit denen sie sich großartig verstanden hat. **e** Nein, sie sagt im Großen und Ganzen nicht. **f** Auf jeden Fall wieder nach England.

3 a sei, bekäme **b** seien, käme

4 Wetter: Sie meinte, das England ein kaltes und verregnetes Land sei. – Es ist fast so wie in Deutschland. Man kann nicht gerade einen Badeurlaub in England machen. Essen: Helga meinte, man könne in England nichts außer Steak and Kidney Pie und Fish and Chips essen. – Sie war ein paar mal zum Essen eingeladen und es war ausgezeichnet. Leute: Helga dachte, dass die Engländer kühl und reserviert seien und dass man nie in Kontakt mit ihnen käme, erst recht nicht, wenn man ihre Art von Humor nicht versteht. – Sie hat viele nette Leute kennen gelernt, mit denen sie sich großartig verstanden hat.

5 Answers will vary.

Test yourself

1 a Helga sagte, dass man in Cornwall sehr gut wandern könne. **b** Außerdem meinte sie, dass sie viele nette Leute kennen gelernt habe. **c** Sie betonte, dass England eine sehr multikulturelle Gesellschaft sei. **d** Sie erklärte, dass die meisten Menschen sehr tolerant seien. **e** Helga sagte, dass sie nächstes Jahr wieder nach England fahren wolle.

2 a -e, -e **b** -e, -em **c** -em **d** -en, -en **e** -em **f** -en, -e, -en

3 a -er **b** -en **c** -en, -e **d** no endings **e** -er, -es **f** -e

4 Ich habe mich weitgehend an die englische Lebensart angepasst, obwohl ich mich bemüht habe, meine deutsche Kultur und Sprache nicht zu vergessen. / Ich weiß, dass sie existieren, aber glücklicherweise sind sie mehr die Ausnahme als die Regel. Manchmal fragen mich die Leute über die typisch deutschen Eigenschaften, wie die deutsche Gründlichkeit oder ob die Deutschen wirklich so früh aufstehen und so hart arbeiten. / Meistens lache ich und sage, dass ich sehr skeptisch bin, was diese typisch deutschen Eigenschaften anbelangt. Ich glaube, man kann sie auch in Menschen anderer Nationalität entdecken.

UNIT 9

Conversation 1

1 a He would like to know more about where he could save energy. **b** She mentions renewable energies: biomass and solar. **c** He switches off his computer and the lights when he leaves his room. He and his family also turn off the radio when they don't need it.

2 a F. Er meint, dass die Politiker und die Industrie mehr unternehmen müssten. **b** R. **c** F. Sie sagt, von Atomkraft sollte man auf Dauer ganz wegkommen. **d** R. **e** R.

3 Zu Hause: Den Computer und das Licht ausmachen, wenn man aus dem Zimmer geht. / Das Radio ausmachen, wenn man es nicht mehr braucht. / Es gibt einen speziellen Zähler, der anzeigt, wie viel Energie man verbraucht./ Auf dem Dach Solarzellen anbringen; Allgemein: Mehr Geld für die Erforschung und Nutzung alternativer Energiequellen ausgeben. / Mehr Biomasse und Sonnenenergie nutzen. / Erneuerbare Energien sind langfristig viel sinnvoller. / Wenn man mit dem Bus fährt, kann man einiges an Energie sparen.

Language discovery 1

1 müssen:... auch die Politiker und die Industrie müssten mehr unternehmen. Abgesehen davon müsste die Sonnenenergie ... **sollen**: Man sollte mehr Geld ... Von Atomkraft sollte man auf Dauer ... **sein**: ... das wäre vielleicht auch eine ganz gute Alternative ....

2 When the first noun ends in -schaft, -tät and -ung, an additional -s is added: Landschaft**s**gärtner, Universität**s**park, Heizung**s**anlage.

Practice 1

1 a der Umweltschutz *protection of the environment* **b** die Biomasse *biomass* **c** das Ozonloch *hole in the ozone layer* **d** die Sonnenenergie *solar energy* **e** der Landschaftspark *landscape park* **f** die Solarzelle *solar cell* **g** der Klimawandel *climate change* **h** die Plastiktüte *plastic bag* **i** das Verpackungsmaterial *packaging (material)*. Also possible: die Bioenergie.

2 a Wenn Sie in der Stadt ihrer Wahl leben könnte, würde sie am liebsten in Mailand leben. **b** Wenn sie im Lotto gewinnen würde, würde sie eine Weltreise machen. **c** Wenn sie in der Vergangenheit leben könnte, würde sie am liebsten in der Antike oder im 19. Jahrhundert leben. **d** Wenn sie eine bekannte Person interviewen könnte, würde sie am liebsten Angelina Jolie interviewen. **e** Wenn sie in einem Film mitspielen könnte, würde sie am liebsten im neuen James Bond-Film mitspielen. **f** Wenn sie für einen Tag Bundeskanzlerin wäre, würde sie mehr Feiertage einführen.

3 Answers will vary.

Listen and understand

1 He doesn't like people waffling about the environment and recycling. He thinks it's all too late anyway and that separation of rubbish is nonsense. He thinks life is too short and he wants to enjoy himself.

2 a Bierdose **b** Nase **c** sinnvolle **d** Container **e** Tasche **f** kurz

3 a-4 **b**-5 **c**-6 **d**-1 **e**-2 **f**-3

4 a Was geht Sie das denn an? **b** Es i doch sowieso alles schon zu spät. **c** Wollen Sie mich auf den Arm nehmen? **d** All dieser ganze Quatsch ... **e** Jetzt lassen Sie mich in Ruhe.

Reading

1 a It wants to decommission all nuclear power plants in Germany. **b** To increase the share of renewable energies to 80% or more. **c** The cost of electricity could increase dramatically. In addition, Germany will be dependent on Russian gas for a long time.

2 a F. Die Bundesregierung beschloss bis 2020 alle Atomkraftwerke abzuschalten. Im Frühjahr 2011 wurden bereits acht Atomkraftwerke abgeschaltet. **b** R. **c** F. Bis 2050 sollen Wohnhäuser nahezu klimaneutral sein. **d** R. **e** R.

3 a 80 % – so hoch soll der Anteil der erneuerbaren Energien an der Stromversorgung im Jahre 2050 sein. **b** 40 % – ist im Moment der Anteil, den Heizungen am gesamten Energieverbrauch haben. **c** 50 % – Frankreich will den Anteil der Atomenergie bis 2025 auf 50 % senken. **d** 15 % – die USA wollen ihren Energieverbrauch bis 2020 um 15 % reduzieren.

4 a ... Energiewende. **b** ... Kohle, Öl und Gas. **c** ... die Biomasse, Wind- und Solarenergie. **d** ... die Atomkraft und Fracking.

Language discovery 2

1 The two sets of sentences illustrate the change of perspective between active and passive structures: In the first pair, the emphasis of the first sentence is on the 'doer', the mechanic. In the second sentence – with a passive structure – it is on the act of repairing. Likewise with the next pair; in the first sentence the federal government, the 'doer', is the main focus. In the second sentence, the emphasis is on the action.

2 a-3 **b**-1 **c**-2

Practice 2

1 a Es wird dunkel. **b** Wenn ich sie wäre, würde ich nicht so viel rauchen. **c** Nächsten Sommer werden wir nach Griechenland fliegen. **d** Das wird viel kosten. **e** Er wurde Politiker. **f** Alle Häuser sollen/sollten energieeffizienter werden.

2 a werden **b** wird **c** werden **d** wird **e** werden

3 a 1871 wurde Berlin zur Hauptstadt des Deutschen Reiches gewählt. **b** 1945 wurde es zerstört. **c** Zwischen 1945 und 1949 wurde Berlin wieder aufgebaut. **d** 1961 wurde die Berliner Mauer gebaut. **e** 1989 wurde die Stadt wiedervereinigt. **f** 2012 wurde das 775. Stadtjubiläum gefeiert.

Conversation 2

1 a He says that people in South America have bigger things than waste to worry about. **b** He is surprised and asks: 'Are you joking?' It all seems strange to him. **c** They should be taken to a special collecting point / recycling centre.

2 a Er hat davon gelesen. **b** Sie hat drei Tonnen zu Hause in ihrer Garage. **c** Das Altpapier kommt in die blaue Tonne. **d** Sie sagt, dass jetzt jeder etwas für die Umwelt tun kann. **e** Man muss Geld bezahlen. **f** Sie kommen in spezielle Container.

3 a Biomüll **b** Verpackungen **c** vierzehntägig **d** zeitaufwendig **e** Sondermüll **f** Altbatterien

4 blaue Tonne: Altpapier, Zeitungen; braune Tonne: Biomüll, Karottenschalen; Gelber Sack: Blechdosen, Konservendosen, Plastiktüten; Container: Batterien, Glasflaschen; Sammelstelle: Lacke, Farben

5 Answers will vary.

Test yourself

1 a müsste **b** sollte **c** wäre, gäbe **d** würde, würden **e** könnte **f** müssten

2 a mit **b** von **c** durch **d** durch **e** von **f** von

3 Also, es gibt eine braune Tonne für Biomüll, eine blaue für Papier und einen Plastiksack für alle Verpackungen, die den Grünen Punkt haben. Alles wird im Wechsel vierzehntägig abgeholt. / Ja, die meisten Leute machen mit. Wenn man nicht mitmacht, muss man saftige Strafen zahlen. Gibt es eigentlich große Unterschiede zwischen Deutschland und England? / Ich glaube, dass Recycling eine sehr sinnvolle Sache ist. Denn wenn wir jetzt nichts für die Umwelt tun, wie sieht dann die Welt für die Kinder in der Zukunft aus? / Natürlich, aber es ist zumindest ein Anfang gemacht.

UNIT 10

Conversation 1

1 a Local and regional papers dominate the news market. **b** It's the most well-known tabloid. **c** Sunday papers play a less important role than in the UK. Many German newspapers do not have a Sunday edition.

2 a Sie berichten über Ereignisse in der Region, haben auch aber Welt- und Wirtschaftsnachrichten. **b** Zum Beispiel die *Süddeutsche Zeitung*, die *Frankfurter Rundschau*, die *Frankfurter Allgemeine Zeitung* und *Die Welt*. **c** Politisch ist die Frankfurter Allgemeine Zeitung eher konservativ. **d** Computerzeitschriften, Magazine für Essen und Trinken und Zeitschriften über Motorsport. **e** Das Nachrichtenmagazin *Der Spiegel* gibt es seit 1947.

3 a Zeitungsmarkt **b** Qualitätsblatt **c** linksliberal **d** Boulevardzeitung **e** erscheinen **f** Nachrichtenmagazine

Language discovery 1

1 a Regional **b** nachrichten **c** zeitungen. In these phrases the hyphen replaces the last part of a compound word when it is the same as in the noun that follows: Lokalzeitungen und Regionalzeitungen; Weltnachrichten und Wirtschaftsnachrichten; Sonntagszeitungen und Wochenzeitungen.

2 a ...which has been on the market since 1974. **b** ...(to) who(m) I gave 100 euros **c** ... whose wife is a journalist.

Practice 1

1 a Der Vorschlag hat viele Vor-und Nachteile. **b** Die Universität bietet sowohl Bachelor- wie Masterkurse an. **c** Die Groß- und Kleinschreibung verursacht vielen Leuten Probleme. **d** Es hängt davon ab, ob ich Früh- oder Spätschicht habe. **e** Probier es ein- oder zweimal. **f** Sie müssen hier ein- und dort aussteigen.

2 a-4 **b**-6 **c**-5 **d**-1 **e**-2 **f**-3

3 a Die Telekom hat einen Handytarif im Angebot, der sehr günstig ist. **b** Das Sportmagazin *Kicker* hat eine neue Internetseite, die sehr gut aussieht. **c** Hier ist das Tablet von Timo, das nur 99 Euro gekostet hat. **d** Das ist die neue App, die von einer Firma in Berlin entwickelt wurde.

4 Answers will vary.

Listen and understand

1 a-3 **b**-3 **c**-2 **d**-2 **e**-3 **f**-2 **g**-1

2 a Hamburg, Bremen und Berlin werden auch Stadtstaaten genannt. **b** Das größte Bundesland ist Bayern. **c** Es liegt in der Mitte von Europa. **d** Der Bundespräsident hat vor allem repräsentative Aufgaben. **e** Das föderalistische Prinzip ist ein Grundpfeiler der politischen Struktur Deutschlands.

3 a Unser erstes Thema heute ist Deutschland. **b** Nun, stellen Sie sich einmal die Europakarte vor ... **c** Wie Sie wissen, besteht Deutschland aus 16 Bundesländern **d** Insgesamt sind es neun Länder .... **e** Aber wie viele Abgeordnete hat der Bundestag eigentlich? **f** Mehr darüber in der nächsten Woche.

Reading

1 a It's generally positive. Germans still believe in a common future for Europe. **b** Scepticism about the Euro has increased. Only 35 % are particularly proud of the common currency. One third of Germans think that they would be better off with the old currency, the Deutschmark. **c** They wish that their professional qualifications or degrees were recognized throughout the whole of Europe.

2 a Das Vertrauen schwindet ... **b** Zwei der wichtigsten Errungenschaften ... **c** Die Skepsis hat sich deutlich verstärkt ... **d** Mittlerweile sind nur noch etwa 35 % besonders stolz auf ... **e** Leute mit geringerem Einkommen. **f** ... unter großem Widerstand ...

3 a F. 60 % der Deutschen unterstützen die Übertragung von mehr Kompetenzen an Brüssel. **b** R. **c** F. Für die Deutschen ist die Möglichkeit, innerhalb Europas ohne Grenzen reisen zu können sehr wichtig. **d** F. Vor allem ältere Leuten sowie Leute mit geringerem Einkommen sind eher skeptisch gegenüber dem Euro. **e** R. **f** R.

4 Pro EU: Man kann ohne Grenzen reisen. / Es gibt die Möglichkeit, in allen Mitgliedsstaaten zu arbeiten. / Die EU-Zusammenarbeit hat Frieden gebracht. / Die EU kann Vorbild für andere Regionen sein. Contra EU: Es gibt Skepsis gegenüber dem Euro. / Viele denken, es ginge ihnen ohne den Euro besser. / Die EU ist zu bürokratisch. / Die Institutionen sind zu weit von den Bürgern entfernt.

Language discovery 2

1 -en is added to Journalist in all cases except the nominative.

2 a krank **b** reich **c** verwandt **d** deutsch **e** fremd **f** verlobt.

Practice 2

1 a Fotografen **b** Student **c** Kollegen **d** Kunde **e** Nachbarn **f** Herrn, Präsidenten **g** Herren

2 a ein Selbständiger, eine Selbständige (a self-employed person) **b** ein Heiliger, eine Heilige (a saint, a holy person) **c** ein Armer, eine Arme (a pauper, a poor person) **d** ein Verrückter, eine Verrückte (a lunatic) **e** ein Bekannter, eine Bekannte (an acquaintance) **f** ein Jugendlicher, eine Jugendliche (an adolescent, a teenager).

3 a Deutschen **b** Bekannte **c** Verlobten **d** Verrückter **e** Verwandter **f** Abgeortnete **g** Jugendlichen

Conversation 2

1 a R. **b** F. Every fourth job in Germany is linked to exports. **c** F. Trading partners are first Europe, then Asia, and the USA in third place.

2 a das produzierende Gewerbe **b** Bereich **c** Motor **d** Maschinenbau **e** chemische Industrie **f** Haushalt **g** Handelspartner **h** Entwicklung

3 a Die chemische Industrie und der Maschinenbau. **b** Mehr als 80 %. **c** Sie sagt, dass der Markt in Deutschland relativ gesättigt sei und dass der Trend im Moment weg vom eigenen Auto und hin zu Carsharing oder öffentlichen Verkehrsmitteln gehe. **d** Nach Asien. **e** Sie denkt, dass sich die Wirtschaft in Europa bald wieder erholen wird.

4 a bekannt sind. **b** abhängig ist. **c** Haushalt ein Auto hat. **d** immer wichtiger geworden ist.

5 Answers will vary.

Test yourself

1 Das ist Herr Franke, ... **a** der als Journalist arbeitet. **b** dessen Frau auch Journalistin ist. **c** dessen Sohn in den USA studiert. **d** der einen roten Ferrari fährt. **e** der meistens italienische Anzüge trägt. **f** den man auf vielen Partys sieht. **g** von dem ich noch €400 bekomme.

2 b Einwohner **c** Demokratie **d** Bundestag **e** Abgeordnete **f** gewählt **g** Macht **h** Bundeskanzler **i** Bundespräsident **j** Aufgaben **k** Export **l** Branchen **m** Handelspartner

3 Das produzierende Gewerbe ist sehr wichtig. Es ist der Motor der deutschen Industrie. / Die chemische Industrie und der Maschinenbau sind auch wichtig. / Ja. Die Autoindustrie zum Beispiel exportiert 80 % ihrer Produkte. Jeder vierte Arbeitsplatz hängt vom Export ab. / Die wichtigsten Handelspartner sind die Länder der EU. Dann kommen Asien und die USA. In den letzten Jahren ist China immer wichtiger geworden. / Ich denke, dass sich die Wirtschaft in Europa bald erholen wird. In den letzten Jahren sind in Deutschland viele neue Arbeitsplätze entstanden. Im Großen und Ganzen bin ich ganz optimistisch.

Listen and understand – Transcripts

UNIT 1 DREI KANDIDATEN STELLEN SICH VOR

 01.02

Moderator	Herzlich willkommen, liebe Zuschauer, zu einer neuen Ausgabe von Super-Preis, das Superquizspiel. Zuerst zu unseren Kandidaten. Kandidat 1. Können Sie sich bitte kurz vorstellen?
Martin	Ja, ich bin der Martin, bin 32, geschieden und komme aus Apolda.
Moderator	Nicht alle Zuschauer werden wissen, wo das liegt. Können Sie uns das kurz erklären?
Martin	Das liegt im Freistaat Thüringen, in der Nähe von Weimar.
Moderator	Gibt es denn etwas Besonderes dort?
Martin	Wir haben ein Bockbierfest dort, das ist ziemlich bekannt.
Moderator	Was machen Sie denn beruflich, Martin?
Martin	Ich bin Krankenpfleger im örtlichen Krankenhaus.
Moderator	Das ist wahrscheinlich ein zeitraubender Job. Bleibt Ihnen denn da noch Zeit für irgendwelche Hobbys?
Martin	Nicht so viel. Aber ich gehe gern ins Kino und fahre sehr gern Ski.
Moderator	So, das war unser erster Kandidat, Martin. Applaus, bitte. Und schnell weiter zu unserer zweiten Kandidatin, Petra.
Petra	Mein Name ist Petra Wunderlich. Ich bin 44 Jahre alt, verheiratet und komme aus Salzburg in Österreich.
Moderator	Ja, Salzburg kennt ja nun fast jeder, Mozart, die Mozartkugeln und so weiter. Was sind Sie denn von Beruf, Petra?
Petra	Ich bin Hotelfachfrau. Mit meinem Mann führe ich eine kleine Pension, die „Pension zur Post". Wir haben 20 Betten.
Moderator	Und was machen Sie in Ihrer Freizeit?
Petra	Nun, viel Zeit bleibt uns nicht, da wir das ganze Jahr über Gäste haben. Ich interessiere mich aber sehr für Geschichte und wenn ich Zeit habe, lese ich.
Moderator	Danke, danke. Applaus, bitte. Schnell zu Kandidaten Nummer 3.
Max	Ja, ich bin der Max, 22 Jahre jung und single. Noch zu haben also ...
Moderator	Und woher kommen Sie?
Max	Ich komme aus Norddeutschland, aus Lübeck.
Moderator	Und was machen Sie beruflich, Max?
Max	Ich bin Student. Ich studiere Mathematik.
Moderator	Und in Ihrer Freizeit? Was für Hobbys haben Sie?
Max	Ich liebe es gefährlich, mache Bungeespringen und in den Ferien gehe ich surfen.
Moderator	Gut. Das war Max. Danke schön. Und damit können wir nun mit der ersten Runde anfangen. Also ...

UNIT 2 WAS MACHT FRAU WOLFRAM?

02.02

Martina	Corinna, du bist 22 Jahre alt, wohnst seit zwei Jahren in München und arbeitest als Kellnerin. Wie sieht eigentlich dein Tagesablauf aus?
Corinna	Es kommt darauf an, ob ich Frühschicht oder Spätschicht arbeiten muss. Wir haben nämlich in der Gaststätte, wo ich arbeite, bis um Mitternacht durchgehend geöffnet. Wenn ich Spätschicht mache, komme ich erst gegen eins, halb zwei nach Hause. Ich stelle mich dann schnell unter die Dusche und gehe sofort ins Bett. Am nächsten Tag stehe ich dann meistens erst um neun oder halb zehn auf. Zum Frühstück trinke ich ein Glas Orangen- oder Grapefruitsaft und manchmal esse ich auch eine Scheibe Toast mit Marmelade oder Honig.
Martina	Da hast du dann ein paar Stunden Freizeit, oder?
Corinna	Ja. Bis vier Uhr nachmittags kann ich machen, was ich will. Einmal in der Woche bringe ich meine Wäsche zum Waschsalon. Ab und zu räume ich mein Zimmer auf. Aber das nimmt nicht allzu viel Zeit in Anspruch.
Martina	Was machst du also mit deiner Freizeit?
Corinna	Zweimal in der Woche – montags und mittwochs – habe ich Englischstunden. Da wir in der Gaststätte so viele Ausländer haben, versuche ich meine Englischkenntnisse aufzufrischen. Sonst gehe ich mit meinem Freund ins Kino oder wir fahren nach Starnberg zum Windsurfen auf dem Starnberger See.
Martina	Und wie oft siehst du deine Eltern?
Corinna	Höchstens viermal im Jahr zu Weihnachten und bei Geburtstagen. Die wohnen ja in Würzburg, was ziemlich weit weg ist.
Martina	Und wie ist es mit dem Essen? Bekommst du deine Mahlzeiten hier im Restaurant umsonst?
Corinna	Oh, ja. Das versteht sich von selbst. In meinem Zimmer habe ich nur eine Kochnische mit einer Heizplatte und einem kleinen Kühlschrank.

UNIT 4 WAS MACHST DU JETZT FÜR EINE ARBEIT?

04.02

Gerd	Du, Heiko! Lange nicht gesehen! Wie geht's dir?
Heiko	Hallo, Gerd! Gut, danke.
Gerd	Und was machst du jetzt für eine Arbeit?
Heiko	Ich unterrichte Deutsch als Fremdsprache im Sprachinstitut in der Herder-Straße.
Gerd	Und wie gefällt dir deine Arbeit?
Heiko	Im Allgemeinen sehr gut. Meine Studenten sind alle motiviert und fleißig, da sie es nötig haben, so schnell wie möglich die deutsche Sprache zu erlernen. Das Einzige, was mir nicht so gut gefällt, ist die Bezahlung.
Gerd	Wenn das so ist, kannst du denn daraus einen richtigen Beruf machen? Oder hast du noch etwas ganz anderes vor?

Heiko	Naja, ich bin natürlich auf der Warteliste für eine Lehramtsstelle. Du weißt ja, dass ich eigentlich Gymnasiallehrer für Deutsch und Latein werden möchte. Und was machst du eigentlich zurzeit?
Gerd	Ich arbeite zurzeit in einem Heim für körperlich und geistig behinderte Kinder. Wie du weißt, bin ich Sozialpädagoge. Es gefällt mir sehr gut, obwohl ich auch oft nachts oder am Wochenende arbeiten muss. Das ist schon anstrengend. Aber ich lerne viel und es ist interessant. Leider habe ich nur einen befristeten Vertrag für 12 Monate.
Heiko	Und was hast du danach vor?
Gerd	Ich weiß noch nicht genau, aber ich hoffe, dass der Vertrag verlängert wird. Wenn nicht, werde ich mich um eine andere Stelle bewerben. Im Moment gibt es relativ viele Jobs für Sozialpädagogen.

UNIT 5 PLÄNE FÜR DEN SOMMER

 05.02

Sebastian	Mensch, ich bin vielleicht froh, dass die Sommerferien übermorgen anfangen!
Jochen	Und ich erst! Was hast du denn eigentlich so geplant?
Sebastian	Also, ich werde meinen Führerschein anfangen. Meine Eltern haben mich endlich in der Fahrschule angemeldet und in zwei Wochen geht's los.
Jochen	Wie viele Stunden glaubst du denn, dass du brauchen wirst?
Sebastian	Naja, zwanzig ist ja so der Durchschnitt – und wenn ich nicht durchfalle, müsste ich meinen Deckel Anfang des neuen Schuljahres schon haben! – Und was hast du denn eigentlich vor?
Jochen	Meine Eltern haben mir versprochen, dass ich meinen dritten Tanzkurs machen kann. Da freue ich mich schon total drauf.
Sebastian	Bist du da etwa immer noch dabei? Ich habe ja auch einen gemacht, vor etwa drei Jahren, aber einer hat mir gereicht. Ich gehe sowieso nur in die Disco und da brauche ich ja so was nicht – höchstens mal bei meiner Hochzeit und bis dahin habe ich wahrscheinlich schon wieder alle Schritte vergessen! Hast du denn eine Partnerin für den Kurs?
Jochen	Ja, du kennst doch die Sybille, oder? Wir haben schon den ersten und zweiten Kurs zusammen gemacht und nach dem dritten wollen wir in den Tanzclub eintreten und auch auf Turniere gehen.
Sebastian	Da muss man doch ziemlich oft trainieren, oder? Glaubst du denn nicht, dass dir das zu viel wird?
Jochen	Ach, außer dem Tanzen und dann noch meinem Schwimmtraining, mache ich eigentlich nichts weiter in meiner Freizeit. Und es ist ja eine gute Gelegenheit, neue Leute kennen zu lernen und sich auch fit zu halten.
Sebastian	Sicherlich. Aber das wäre mir ehrlich gesagt zu viel. So eingebunden zu sein, würde mir überhaupt nicht gefallen. Ich persönlich ziehe es vor, meine Freizeit flexibel zu gestalten. Außerdem bin ich eher kulturinteressiert – Sport hat mich eigentlich schon immer gelangweilt.

UNIT 7 UND WIE KOMME ICH ZU MEINEM HOTEL?

07.02

Silke	Ich hätte eine Frage, bitte. Wie komme ich am besten in die Stadt?
Dame	Mit dem Bus. Vom Flughafen fahren Sie mit der 109 bis zum Bahnhof Zoo.
Silke	Und wie teuer wär's mit einem Taxi?
Dame	Das würde Sie ungefähr das Zehnfache der Busfahrt kosten. Wenn Sie aber viel Gepäck haben, lohnt es sich vielleicht, mit einem Taxi zu fahren.
Silke	Nein, viel Gepäck habe ich nicht. Bloß muss ich vom Bahnhof Zoo noch ein bisschen weiter fahren. Mein Hotel liegt nämlich in der Güntzelstraße.
Dame	Kein Problem! Vom Zoo sind es nur drei U-Bahn-Stationen bis zur Güntzelstraße.
Silke	Wo ist die Bushaltestelle?
Dame	Durch diesen Ausgang, dann nach links. Zirka 50 Meter geradeaus. Da sehen Sie dann die Haltestelle auf der rechten Seite.
Silke	Und wo kann ich eine Fahrkarte lösen?
Dame	Im Bus beim Fahrer.

UNIT 8 AUSBILDUNG IN DEUTSCHLAND UND GROSSBRITANNIEN – EIN VERGLEICH

08.02

Martin	Ja, was die typisch deutschen Eigenschaften angeht, glaubst du, dass die Engländer wirklich so verschieden von den Deutschen sind?
Darren	Wahrscheinlich nicht. Aber die Kultur und die Mentalität sind irgendwie doch unterschiedlich. Ich finde zum Beispiel, dass dieses Klischee von der deutschen Gründlichkeit gar nicht so falsch ist.
Martin	Tatsächlich? Das musst du mir aber näher erläutern!
Darren	Naja, nimm doch nur mal die Ausbildung hier in Deutschland: man muss in diesem Land nicht unbedingt Abitur gemacht haben, um eine gute Stellung zu bekommen. Wer Hauptschulabschluss oder mittlere Reife gemacht hat, bekommt in der Lehre eine gründliche Ausbildung, sowohl praktisch als auch theoretisch, und macht eine richtige Abschlussprüfung, die ihm einen guten Start ins Berufsleben gibt.
Martin	Aber ist das in England nicht genauso?
Darren	Es ist weniger streng geregelt. Natürlich, wenn man A-Levels oder einen Universitätsabschluss hat, macht man zumeist ein gutes Training, aber ansonsten haben die Leute nicht so eine gründliche Ausbildung. Ich meine, in Deutschland macht man ja sogar als Verkäufer in einer Bäckerei oder Metzgerei eine dreijährige Ausbildung! Das gibt es in England kaum.

Martin	Und wie sieht es mit der Schulbildung in England aus?
Darren	Ja, die ist schon sehr gut. Aber zum Beispiel habe ich festgestellt, dass man in Deutschland Fremdsprachen viel mehr fördert, was ja heutzutage ungeheuer wichtig ist. Und dann finde ich auch, dass hier so viel Wert auf Qualifikationen gelegt wird.
Martin	Da hast du allerdings Recht!
Darren	Aber die Gründlichkeit erstreckt sich nicht nur auf den Arbeitsbereich. Ich finde, dass die Deutschen im Allgemeinen ihre Freizeitaktivitäten viel systematischer angehen als die Engländer. Sehr viele Leute betreiben ihr Hobby in einem Club und Talente werden sofort gefördert.
Martin	Mmmh ... ich weiß nicht so recht. Das ist zwar alles nicht ganz falsch, was du da festgestellt hast. Aber ich bin doch sehr skeptisch, was diese typisch deutschen Eigenschaften angeht. Sicherlich ist da ein Körnchen Wahrheit dran, aber ich glaube, man kann all diese Eigenschaften auch bei Menschen anderer Nationalität feststellen.
Darren	Na, ich bin nicht so sicher! Du erscheinst mir zwar auch nicht wie der typische Deutsche.

UNIT 9 ROLAND – DER UMWELTFLEGEL

 09.02

Bürgerin	Entschuldigung, aber warum werfen Sie denn Ihre leere Bierdose auf die Wiese? Da vorne ist doch ein Abfalleimer!
Roland	Häh? Was geht Sie das denn an?
Bürgerin	Also, Sie haben vielleicht eine Auffassung – wenn jeder so denken würde wie Sie, dann würden wir bald im Müll ersticken und der Park wäre eine Müllhalde.
Roland	Ach, sind Sie etwa auch so einer, der dauernd von Umwelt und Recycling schwafelt? Davon habe ich die Nase schon lange voll. Wem nützt das denn überhaupt? Ist doch sowieso alles schon zu spät. Und dieser ganze Quatsch mit dieser Müllsortierung.
Bürgerin	Recycling ist eine sehr sinnvolle Sache – wenn wir jetzt nichts für die Umwelt tun, wie sieht denn dann das Leben für unsere Kinder aus? Und wenn wir schon von Recycling reden: Dosen werden jetzt auch getrennt gesammelt!
Roland	Wollen Sie mich jetzt auf den Arm nehmen? Soll ich jetzt etwa zum Container rennen, nur um eine einzige Blechdose wegzuwerfen?
Bürgerin	Sie könnten die Dose ja in Ihre Tasche packen und später entsorgen. Damit hätten Sie zum einen die Wiese sauber gehalten und zum anderen 'was für die Umwelt getan.
Roland	Wenn Sie glauben, dass Sie mich bekehren können, haben Sie sich getäuscht. Das Leben ist kurz genug und ich will mich amüsieren. Für Ihre Moralpredigten habe ich keine Zeit. Und jetzt lassen Sie mich in Ruhe!

10.02

Unser erstes Thema heute ist Deutschland. Sie wissen sicherlich, dass Deutschland mit seinen über 81,5 Millionen Einwohnern der bevölkerungsreichste Staat in Europa ist – sieht man einmal von Russland ab – aber wie ist das flächenmäßig? Ist Deutschland auch größer als Großbritannien, größer als Frankreich? Nun, stellen Sie sich einmal die Europakarte vor – Deutschland in der Mitte, Großbritannien als Insel – nun, es ist tatsächlich um einiges größer als Großbritannien aber im Vergleich zu Frankreich – nun, da kann man zu Recht von der „Grande Nation" sprechen: mit 543 000 km² ist es mehr als doppelt so groß wie Großbritannien und auch um einiges größer als Deutschland.

Von der Bevölkerungsdichte her leben wir hier also ziemlich zusammengedrängt, verglichen mit unseren europäischen Nachbarn. Aber wer sind eigentlich unsere Nachbarn? Haben Sie schon mal darüber nachgedacht, mit wie vielen Ländern Deutschland eine Grenze hat? Nun, wahrscheinlich fangen Sie jetzt an zu zählen, Dänemark im Norden, Polen ja … Lassen Sie sich ein wenig Zeit und in der Zwischenzeit wenden wir uns unseren eigenen Ländern zu. Wie Sie wissen, besteht Deutschland ja aus 16 Bundesländern, einschließlich der Stadtstaaten Hamburg und Bremen und auch Berlin. Doch wissen Sie auch, welches Bundesland flächenmäßig am größten ist? Nun, ich nehme an, dass dies viele unserer süddeutschen, genauer unserer bayrischen Hörer wissen werden, denn tatsächlich ist Bayern das größte Bundesland.

Aber lassen Sie uns auf unser Problem zurückkommen, mit wie vielen Staaten Deutschland eine gemeinsame Grenzen hat, und wenn Sie mittlerweile mit dem Zählen aufgehört haben und bei 10 angekommen sind … dann haben Sie sich verzählt! Insgesamt sind es nämlich neun Länder: Dänemark im Norden, die Niederlande, Belgien, Luxemburg und Frankreich im Westen, die Schweiz und Österreich im Süden und die Tschechische Republik und Polen im Osten.

Diese einzigartige Mittellage Deutschlands war historisch natürlich nicht ganz unproblematisch, womit wir auch bei einem anderen Thema angelangt wären: der Politik.

Sie werden wissen, dass die wichtigsten politischen Entscheidungen im Bundestag – unserem Parlament – gefällt werden. Aber wie viele Abgeordnete hat der Bundestag eigentlich? Mehr als 500? Weniger als 500? Nun, es sind weit mehr: 656. Und durch unser Wahlsystem kann die Anzahl sogar noch steigen. Und diese 656 Abgeordneten wählen dann den Bundeskanzler, der dann seine Minister benennt und somit die größte politische Macht besitzt. Der Bundespräsident – anders als zum Beispiel in den USA – hat dagegen weitgehend nur repräsentative Aufgaben. Diese Reduzierung der Macht lag den Vätern unseres Grundgesetzes besonders am Herzen, genauso wie ein anderer Aspekt: das föderalistische Prinzip, das ein Grundpfeiler unserer politischen Struktur ist. Aber darüber mehr in der nächsten Woche.

So, damit sind wir zum Ende unseres ersten Teiles gekommen, und bevor Sie uns, liebe Zuhörerinnen und Zuhörer, direkt anrufen können – spielen wir schnell noch ein paar Takte Musik …

Common irregular verbs

Here is a list of commonly used irregular verbs in German, most of which are featured in *Enjoy German*. It is not intended to be complete, but should help you to familiarize yourself with the most important forms.

*indicates that these verbs normally form their perfect tense with **sein**.

infinitive	present tense vowel change 3rd person sing.	simple past	past participle
anfangen *to start*	fängt an	fing an	angefangen
anrufen *to telephone*		rief an	angerufen
aufstehen *to get up*		stand auf	aufgestanden*
beginnen *to begin*		begann	begonnen
bieten *to offer*		bot	geboten
binden *to bind, tie*		band	gebunden
bleiben *to stay*		blieb	geblieben*
brechen *to break*	bricht	brach	gebrochen
brennen *to burn*		brannte	gebrannt
bringen *to bring*		brachte	gebracht
denken *to think*		dachte	gedacht
einladen *to invite*	lädt ein	lud ein	eingeladen
empfehlen *to recommend*	empfiehlt	empfahl	empfohlen
entscheiden *to decide*		entschied	entschieden
essen *to eat*	isst	aß	gegessen
fahren *to go (by vehicle), to drive*	fährt	fuhr	gefahren*
fallen *to fall*	fällt	fiel	gefallen*
finden *to find*		fand	gefunden
fliegen *to fly*		flog	geflogen*
geben *to give*	gibt	gab	gegeben
gehen *to go*		ging	gegangen*
gelingen *to succeed*		gelang	gelungen*
gelten *to be regarded*	gilt	galt	gegolten
geschehen *to happen*	geschieht	geschah	geschehen*
haben *to have*		hatte	gehabt
halten *to hold, keep*	hält	hielt	gehalten
heißen *to be called*		hieß	geheißen
helfen *to help*	hilft	half	geholfen
kennen *to know, be acquainted with*		kannte	gekannt
kommen *to come*		kam	gekommen*
lassen *to let, to leave*	lässt	ließ	gelassen
laufen *to run, walk*	läuft	lief	gelaufen*
leiden *to suffer*		litt	gelitten

liegen *to lie*		lag	gelegen*
nehmen *to take*	nimmt	nahm	genommen
nennen *to name*		nannte	genannt
raten *to advise*	rät	riet	geraten
reißen *to tear*		riss	gerissen
reiten *to ride*		ritt	geritten*
rennen *to run*		rannte	gerannt*
riechen *to smell*		roch	gerochen
schaffen *to create*		schuf	geschaffen
scheinen *to seem; to shine*		schien	geschienen
schlafen *to sleep*	schläft	schlief	geschlafen
schlagen *to hit*	schlägt	schlug	geschlagen
schließen *to shut, close*		schloss	geschlossen
schneiden *to cut*		schnitt	geschnitten
schreiben *to write*		schrieb	geschrieben
schwimmen *to swim*		schwamm	geschwommen*
sehen *to see*	sieht	sah	gesehen
sein *to be*	ist	war	gewesen*
singen *to sing*		sang	gesungen
sitzen *to sit*		saß	gesessen
sprechen *to speak*	spricht	sprach	gesprochen
springen *to jump*		sprang	gesprungen*
stehen *to stand*		stand	gestanden
steigen *to climb, to rise*		stieg	gestiegen*
sterben *to die*	stirbt	starb	gestorben*
tragen *to carry, wear*	trägt	trug	getragen
treffen *to meet*	trifft	traf	getroffen
treiben *to do (esp. sport)*		trieb	getrieben
treten *to step*	tritt	trat	getreten*
trinken *to drink*		trank	getrunken
tun *to do*		tat	getan
verbergen *to hide*	verbirgt	verbarg	verborgen
vergessen *to forget*	vergisst	vergaß	vergessen
vergleichen *to compare*		verglich	verglichen
verlieren *to lose*		verlor	verloren
vermeiden *to avoid*		vermied	vermieden
wachsen *to grow*	wächst	wuchs	gewachsen*
waschen *to wash*	wäscht	wusch	gewaschen
werben *to advertise*	wirbt	warb	geworben
werden *to become*	wird	wurde	geworden*
werfen *to throw*	wirft	warf	geworfen
wissen *to know*	weiß	wusste	gewusst
ziehen *to move*		zog	gezogen*
zwingen *to force, compel*		zwang	gezwungen

Glossary of grammatical terms

This glossary covers the most important grammar terminology used in this book.

adjectives

Adjectives are used to provide more information about nouns. In English they can stand on their own after a verb, such as *to be* or *to seem*, or they can appear in front of a noun: *The car is new. The new car wasn't cheap.* Note that in German endings are needed on adjectives that come before a noun:
Das Auto ist *neu*. Das *neue* Auto war nicht billig.

adverbs

Adverbs provide more information about a) verbs: *Wayne ran **quickly** down the stairs* and b) adjectives: *I was **completely** exhausted.*

In English, adverbs often (but not always) end in *-ly*.

In German, adverbs often have the same form as adjectives:
Deine Arbeit ist *gut*.   *Your work is **good**.*
Du hast das sehr *gut* gemacht.   *You did that very **well**.*

articles

In German there are three definite articles: **der** (masculine), **die** (feminine) and **das** (neuter). The indefinite articles are **ein** (masculine), **eine** (feminine) and **ein** (neuter). (See also **gender**.)

auxiliary verbs

Auxiliary verbs are used as a support to the main verb, e.g. *I **am** working; he **has** gone.* The most important verbs in German are **haben**, **sein** and **werden**. These are used in the formation of the present perfect tense and of the passive:
Ich *habe* gerade einen sehr guten Film gesehen.   *I **have** just seen a good film.*
Die neue Schule *wurde* 2014 gebaut.   *The new school **was** built in 2014.*

cases

The four cases in German are: *the nominative, the accusative, the genitive* and *the dative*. Cases are used in German to express relationships between the various parts of the sentence.

Nominative – this is the case that indicates the subject of the sentence.
Der *Mann* kauft einen Computer.   *The **man** buys a computer.*

Accusative – this is the case that indicates the direct object of the sentence:
Der Mann kauft *einen Computer*.   *The man buys **a computer**.*

Dative – this is the case that indicates the indirect object of the sentence:

Wir haben den Computer *meinem Bruder* gegeben.   *We gave the computer **to my brother**.*

Genitive – this is the case that indicates possession:

Das ist der Computer *meines Bruders*.   *That's **my brother's** computer.*

Note that **prepositions** in German are followed by the accusative, dative or genitive case.

comparative

When we make comparisons, we need the comparative form of the adjective. In English this usually means adding *-er* to the adjective or putting *more* in front of it: *This shirt is cheap**er** than that one. This blouse is **more** expensive than that one.*

In German -er is added to the adjective to form the comparative:

Dieses Hemd ist *billiger* als das da. Diese Bluse ist *teurer* als die da.

(See also **superlative**.)

conditional

The conditional mood is used to express a hypothetical situation or state which is subject to a condition. For instance, the sentence *Peter would visit his mother, if he had a car* tells us that Peter does not visit his mother and that he doesn't have a car (real situations). For him to visit his mother (as yet a hypothetical situation) he would have to have a car (condition). The conditional in German follows a similar pattern, using subjunctive forms of the verbs:

Peter *würde* seine Mutter *besuchen*, wenn er ein Auto *hätte*.

conjunctions

Conjunctions join words or clauses together. In German, a distinction is made between *co-ordinating conjunctions* and *subordinating conjunctions*. Co-ordinating conjunctions such as **und** *and*, **aber** *but* and **oder** *or* simply join two main clauses together and do not affect the word order:

Anna kommt aus München und ist 21 Jahre alt.   *Anna comes from Munich and is 21 years old.*

Subordinating conjunctions include such words as **wenn** *when(ever)*, *if*, **weil** *because*, **obwohl** *although* and **seitdem** *since* and send the verb to the end of the clause:

Er kann nicht kommen, *weil* er krank ist.   *He can't come, **because** he is ill.*

Other subordinating conjunctions are: **während** *while*, **nachdem** *after*, **da** *as*, **ob** *whether* and **dass** *that*. (See also **subordinate clause**.)

demonstratives

Words such as *this, that, these, those* are called demonstratives or *demonstrative adjectives*:

Dieses Buch ist interessant.   ***This** book is interesting.*
Diese Übungen sind sehr schwierig.   ***These** exercises are very difficult.*

In German **dieser** (masculine), **diese** (feminine and plural), **dieses** (neuter) are the most commonly used demonstratives.

gender

In German, there are three genders, *masculine*, *feminine* and *neuter*: **der Tisch** *the table*, **die Lampe** *the lamp*, **das Haus** *the house*. In German, nouns have a gender irrespective of sex. For instance, the gender of the word for *girl* (**das Mädchen**) is neuter.

imperative

The imperative is the form of the verb used to give orders or commands: *Help me, please*. In German, there are three main forms of the imperative, because of the various forms of address. **Helfen Sie mir, bitte!** (**Sie** form); **Hilf mir, bitte!** (**du** form); **Helft mir, bitte!** (**ihr** form).

infinitive

The infinitive is the form of the verb that you will find entered in the dictionary. In English, the infinitive is usually preceded by the word *to*, e.g. *to go*, *to play*. In German, the infinitive usually ends in **-en**: **gehen** *to go*, **spielen** *to play*, **machen** *to do*, etc.

irregular verbs

see **verbs**

Konjunktiv I, Konjunktiv II

see **subjunctive**

modal verbs

Verbs which express concepts such as permission, obligation, possibility, etc. (*can*, *must*, *may*) are referred to as modal verbs. Verbs in this category cannot in general stand on their own. Modal verbs in German include **wollen** *to want to*, **können** *to be able to*, **dürfen** *to be allowed to*.

nouns

Nouns are words like *house* **Haus**, *bread* **Brot** and *beauty* **Schönheit**. They are often called 'naming words'. A useful test of a noun is whether you can put *the* in front of it: e.g. *the house*, *the bread*. Nouns in German have one of three genders and take a capital letter.

object

The term object expresses the 'receiving end' relationship between a noun and a verb. Look at the following sentence:

Der Hund biss den Postboten.   *The dog bit the postman.*

The postman is said to be the object of the sentence, as he is at the receiving end of the action.

Sentences such as: *My mother gave my wife an expensive ring* have both a direct object (*an expensive ring*) and an indirect object (*my wife*) – indirect because the ring was given to my wife. In German the direct object requires the accusative case and the indirect object the dative case: **Meine Mutter gab *meiner* Frau** (dative) ***einen teuren* Ring** (accusative).

(See also **subject**.)

passive voice

Most actions can be viewed in two different ways:
1 *The dog bit the postman.* Active voice
2 *The postman was bitten by the dog.* Passive voice

In German you will also find both the active and passive voice. The passive is normally formed with the verb **werden** rather than with the verb **sein**:

1 **Der Hund biss den Postboten.**

2 **Der Postbote *wurde* vom Hund gebissen.**

personal pronouns

Personal pronouns refer, as their name suggests, to persons. In German they are: **ich** *I*; **du** *you* (informal singular), **Sie** *you* (formal singular); **er**, **sie**, **es** *he, she, it*; **wir** *we*; **ihr** *you* (informal plural), **Sie** *you* (formal plural); **sie** *they*. (See also **pronouns**.)

plural

see **singular** and **plural**

possessives

Words such as **mein** *my*, **dein** *your* (informal), **Ihr** *your* (formal), **ihr** *her*, **sein** *his* are given the term *possessives* or *possessive adjectives*, because they indicate who something belongs to.

prepositions

Words like **in** *in*, **auf** *on*, **zwischen** *between*, **für** *for* are called prepositions. Prepositions often tell us about the position of something. They are normally followed by a noun or a pronoun:
a *This present is **for** you.*
b ***Despite** the weather I am going to walk.*
c *Your book is **on** the table.*

In German prepositions require the use of a **case**, such as the accusative, genitive or dative:
a **Dieses Geschenk ist *für dich*.** (accusative)
b ***Trotz des* Wetters gehe ich zu Fuß.** (genitive)
c **Dein Buch liegt *auf dem Tisch*.** (dative)

pronouns

Pronouns fulfil a similar function to nouns and often stand in the place of nouns mentioned earlier.

Die *Lampe* ist modern. *Sie* ist hässlich.   *The **lamp** (noun) is modern. **It** (pronoun) is ugly.*

Note that in German the pronoun has to be the same gender as the noun which it stands for (**die Lampe** → **sie**). (See **nouns**.)

relative clauses

Relative clauses are subordinate clauses which usually provide more information about a noun or phrase in the main clause. (See **subordinate clause**.) They are usually introduced by a relative pronoun, a word like *whom, whose,* etc. in English and like **der**, **deren**, etc. in German:
Kennst du *den* Mann, den wir in der Bäckerei gesehen haben?   *Do you know the man (whom) we saw in the bakery?*
Die Frau, *deren* Mann mit mir arbeitet, hatte gestern einen Unfall gehabt.
The woman whose husband works with me had an accident yesterday.

Note that it is not possible in German, as it often is in English, to omit the relative pronoun.

singular and plural

The terms singular and plural are used to make the contrast between 'one' and 'more than one': *book/books* **Buch/Bücher**, *dog/dogs* **Hund/Hunde**; *hat/hats* **Hut/Hüte**.

Most plural forms in English are formed by adding an -*s*, but not all: *child/children, woman/women, mouse/mice.*

There are many different plural forms in German. Here are just three: **Kind/Kinder**, **Frau/Frauen**, **Maus/Mäuse**.

Some nouns do not normally have plurals and are said to be uncountable: **das Obst** *fruit*; **die Luft** *air.*

subject

The term 'subject' expresses a relationship between a noun and a verb. Look at the sentence *The dog bit the postman.* Here *the dog* is said to be the subject of the verb *to bite*, because it is the dog that is doing the biting. In German the subject of the sentence needs to be in the nominative case: ***Der Hund* biss den Postboten.**

subjunctive

The subjunctive mood has all but disappeared from use in modern English. It appears in set expressions, such as *If I were you* and *God forbid.* In German there are two forms of the subjunctive:

  a Konjunktiv I which is formed from the present tense form of the verb and which is mainly used in reported speech.
Christiane hat gesagt, dass Florian jetzt mit Birgit verheiratet *sei*.
Christiane said that Florian is now married to Birgit.

  b Konjunktiv II which is formed from the past simple form of the verb and which is mainly used for indicating that an activity, event or state is hypothetical, possible or perhaps not true.
Ich *würde* mich freuen, wenn du kämest.   *I would be glad if you came.*

subordinate clauses

Subordinate clauses are linked to a main clause and normally can't stand on their own: *He goes home **because it is late***.

In German subordinating clauses are usually introduced by a subordinating conjunction (**dass, weil,** etc.):
Er geht nach Hause, *weil es spät ist*.

Other types of subordinate clauses covered in this book are **relative clauses** and **indirect questions**:
Weißt du, *wer* **heute Abend kommt?**   *Do you know who is coming this evening?*

A subordinate clause is separated from the main clause by a comma or commas.

superlative

The superlative is used for the most extreme version of a comparison:
  a *This shirt is the **cheapest** of all.*
  b *This blouse is the **most** expensive of all.*

The superlative in German follows a similar pattern:
  a **Dieses Hemd ist das** *billigste* **von allen.**
  b **Diese Bluse ist die** *teuerste* **von allen.**

(See also **comparative.**)

tense

Most languages use changes in the verb form to indicate an aspect of time. These changes in the verb are traditionally referred to as tense, and the tenses may be *present, past* or *future*. Tenses are often reinforced with expressions of time:
Present: **Heute bleibe ich zu Hause.**   ***Today*** *I am staying at home.*

Past: ***Gestern* bin ich nach London gefahren./Gestern fuhr ich nach London.**
Yesterday *I went to London.*

Future: *Morgen* werde ich nach Berlin fliegen.   *Tomorrow* *I'll be flying to Berlin.*

The German tenses dealt with in this book are *the present* (**das Präsens**), *the simple past* (**das Präteritum**), *the present perfect tense* (**das Perfekt**) and *the future tense* (**das Futur**).

verbs

Verbs often communicate actions, states and sensations. So, for instance, the verb *to play* **spielen** expresses an action, the verb *to exist* **existieren** expresses a state and the verb *to see* **sehen** expresses a sensation. A verb may also be defined by its role in the sentence or clause and usually has a **subject**. It may also have an **object**.

Verbs in German can be *regular* (often called *weak verbs*), or *irregular* (*strong* or *mixed verbs*). A list of the most common irregular verbs is provided in the previous part of this reference section.

German–English glossary

This glossary is intended to help you recall and use some of the most important words that you have met during the course. It is not intended to be comprehensive.

~ indicates that this verb or its root form can be found in the list of **Common irregular verbs**.

/ indicates that a verb is separable (e.g. **ab/bauen**).

With job titles, nationalities, etc., the female version is usually given in an abbreviated form, e.g. **der Akademiker (-)/die -in**. In the plural, feminine nouns ending in **-in** add **-nen**, e.g. **die Akademikerin**, **die Akademikerinnen**.

Abkürzungen *Abbreviations:*

acc. – accusative

adj. n. – adjectival noun

coll. – colloquial

dat. – dative

neut. – neuter

gen. – genitive

plur. – plural

wk. n. – weak noun

ab und zu   *now and again*
ab/fahren~   *to depart*
die Abfahrt (-en)   *departure*
die Abgase   (plur.) *exhaust fumes*
der/die Abgeordnete (-n) (adj. n.)   *member of parliament*
abgesehen von (+ dat.)   *apart from*
ab/hängen von (+ dat.)   *to depend on*
abhängig von (+ dat.)   *dependent on*
ab/holen   *to pick up, collect*
das Abitur   *school-leaving examination, taken at age 18+*
ab/legen   *to sit, take (an exam)*
ab/räumen   *to clear up/away*
ab/schaffen   *to abolish, get rid of*
ab/schließen~   *to finish (one's studies)*
der Abschluss (-¨e)   *leaving exam*
die Abteilung (-en)   *department*
ab/waschen   *to wash up, do the dishes*
achtlos   *heedless(ly), without caring*
ähnlich   *similar(ly)*
der Akademiker (-)/die -in   *graduate*
akkurat *precise, meticulous*
der/die Alkoholkranke (-n) (adj. n.)   *person who is ill from alcohol-related problems*
allerhand   *all sorts (of things)*

allgemein   *general*
im Allgemeinen   *in general*
allzu viel   *too much*
als Nächstes   *next*
das Alter   *age*
die Ampel (-n)   *traffic lights*
an/belangen   *to concern*
Was ... anbelangt, ...   *in so far as ... is concerned*
an/bieten~   *to offer*
andere   *other, different*
andere Länder, andere Sitten   *when in Rome, do as the Romans do; lit. different countries, different customs*
anders   *different(ly)*
anderthalb   *one and a half*
an/erkennen~   *to recognize*
an/fallen~   *to come up (of work)*
der Anfang (-¨e)   *beginning*
von Anfang an   *from the start*
an/fangen   *to begin, commence*
der Anfängerkurs (-e)   *beginners course*
an/gehen~   *to concern*
Das geht dich nichts an.   *That doesn't concern you.*
der/die Angestellte (-n)   (adj. n.)   *employee*

die Anglistik   *English language and literature*
die Angst (-¨e)   *fear, anxiety*
an/kommen~   *to arrive*
    gut ankommen   *to be well received*
die Ankunft (-¨e)   *arrival*
der Anlass (-¨e)   *occasion, reason*
an/melden   *to register*
annähernd   *almost*
an/nehmen~   *to assume*
sich an/passen an (+ acc.)   *to adapt to*
sich etwas an/schauen   *to watch, look at*
    something
anschließend   *afterwards, subsequently*
ansonsten   *otherwise*
der Anspruch (-¨e) auf (+ acc.)   *right to*
    in Anspruch nehmen~   *to take up (of time,*
    energy, etc.)
anstatt (+ gen.)   *instead of*
der Anteil (-e)   *proportion*
an/wachsen~   *to grow, increase*
der Anwärter/die -in   *candidate (for a job)*
die Anzahl   *number*
die Arbeitsagentur (-en)   *job centre*
arbeitsam   *hard-working*
die Arbeitslosigkeit   *unemployment*
der Arbeitsplatz (-¨e)   *workplace; job*
der Architekt (wk. n.)/die -in   *architect*
sich ärgern (über + acc.)   *to be annoyed (about)*
der Arm (-e)   *arm*
    jdn auf den Arm nehmen~   *to pull someone's*
    leg (coll.)*
der Artikel (-)   *article*
die Ärztekammer (-n)   *chamber of doctors*
der Assistent (wk. n.)/die -in   *assistant*
atmen   *to breathe*
die Atomkraft   *nuclear power*
die Auffassung (-en)   *view, attitude*
auf/frischen   *to freshen up, to polish up*
auf/geben~   *to drop, give up*
auf/hören   *to stop, cease*
auf/polieren   *to brush up*
auf/räumen   *to clear up*
aufregend   *exciting*
der Aufschwung (-¨e)   *upswing*
auf/stehen~   *to get up*
der Aufwand (-¨e)   *expense (in time/money)*
aufwendig   *lavish*
die Ausbildung (-en)   *training*
ausfallen lassen~   *to skip*
der Ausflug (-¨e)   *excursion, trip*
aus/führen   *to export*
ausführlich   *detailed*
die Ausgabe (-n)   *edition*
der Ausgang (-¨e)   *exit, way out*

aus/geben~   *to spend (of money)*
aus/gehen~   *to go out*
ausgepumpt (coll.)   *exhausted*
ausgiebig   *thoroughly*
die Auskunft (-¨e)   *information*
der Ausländer/die -in   *foreigner*
aus/machen   *to switch/turn off*
die Ausnahme (-n)   *exception*
sich aus/schließen~   *to exclude oneself*
aus/sehen~   *to look (like)*
außer (+ dat.)   *besides, except (for)*
außerhalb (+ gen.)   *outside (of a town)*
sich aus/sprechen~ für (+ acc.)   *to speak in*
    favour of
die Ausstellung (-en)   *exhibition*
sich aus/tauschen   *to exchange views*
aus/treten~ aus (+ dat.)   *to leave (a club, a*
    society, etc.)*

der Badeurlaub (-e)   *swimming holiday*
die Bahn (-en)   *railway*
    mit der Bahn   *by rail*
der Bahnhof (-¨e)   *station*
bald   *soon*
die Banklehre (-n)   *banking apprenticeship*
die Batterie (-n)   *battery*
der Bauingenieur (-e)/die -in   *civil engineer*
(das) Bayern   *Bavaria*
beabsichtigen   *to intend*
der Beamte (-) (adj.n)/die Beamtin   *civil servant*
bedauern   *to regret*
bedeuten   *to mean*
die Bedeutung (-en)   *importance*
beeindruckend   *impressive*
begegnen (+ dat.)   *to encounter*
sich begeistern für (+ acc.)   *to be enthusiatic*
    about
behindert   *disabled*
das Beispiel (-e) (für + acc.)   *example (of)*
bekannt   *well-known*
der/die Bekannte (-n) (adj. n.)   *acquaintance*
bekehren   *to convert (someone)*
bekommen~   *to get, to receive*
belasten   *to strain, burden*
belegen   *to occupy (a room)*
sich bemühen   *to make an effort, try*
benennen~   *to name, appoint*
benutzen   *to use*
das Benzin   *petrol, gasoline*
bequem   *comfortable; convenient(ly)*
bereits   *already*
der Berg (-e)   *mountain*
berichten   *to report*
der Beruf (-e)   *job, profession*

Was sind Sie von Beruf?   *What job do you do?*

berufstätig   *(gainfully) employed*

beschäftigen   *to employ*

sich beschäftigen mit (+ dat.)   *to concern oneself with*

Bescheid wissen (über + acc.)   *to know (about)*

die Besichtigung (-en)   *sightseeing*

der Besitzer (-)/die Besitzerin (-nen)   *owner*

die Besorgnis (-se)   *concern*

bestätigen   *to confirm*

bestehen~   *to exist, to be; to pass (an exam)*

bestellen   *to order*

besuchen   *to visit*

betonen   *to emphasize, to stress*

betreiben~   *to pursue; do; to run (a business, company)*

der Betrieb (-e)   *business, factory*

die Bevölkerung (-en)   *population*

die Bevölkerungsdichte (-n)   *population density*

bevölkerungsreich   *densely populated*

die Bewältigung (-en)   *overcoming*

sich bewerben~ (um + acc.)   *to apply (for)*

der Bewerber (-) /die -in   *applicant*

bewusst   *conscious*

die Bezahlung   *pay*

beziehungsweise   *alternatively, or*

bezüglich (+ gen.)   *concerning, with regard to*

bezweifeln   *to doubt*

die Bibliothek (-en)   *library*

der Bienenhonig   *(bee) honey*

bieten~   *to offer*

das Bild (-er)   *picture, image*

bilden   *to form, to constitute*

die Bildung   *education*

binden~   *to bind*

die Biologie   *biology*

die Biomasse (-n)   *biomass*

das Blatt (-¨er)   *leaf; sheet, newspaper*

blau   *blue*

der Blick (-e)   *view, glance*

die Boulevardzeitung (-en)   *tabloid*

die Branche (-n)   *sector, industry*

brechen~   *to break*

der Brite (wk.n.)/die -in   *Briton*

die Brücke (-n)   *bridge*

das Buch (-¨er)   *book*

die Buche (-n)   *beech (tree)*

bummeln   *to stroll*

der Bundeskanzler/die -in   *Federal Chancellor*

das Bundesland (-¨er)   *federal state*

der Bundespräsident (wk.n.)/die -in   *Federal President*

der Bundestag   *Federal Parliament*

der Bürger (-)/die -in   *citizen*

das Büro (-s)   *office*

die Bushaltestelle (-n)   *bus stop*

der Chef (-s)/die -in   *boss, head*

die Chemie   *chemistry*

circa   *about, approximately*

der Computer (-)   *computer*

dabei sein~   *to be there; to be in the process of*

das Dach (-¨er)   *roof*

dagegen   *against that; on the other hand*

danach   *after that, then*

danken (+ dat)   *to thank*

dann   *then*

auf Dauer   *in the long term*

der Deckel (-) lid; (coll.)   *driving licence*

denken~   *to think*

deswegen   *therefore, for this reason*

deutlich   *clear(ly), significant(ly)*

dicht   *densely; closely*

der Dienst (-e)   *service*

der Dienstleistungssektor (-en)   *service sector*

das Ding (-e)   *thing*

die Diplomarbeit (-en)   *thesis*

der Direktor (wk. n.)/die -in   *director, head teacher*

diskutieren   *to discuss*

der Dokumentarfilm (-e)   *documentary (film)*

der Dom (-e)   *cathedral*

doppelt so ... wie   *twice as ... as*

das Dorf (-¨er)   *village*

da ist 'was dran   *there's some truth in that*

durch/fallen~   *to fail (a test or exam)*

durch/führen   *to conduct; carry out*

durchgehend   *all day, all the time*

der Durchschnitt (-e)   *average*

dürfen   *to be allowed to*

die Dusche (-n)   *shower*

sich unter die Dusche stellen   *to take a shower*

die Ecke (-n)   *corner*

um die Ecke   *around the corner*

egal   *all the same*

eher   *rather*

ehrlich gesagt   *quite honestly*

die Eiche (-n)   *oak tree*

eigen   *own (adj.)*

die Eigenschaft (-en)   *characteristic*

eigentlich   *actual(ly)*

ein/atmen   *to breathe in*

eindeutig   *clear(ly), unambiguous(ly)*

einfach   *simple, simply*

ein/führen   *to introduce*

eingebunden   *tied, constrained, bound*

die Einheit (-en)   *unity*

ein/kaufen *to shop*
das Einkommen (-) *income*
ein/laden~ *to invite*
die Einladung (-en) *invitation*
ein/richten *to arrange, to furnish*
die Einschätzung (-en) *estimation*
einschließlich (+ gen.) *inclusive of, including*
ein/sehen~ *to recognize, acknowledge*
ein/sparen *to save*
ein/treten~ (in + acc.) *to join*
die Einwirkung (-en) (auf + acc.) *effect (on)*
der Einwohner (-)/die -in *inhabitant*
einzigartig *unique*
empfehlen~ *to recommend*
die Energie (-n) *energy*
die Energiequelle (-n) *source of energy*
die Energiesparlampe (-n) *energy-saving bulb*
die Englischkenntnisse (plur.) *knowledge of
   English*
entdecken *to discover*
enthalten~ *to contain, to include*
entlassen~ *to dismiss*
entscheiden~ *to decide*
sich entschuldigen *to apologize*
entsorgen *to dispose of (waste)*
sich entspannen *to relax*
entsprechend *corresponding, respective*
die Entwicklung (-en) *development, trend*
meines Erachtens *in my opinion*
erbringen~ *to provide*
das Ereignis (-se) *event*
die Erfahrung (-en) *experience*
erforderlich *necessary*
die Erforschung (-en) *research*
ergänzen *to complete*
das Ergebnis (-se) *result*
sich erinnern an (+ acc.) *to remember*
erklären *to explain, to clarify*
erledigen *to deal with, attend to*
sich ernähren von (+ dat.) *to feed oneself on,
   live on*
die Ernährung *nutrition*
ernennen~ *to appoint*
erneuerbar *renewable*
erreichen *to reach*
die Errungenschaft (-en) *achievement*
erscheinen~ *to appear*
erst *first; only, not until*
ersticken *to suffocate*
sich erstrecken auf (+ acc.) *to stretch to,
   extend to*
der/die Erwachsene (-n) (adj. n.) *adult*
erzeugen *to generate, to produce*
essen~ *to eat*

das Exemplar (-e) *copy*
der Export (-e) *export*
der EZ-Zuschlag (-̈e) *single room supplement*

fahren~ *to go (in a vehicle), drive*
die Fahrerei *travelling backwards and forwards*
die Fahrerlaubnis (-se) *licence to drive*
die Fahrschule (-n) *driving school*
der Fall (-̈e) *case; fall*
   auf keinen Fall *under no circumstances; lit. in
   no case*
die Farbe (-n) *colour, paint*
fast *almost*
Feierabend machen *to finish work*
feiern *to celebrate*
fern/sehen~ *to watch TV*
fertig *finished, ready*
das Fest (-e) *party, celebration*
die Festspiele (neut. plur.) *festival*
fest/stellen *to ascertain*
finden~ *to find, to consider*
flächenmäßig *in area*
der Flegel (-) *lout*
fleißig *hard-working, industrious*
fließend *fluent(ly)*
der Flughafen (-̈) *airport*
das Flugzeug (-e) *plane*
folgen (+ dat.) *to follow*
der Folgeschaden (-̈) *harmful effect*
die Forderung (-en) *demand*
der/die Fortgeschrittene (-n) (adj. n.) *advanced
   learner*
der Fotograf (wk. n.)/die -in *photographer*
der Franzose (wk. n.)/die Französin *Frenchman/
   Frenchwoman*
freizügig *liberal, permissive*
die Fremdsprache (-n) *foreign language*
sich freuen (über + acc.) *to be glad (about)*
sich freuen auf (+ acc.) *to look forward to*
froh *glad*
führen *to lead, to conduct; to run (a business etc.)*
der Führerschein (-e) *driving licence*
die Führung (-en) *guided tour*
der Fuß (-̈e) *foot*
   zu Fuß *on foot*

gar nicht *not at all*
der Gast (-̈e) *guest*
die Gaststätte (-n) *restaurant, inn*
das Gebäude (-) *building*
geben~ *to give*
geboren *born*
   Wann bist du geboren? *When were you born?*
Gebrauch machen von (+ dat.) *to make use of*

der Geburtstag (-e)   *birthday*
gefährlich   *dangerous*
gefallen~ (+ dat.)   *to be pleasing*
  Es gefällt mir.   *I like it.*
das Gefühl (-e)   *feeling*
gehören   *to belong*
die Geisteswissenschaften   *Humanities*
geistig   *mental(ly)*
der Geldmangel   *lack of money*
die Gelegenheit (-en)   *opportunity*
gelegentlich   *occasionally*
das Gelenk (-e)   *joint*
gelingen~   *to succeed*
  Es ist uns nicht gelungen, ...   *We didn't*
  succeed in ... We didn't manage to ...
gelten~ als   *to be regarded as*
gemächlich   *leisurely*
genau   *exact(ly), precise(ly)*
genau(er) hinschauen   *to take a close(r) look*
geöffnet   *open*
das Gepäck   *luggage*
gepflegt   *well-kept*
geradeaus   *straight on*
geregelt   *regulated*
die Gesamtnote (-n)   *final mark, classification*
geschädigt   *damaged*
die Geschäftsreise (-n)   *business trip*
geschehen~   *to happen*
das Geschenk (-e)   *present*
die Geschichte (-n)   *history; story*
geschieden   *divorced*
das Geschirr   *crockery, dishes*
der Geschmack (-¨er)   *taste*
gesellig   *sociable*
die Gesellschaft (-en)   *society*
das Gesetz (-e)   *law*
gestalten   *to arrange, form, shape*
gestresst   *stressed*
gesundheitlich   *from the health point of view*
gewöhnen   *to familiarize*
  an etwas gewöhnt sein   *to be used to*
  something
gewöhnlich   *usually*
der Glascontainer (-)   *glass container*
glauben (+ dat.)   *to believe (a person)*
die Globalisierung   *globalization*
das Glück   *(good) fortune*
  Glück haben   *to be lucky*
glücklicherweise   *fortunately*
gratulieren (+ dat.)   *to congratulate*
die Grenze (-n)   *border, frontier*
großartig   *magnificent(ly) splendid(ly)*
der Grund (-¨e)   *reason*
gründen   *to found*

das Grundgesetz   *Basic Law (constitution of the*
  Federal Republic)
gründlich   *thorough*
die Gründlichkeit   *thoroughness*
der Grundpfeiler (-)   *cornerstone*
der Grüne Punkt   *lit. the Green Dot (sign on*
  products to indicate that a wrapping should
  be recycled)
günstig   *cheap, good value for money*
der Gymnasiallehrer (-)/die -in   *grammar*
  school teacher
das Gymnasium (Gymnasien)   *(German)*
  grammar school

halbtags   *part-time (lit. half days)*
halten~ von (+ dat.)   *to think of*
die Haltestelle (-n)   *(bus, train, tram) stop*
die Hand (-¨e)   *hand*
der Handel   *trade*
handeln   *to trade*
der Hauptschulabschluss (-¨e)   *secondary-school*
  leaving exam after nine years of schooling
die Hauptschule (-n)   *secondary school*
heiter   *funny; cheerful; bright*
  Das kann ja heiter werden!   *That will be fun!*
  (ironic)
die Heizplatte (-n)   *hotplate*
die Heizung (-en)   *heating*
helfen~ (+ dat.)   *to help*
der Herr (-en) (wk. n)   *gentleman*
her/stellen   *to produce, manufacture*
das Herz (-en) (wk. n.)   *heart*
die Hilfe (-n)   *help, assistance, aid*
der Hin- und Rückflug (-¨e)   *return flight*
hin/schauen   *to look (at)*
hinterher   *afterwards*
hin/weisen auf (+ acc.)   *to point out*
die Hochschule (-n)   *institution of Higher*
  Education
höchstens   *at the most*
die Hochzeit (-en)   *wedding*
die Hoffnung (-en)   *hope*
der Honig   *honey*
hören   *to hear, to listen to*

immer   *always*
immerhin   *all the same, nevertheless*
der Industriekaufmann/die -frau   *person with*
  three years' business training
die Industrienation (-en)   *industrialized nation*
das Ingenieurwesen   *engineering*
insgesamt   *in total, in all*
sich interessieren (für + acc.)   *to be interested in*
Italienisch   *Italian (language)*

das Jahr (-e)   *year*
  vor zwei Jahren   *two years ago*
  zweimal im Jahr   *twice a year*
das Jahrhundert (-e)   *century*
jammern   *to moan, to whine*
je   *in each case*
je nach (+ dat.)   *depending on*
jedenfalls   *in any case*
jeder/-e/-es   *each, every*
jeweils   *in each instance*
der Journalist (-en) (wk. n.)/die -in   *journalist*
der/die Jugendliche (-n) (wk. n.)   *young person*
der Junge (-n) (wk. n.)   *boy*
(die) Jura   *Law*

der Kaffee (-s)   *coffee*
die Kammer (-n)   *chamber*
der Kandidat (-en) (wk. n.)/die -in   *candidate*
der Kater (coll.)   *hangover; tomcat*
kaufen   *to buy*
der Kegelclub (-s)   *bowling club*
die Kehrseite (-n)   *the other side*
der Kellner (-)/die -in   *waiter/waitress*
kennen lernen   *to get to know*
die Kernenergie   *nuclear energy*
die Kiste (-n)   *box, old banger (car)*
klappen   *to turn out all right*
klar   *clear*
das Klischee (-s)   *cliché*
kochen   *to cook, to make (coffee)*
die Kochnische (-n)   *kitchenette; lit. cooking niche*
der Kollege (-n) (wk. n.)/die -in   *colleague*
komisch   *funny, strange*
  Das hört sich komisch an.   *That sounds strange.*
die Konkurrenz   *competition*
konkurrenzfähig   *competitive, viable*
können   *to be able to*
das Körnchen (Wahrheit)   *grain (of truth)*
körperlich   *physically, bodily*
kosten   *to cost*
die Kosten (plur.)   *cost(s)*
kostspielig   *expensive*
die Kraft (-¨e)   *force, power*
der Krankenpfleger (-)   *male nurse*
die Krankenschwester (-n)   *female nurse*
die Krankheit (-en)   *disease, illness*
der Krebs   *cancer*
der Kreislauf (-¨e)   *circulatory system*
die Kreuzung (-en)   *crossroads*
der Krieg (-e)   *war*
der Kühlschrank (-¨e)   *refrigerator*
kulturinteressiert   *interested in the arts*

sich kümmern um (+ acc.)   *to take care of, look after, concern oneself with*
der Kunde (-n) (wk. n.)/die Kundin   *customer, client*
die Kunst (-¨e)   *art*
die Kur (-en)   *cure (at a spa)*
kursiv   *in italics*

das Labor (-s/-e)   *lab*
der Lack (-e)   *varnish*
der Laden (-¨)   *shop*
das Land (-¨er)   *country; federal state*
die Landschaft (-en)   *scenery*
der Landwirt (-e)   *farmer*
lang   *long*
langfristig   *long-term, in the long run*
langjährig   *of many years*
langsam   *slow(ly)*
längst   *long since*
langweilig   *boring*
  Wird Ihnen nicht manchmal langweilig?   *Don't you get bored sometimes?*
die Laufbahn (-en)   *career*
laufen~   *to run, walk*
  auf dem Laufenden sein   *to be up to date*
laut   *loud, noisy*
lebendig   *lively*
die Lebensart (-en)   *way of life*
der Lebenslauf (-¨e)   *CV*
die Leberzirrhose (-n)   *cirrhosis of the liver*
legen   *to lay, put*
leiden~   *to suffer*
leid tun~   *to be sorry*
  Es tut mir leid   *I am sorry*
die Leistung (-en)   *performance, achievement; what is included (in a package holiday)*
die Leistungsanforderung (-en)   *demands on performance*
der Leistungsdruck   *pressure to perform, to work harder*
lieben   *to love*
lieber   *preferable*
  Ich gehe lieber ins Kino.   *I prefer to go to the cinema.*
liegen~ (in + dat.)   *to lie (in); to be situated (in)*
liegen bleiben~   *to be left over, undone*
links   *on the left*
  Gehen Sie nach links.   *Go left.*
der/das Liter (-)   *litre*
sich lohnen   *to be worthwhile*
lösen   *solve; to obtain (a ticket)*
los/gehen~   *to start, set off*
die Luft (-¨e)   *air*
Lust haben   *to feel like, to want to*

die Macht (-¨e)   *power*
das Mädchen (-)   *girl*
die Mahlzeit (-en)   *meal*
die Malerei   *painting*
manche   *some*
manchmal   *sometimes*
marktdominierend   *dominating the market*
die Marmelade (-n)   *jam*
die Maßnahme (-n)   *measure*
die Mathematik   *mathematics*
die Medaille (-n)   *medal*
   die Kehrseite der Medaille   *on the other side of the coin*
die Medien (plur.)   *media*
die Mehrheit (-en)   *majority*
die Mehrwegflasche (-n)   *reusable bottle*
meinen (zu + dat.)   *to think about, to have an opinion on*
die Meinung (-en)   *opinion*
meistens   *mostly*
die Menge (-n)   *quantity*
die Mensa (Mensen)   *refectory, university dining hall*
der Mensch (-en) (wk. n.)   *human being, person*
   Mensch!   *wow!*
merkwürdig   *strange, peculiar*
der/das Meter (-)   *metre*
der Metzger (-)/die -in   *butcher*
die Metzgerei (-en)   *butcher's (shop)*
die Minderheit (-en)   *minority*
der Mindestlohn (-¨e)   *minimum wage*
miteinander   *with one another*
mit/gehen~   *to go along with*
das Mitglied (-er)   *member*
mit/machen   *to take part, to participate*
der Mittag   *midday*
   zu Mittag essen~   *to have lunch*
mittags   *midday, lunchtime*
die Mitte (-n)   *middle, centre*
der Mittelpunkt (-e)   *centre*
(die) Mitternacht   *midnight*
die mittlere Reife   *secondary-school-leaving certificate taken after ten years of schooling*
der Modellbau   *model-building*
mögen   *to like*
die Möglichkeit (-en)   *possibility*
die Moralpredigt (-en)   *(moralizing) lecture*
motiviert   *motivated*
der Müll   *rubbish, garbage*
der Mülleimer (-)   *rubbish bin*
die Mülltrennung   *separation of waste*
der Mund (-¨er)   *mouth*
die Musik   *music*
müssen   *to have to, must*
die Muttersprache (-n)   *mother tongue*

der Nachbar (-n) (wk. n.)/die -in   *neighbour*
die Nachfrage (-n)   *demand*
die Nachrichtensendung (-en)   *news broadcast*
das Nachschlagewerk (-e)   *reference work*
nach/sehen~   *to have a look*
der Nachteil (-e)   *disadvantage*
der Nachweis (-e)   *proof, evidence*
   einen Nachweis erbingen   *to produce evidence*
die Nadel (-n)   *needle*
die Nähe   *proximity*
in der Nähe (von + dat.)   *near*
nahezu   *nearly*
der Name (wk. n.)   *name*
nämlich   *lit. namely; you see*
die Nase (-n)   *nose*
   die Nase voll haben (coll.)   *to have had enough*
natürlich   *natural(ly), of course*
die Naturwissenschaft (-en)   *natural science*
nehmen~   *to take*
nervenaufreibend   *nerve-racking*
neulich   *recently*
der Nichtraucher (-) / die -in   *non-smoker*
nie   *never*
niedrig   *low*
normalerweise   *normally*
die Note (-n)   *mark, grade*
nötig   *necessary*
notwendig   *necessary*
nur   *only*
nutzen   *to use*
die Nutzung (-en)   *usage, use*

offen   *open, open-minded*
die Öffentlichkeit   *public*
oft   *often*
öfters   *fairly often*
ordentlich   *tidy*
die Ordnung   *order, orderliness, tidiness*
ordnungsliebend   *liking to see things neat and tidy*
der Ort (-e)   *place*
die Ostseeküste   *Baltic Coast*

die Partnerstadt (-¨e)   *twin town*
passen   *to match*
passieren   *to happen*
pendeln   *to commute*
die Pension (-en)   *guesthouse, pension*
der Personalberater (-)/die -in   *personnel consultant*
das Pflanzenöl (-e)   *vegetable oil*
das Plätzchen (-)   *biscuit, cookie*

die Podiumsdiskussion (-en) *panel discussion*
der Politiker (-)/die -in *politician*
der Polizist (-en) (wk. n.)/die -in *police officer*
das Praktikum (die Praktika) *work placement*
der Präsident (-en) (wk. n.)/die -in *president*
das Problem (-e) *problem*
die Prüfung (-en) *examination*
der Punkt (-e) *point, full stop, dot*

der Quatsch (coll.) *nonsense*

der Rand (-¨er) *edge*
raten~ (+ dat.) *to advise*
die Ratesendung (-en) *panel game, quiz show*
die Realschule (-en) *school geared to the*
   mittlere Reife *exam (roughly equivalent to*
   16+ school-leaving exam)
das Recht (-e) (auf + acc.) *right (to)*
das Recht *law*
recht haben *to be right*
rechts *on the right*
   nach rechts *to the right*
recyceln *to recycle*
das Recycling *recycling*
die Redaktion (-en) *editorial staff*
reden (über + acc.) *to talk (about)*
die Regel (-n) *rule*
regelmäßig *regular(ly)*
regeln *to regulate, to settle*
regional *regional(ly)*
reichen *to suffice*
   Das hat mir gereicht. *That was enough for me.*
die Reihe (-n) *series*
rein *pure, clean*
reinigen *to clean*
die Reisebegleitung (-en) *accompanied tour,*
   lit. tour accompaniment
der Reiseleiter (-) *courier*
reiselustig *keen on travelling*
der Reiseverlauf (-¨e) *tour plan; lit.: tour course*
das Reiseziel (-e) *destination*
der Renner (-) *hit*
renovieren *to renovate*
der Rentner (-)/die -in *pensioner*
der Richter (-)/die -in *judge*
richtig *right, correct*
die Richtung (-en) *direction*
der Rohstoff (-e) *raw material*
die Rolle (-n) *role*
die Ruhe *peace, quiet*
rund *around*
die Runde (-n) *round (n)*
die Sache (-n) *thing, matter*

der Saft (-¨e) *juice*
sagenhaft *legendary, incredible*
die Sammelstelle (-n) *collecting point*
sauber *clean*
sauber machen *to clean*
das Sauerkraut *sauerkraut, pickled cabbage*
schädigen *to harm, damage*
schaffen (coll.) *to manage*
schaffen~ *to create*
der Schalter (-) *ticket window*
schätzen *to appreciate, estimate*
schauen (auf + acc.) *to look (at)*
die Scheibe (-n) *slice*
die Schicht (-en) *work shift*
   die Frühschicht (-en) *early shift*
   die Spätschicht (-en) *late shift*
schlafen~ *to sleep*
schlecht *bad*
schließen~ *to shut, close*
schließlich *after all, finally*
schlimm *bad, severe*
der Schluss (-¨e) *end*
zum Schluss *finally*
der Schnitt (-e) *average*
schon *already*
schrecklich *terrible*
der Schreibtisch (-e) *desk*
der Schreiner (-)/die -in *carpenter*
die Schreinerlehre (-n) *carpentry apprenticeship*
der Schritt (-e) *step*
der Schutz *protection*
der Schwerpunkt (-e) *focus, main area/subject*
die Schwiegereltern (plur.) *parents-in-law*
schwierig *difficult*
die Schwierigkeit (-en) *difficulty*
der Schwimmunterricht *swimming lessons*
das Schwindelgefühl (-e) *feeling of dizziness*
schwinden *to shrink, to fade*
der See (-n) *lake*
die See (-n) *sea*
die Seehöhe *sea level*
die Sehenswürdigkeit (-en) *sight (worth seeing)*
die Seite (-n) *side; page*
selbstständig *self-employed; independent*
selbstverständlich *natural(ly), self-evident*
selten *rare(ly)*
das Semester (-) *semester*
das Seminar (-e) *seminar*
senden *to broadcast*
der Sender (-) *(radio/TV) station*
setzen *to put, place*
sicher *safe, secure; sure(ly), certain(ly)*
sicherlich *certainly, undoubtedly*

der Sinn (-e)   *sense*
Ski fahren~   *to go skiing*
sofort   *immediately*
sogar   *even*
die Solarenergie (-n)   *solar energy*
die Solarzelle (-n)   *solar cell*
der Soldat (-en) (wk. n.)/die -in   *soldier*
sollen   *ought, should*
der Sondermüll   *hazardous waste*
sonnabends   *on Saturdays*
die Sonne (-n)   *sun*
die Sonnenenergie (-n)   *solar energy*
sonst   *otherwise*
die Sorge (-n)   *worry*
sich Sorgen machen   *to worry*
Machst du dir keine Sorgen?   *Don't you worry?*
sowieso   *anyway, in any case*
sowohl ... als   *as well as*
der Sozialarbeiter (-)/die -in   *social worker*
der Sozialpädagoge (-n) (wk. n.)/die
   -pädagogin   *person with a degree in Social
   Education*
der Spaß (-¨e)   *fun*
   Es macht mir Spaß   *I enjoy it*
speziell   *special(ly)*
spielen   *to play*
der Spitzenreiter (-)   *leader, front runner*
Sport treiben   *to do sports*
sprechen~   *to speak*
das Staatsexamen (-)   *state exam; similar to a
   degree*
ständig   *constant(ly)*
die Stange (-n)   *stick, bar*
   eine schöne Stange Geld   *a small fortune*
stark   *strong(ly)*
der Starnberger See   *large lake near Munich*
statt/finden~   *to take place*
staunen (über + acc.)   *to be amazed (at)*
stehen~   *to stand*
steigen~   *to rise*
sich steigern   *to increase*
stellen   *to put, place*
die Stellung (-en)   *position, job*
sterben~   *to die*
stimmen   *to be correct*
der Stoff (-e)   *substance*
die Störung (-en)   *disturbance*
die Straßenbahn (-en)   *tram*
streng   *strict(ly)*
stressfrei   *free of stress*
stricken   *to knit*
der Strom   *electricity*
der Student (-en) (wk. n.)/die -in   *student*

der Studienabschluss (-¨e)   *roughly equivalent to
   a degree; lit. end of studies*
der Studienplatz (-¨e)   *university place*
die Studienzeit (-en)   *period of study*
die Stunde (-n)   *hour, lesson*
suchen   *to search, to look for*
die Süßigkeit (-en)   *sweet things, confectionery*
der Supermarkt (-¨e)   *supermarket*

die Tabellenkalkulation (-en)   *spreadsheets*
der Tagesablauf (-¨e)   *daily routine*
die Tageszeitung (-en)   *daily paper*
der Tanzclub (-s)   *dance club*
tanzen   *to dance*
der Tanzkurs (-e)   *dancing classes*
sich täuschen   *to be wrong, to be mistaken*
der Teelöffel (-)   *teaspoon*
der Teil (-e)   *part*
teilen   *to share*
teuer   *dear, expensive*
die Textverarbeitung   *word processing*
das Theaterstück (-e)   *play, drama*
das Thema (Themen)   *subject, topic*
(das) Thüringen   *Thuringia – one of the sixteen
   German Länder (states)*
toll (coll.)   *fantastic, great*
der Tourist (-en) (wk. n.)/die -in   *tourist*
der Traum (-¨e)   *dream*
treffen~   *to meet*
trennen   *to separate*
der Trost   *consolation, comfort*
tun~   *to do*
das Turnier (-e)   *tournament*
typisch   *typical(ly)*

die U-Bahn (-en) (= Untergrundbahn)   *tube,
   subway*
über/einstimmen (mit + dat.)   *to agree (with)*
überfüllt   *overcrowded*
überhaupt nicht   *not at all*
übermorgen   *the day after tomorrow*
die Übernachtung (-en)   *overnight stay*
übernehmen~   *to take on*
überprüfen   *to check (over)*
überregional   *national, nationwide*
übersetzen   *to translate*
übertreiben~   *to exaggerate*
übrigens   *by the way*
umfassend   *comprehensive*
die Umfrage (-n)   *survey, opinion poll*
die Umgänglichkeit (-en)   *friendliness, sociability*
die Umgebung (-en)   *surrounding area*
um/gehen mit (+ dat.)   *to deal with*

umsonst   *free of charge*

umweltbewusst   *conscious of the environment*

der Umweltflegel (-)   *lout (in environmental matters)*

das Umweltministerium   *Ministry of the Environment*

der Umweltschutz   *environmental protection*

unbedingt   *definitely, at all costs*

unbemerkt   *unnoticed*

ungeheuer   *huge(ly), immense(ly)*

unheimlich viel   *a huge amount*

das Unrecht (-e)   *injustice*

sich unterhalten~ (über + acc.)   *to talk (about)*

die Unterhaltung   *entertainment*

die Unterhaltungsserie (-n)   *serial*

der Untermieter (-)   *lodger*

unternehmen~   *to do, undertake*

der Unterricht   *instruction, lessons*

unterrichten   *to teach, instruct*

unterschiedlich   *different(ly), varying*

der Untertitel (-)   *subtitle*

unterwegs sein   *to be away, to be on a trip*

unvergleichlich   *incomparably*

der Urenkel (-)/die -in   *great-grandchild*

der Urlaub (-e)   *holiday, vacation*

der Urlauber (-)   *holidaymaker*

die Veranstaltung (-en)   *event*

die Verantwortung (-en)   *responsibility*

verbessern   *to improve*

verbieten~   *to prohibit, to ban*

verbinden~   *to join, combine*

das Verbot (-e)   *ban*

verbringen~   *to spend (time)*

verdienen   *to earn*

die Verfassung (-en)   *constitution*

verfassungsgemäß   *constitutional*

zur Verfügung stehen   *to be available, at one's disposal*

vergangen   *past*

die Vergangenheit (-en)   *past*

vergessen~   *to forget*

der Vergleich (-e)   *comparison*

   im Vergleich (zu/mit + dat.)   *compared (to/with)*

vergleichen~   *to compare*

die Verhandlung (-en)   *negotiation*

verhängen   *to impose (a ban)*

verheiratet   *married*

der Verkehr   *traffic*

das Verkehrsamt (-¨er)   *tourist information office*

verkennen~   *to fail to appreciate, recognize*

der Verlag (-e)   *publishing company*

verlangen   *to demand*

   Das ist zu viel verlangt.   *That is asking too much.*

verlängern   *to extend*

verlassen~   *to leave*

verlieren~   *to lose*

vermeiden~   *to avoid*

vermitteln   *to give, provide; to arrange, mediate*

die Verpackung (-en)   *wrapping, packaging*

verpesten   *to pollute*

verpflichten   *to oblige, commit*

verplanen   *to book up completely, to plan every minute*

verregnet   *rainy, wet, spoilt by rain*

verrückt   *mad, insane*

verschieden   *various, different*

die Versicherungsfirma (-firmen)   *insurance company*

versprechen~   *to promise*

das Verständnis   *understanding*

verstärken   *to reinforce, to increase*

sich mit jemandem verstehen   *to get along with somebody*

der Versuch (-e)   *experiment, attempt*

versuchen   *to try*

vertauschen   *to exchange; to mix up*

der Vertrag (-¨e)   *contract*

das Vertrauen   *trust*

vertraut sein (mit + dat.)   *to be familiar (with)*

der/die Verwandte (-n) (adj. n.)   *relative*

verwenden   *to use*

verzählen   *to miscount*

vierzehntägig   *fortnightly*

verzichten auf (+ acc.)   *to do without*

das Volk (-¨er)   *people, nation*

voll   *full*

vollkommen   *complete(ly)*

vor allem   *above all*

vor/behalten~   *to reserve (the right)*

vor/bereiten~   *to prepare*

die Vorbereitung (-en)   *preparation*

das Vorbild (-er)   *role model, example*

vorher   *in advance, beforehand*

vor/kommen~   *to occur*

die Vorlesung (-en)   *lecture*

der Vorlesungssaal (-säle)   *lecture theatre*

die Vorliebe (-n)   *preference*

vor/nehmen~   *to plan, to undertake something*

der Vorsatz (-¨e)   *intention, resolution*

vor/schlagen~   *to suggest, propose*

die Vorschrift (-en)   *regulation*

vor/stellen   *to introduce*

sich (etwas) vor/stellen   *to imagine (something)*

der Vorteil (-e)   *advantage*
das Vorurteil (-e)   *prejudice*
vor/ziehen~   *to prefer*
wachsen~   *to grow*
die Wahrheit (-en)   *truth*
wahrscheinlich   *probably*
der Wald (-¨er)   *forests*
wandern   *to ramble, hike*
warnen (vor + dat.)   *to warn (against)*
was für …?   *what kind of …?*
die Wäsche   *laundry, washing*
waschen~   *to wash*
der Waschsalon (-s)   *launderette*
im Wechsel   *alternating*
weder … noch   *neither … nor*
weg/kommen~ (von + dat.)   *to get away from*
(das) Weihnachten   *Christmas*
weitaus   *by far, much*
weiter   *further*
weitgehend   *largely, to a large extent*
die Welt (-en)   *world*
weltbekannt   *famous throughout the world*
der Weltmeister (-)   *world champion*
werden~   *to become*
die Werkstatt (-¨en)   *workshop*
die Werkzeugmaschine (-n)   *machine tool*
der Wert (-e)   *value*
wert   *worth*
wichtig   *important*
widersprechen~   *to contradict*
der Widerstand (-¨e)   *resistance, opposition*
wiedervereinigt   *re-united*
wieder/verwerten   *to recycle*
wie viel?   *how much, how many*
willkommen   *welcome*
wirken   *to appear, seem*
die Wirtschaft (-en)   *economy*
wirtschaftlich   *economic/ally*
das Wirtschaftsklima   *economic climate*
das Wirtschaftswunder (-)   *economic miracle*
wissen~   *to know (a fact)*
der Wissenschaftler (-)/die -in   *scientist, scholar, academic*

die Witwe (-n)   *widow*
der Witz (-e)   *joke*
die Woche (-n)   *week*
wohin?   *where … to?*
sich wohl/fühlen   *to feel at home*
wollen   *to want to, intend to*
womöglich   *where possible*
das Wörterbuch (-¨er)   *dictionary*
wunderschön   *really beautiful*

die Zahl (-en)   *number*
zählen   *to count*
der Zähler (-)   *meter*
zeigen   *to show*
zeitaufwendig   *time-consuming*
eine Zeit lang   *for a while*
der Zeitmangel   *lack of time*
zeitraubend   *time-consuming*
die Zeitschrift (-en)   *journal, magazine*
ziehen~   *to move; to pull*
ziemlich   *fairly*
der Zivildienst   *community service (instead of military service)*
zuerst   *at first*
zufrieden   *satisfied, content*
der Zug (-¨e)   *train*
  im Zuge von (+ dat.)   *in the wake of*
zugänglich   *approachable*
zu/hören (+ dat.)   *to listen to*
die Zukunft   *future*
zuletzt   *at last, finally*
zu/machen   *to close*
die Zumutung (-en)   *imposition*
zunächst   *first, initially*
zurückhaltend   *restrained, reserved*
der Zustand (-¨e)   *state*
die Zusteigemöglichkeit (-en)   *pick-up point; lit. getting-on possibilities*
zuverlässig   *reliable*
die Zuverlässigkeit (-en)   *reliability*
zwar   *admittedly*
die Zweigstelle (-n)   *branch, subsidiary*
in der Zwischenzeit   *in the meantime*

English–German glossary

This glossary is not intended to be comprehensive. It does not contain many of the more basic words generally learned at the beginner's level.

~ indicates that this verb or its root form can be found in the list of **Common irregular verbs**.

/ indicates that a verb is separable (e.g. **an/kommen**).

With job titles, nationalities, etc., the female version is usually given in an abbreviated form, e.g. **der Akademiker (-)/die -in**. In the plural, feminine nouns ending in **-in** add **-nen**, e.g. **die Akademikerin**, **die Akademikerinnen**.

Abkürzungen *Abbreviations*

acc. – accusative

adj. n. – adjectival noun

coll. – colloquial

dat. – dative

neut. – neuter

gen. – genitive

plur. – plural

wk. n. – weak noun

to abolish ab/schaffen
about circa, ungefähr
achievement die Leistung (-en), die Errungenschaft (-en)
acquaintance der/die Bekannte (-n) (adj.n.)
actual(ly) eigentlich
admittedly zwar
adult der/die Erwachsene (-n) (adj.n.)
advantage der Vorteil (-e)
to advise raten~ (+ dat.)
afterwards nachher, hinterher
age das Alter
ago – two years ago vor – vor zwei Jahren
to agree (with) überein/stimmen (mit + dat.)
aid die Hilfe (-n)
air die Luft (-̈e)
airport der Flughafen (-̈)
almost fast
already schon, bereits
always immer
apart from abgesehen von (+ dat.)
to apologize sich entschuldigen
to appear erscheinen~; aus/sehen, wirken

applicant der Bewerber (-)/die -in
to apply for sich bewerben~ (um + acc.)
to appoint benennen
approachable zugänglich
approximately circa, ungefähr
architect der Architekt (-en) (wk. n.)/die -in
arm der Arm (-e)
arrival die Ankunft (-̈e)
to arrive an/kommen~
art die Kunst (-̈e)
to ascertain fest/stellen
assistance die Hilfe (-n)
to assume an/nehmen~
attempt der Versuch (-e)
autumn der Herbst (-e)
average der Durchschnitt (-e)
to avoid vermeiden~

bad schlimm, schlecht
ban das Verbot (-e)
bank die Bank (-en)
battery die Batterie (-n)
to be able können

to be amazed (at)   staunen (über + acc.)

to be interested in   sich interessieren (für + acc.)

to be right   recht haben

beach   der Strand (-̈e)

to become   werden~

beginning   der Anfang (-̈e)

to believe   glauben (+ dat.)

to believe in   glauben an (+ acc)

to belong   gehören (+ dat.)

birthday   der Geburtstag (-e)

biscuit, cookie   das Plätzchen (-)

black   schwarz

blue   blau

body   der Körper (-)

to book   reservieren, buchen

border   die Grenze (-n)

boring   langweilig

born – When were you born?   geboren – Wann
     bist du geboren?

boss   der Chef (-s)/die -in

boy   der Junge (-n) (wk. n.)

boyfriend   der Freund (-e)

to break   brechen~

to breathe   atmen

bridge   die Brücke (-n)

to bring   bringen~

to broadcast   senden

building   das Gebäude (-)

to burn   brennen~

bus stop   die Bushaltestelle (-n)

business trip   die Geschäftsreise (-n)

butcher's (shop)   die Metzgerei (-en)

to buy a ticket   eine Fahrkarte lösen

by the way   übrigens

to call   rufen~; (phone) an/rufen~

can (to be able to)   können

cancer   der Krebs

capital   die Hauptstadt (-̈e)

career   die Laufbahn (-en)

carpenter   der Schreiner (-)/die -in

carpet   der Teppich (-e)

to carry   tragen~

case; in any case   der Fall (-̈e); jedenfalls

cathedral   der Dom (-e)

cause   die Ursache (-n)

to cause   verursachen

cautious   vorsichtig

to celebrate   feiern

centre   die Mitte (-n); der Mittelpunkt (-e)

century   das Jahrhundert (-e)

certain(ly)   sicher

characteristic   die Eigenschaft (-en)

Christmas   (das) Weihnachten

cinema – to go to the cinema   das Kino (-s); ins
     Kino gehen

citizen   der Bürger (-)/die -in

civil servant   der Beamte (-) (adj.n) / die Beamtin

to clean   reinigen, putzen, sauber machen

clean   sauber, rein

to clear up   auf/räumen

clear(ly)   klar, deutlich

client   der Kunde (-n) (wk. n.)/die Kundin

climate   das Klima (-s)

to close   schließen~, zu/machen

cloud   die Wolke (-n)

cold   kalt

colleague   der Kollege (-n) (wk. n.)/die -in

colour   die Farbe (-n)

to combine   verbinden~

comfortable   bequem

to commute   pendeln

company   die Gesellschaft (-en), die Firma (Firmen)

to compare   vergleichen~

comparison   der Vergleich (-e)

to compel   zwingen~

competition   die Konkurrenz

competitive   konkurrenzfähig

to complete   ergänzen

complete(ly)   vollkommen

computer   der Computer (-)

to conduct   führen, leiten

to confirm   bestätigen

to congratulate   gratulieren (+ dat.)

conscious(ly)   bewusst

constant(ly)   ständig

constitution   die Verfassung (-en)

contain   enthalten~

contract   der Vertrag (-̈e)

to contradict   widersprechen~

to cook   kochen

copy   das Exemplar (-e)

corner   die Ecke (-n)

correct   richtig

to cost   kosten

cost(s)   die Kosten (plur.)

to count   zählen

country   das Land (-̈er)

to create   schaffen~

crockery   das Geschirr

crossroads   die Kreuzung (-en)

current   der Strom (-̈e)

customer   der Kunde (-n) (wk. n.)/die -in

to cut   schneiden~

CV   der Lebenslauf (-̈e)

to damage   schädigen

damaged   geschädigt

to dance   tanzen
dangerous   gefährlich
dear   teuer; lieb
to decide   entscheiden~
demand   die Nachfrage (-n)
to demand   verlangen
to depart   ab/fahren~
department   die Abteilung (-en)
department store   das Kaufhaus (-¨er), das
   Warenhaus (-¨er)
departure   die Abfahrt (-en)
to depend on   ab/hängen von (+ dat.)
dependent on   abhängig von (+ dat.)
depending on   je nach
desk   der Schreibtisch (-e)
development   die Entwicklung (-en)
dictionary   das Wörterbuch (-¨er)
to die   sterben~
different   verschieden
different from   anders als
difficult   schwierig
difficulty   die Schwierigkeit (-en)
direction   die Richtung (-en)
director   der Direktor (-en) (wk. n.)/die -in
disabled   behindert
disadvantage   der Nachteil (-e)
to discover   entdecken
to discuss   diskutieren
disease   die Krankheit (-en)
dishes   das Geschirr
to dismiss (sack)   entlassen~
to disturb   stören
disturbance   die Störung (-en)
divorced   geschieden
to do   machen, tun~
to doubt   zweifeln, bezweifeln
dream   der Traum (-¨e)
to dream   träumen
to drive   fahren~

each   jeder/-e/-es
ear   das Ohr (-en)
to earn   verdienen
economic/ally   wirtschaftlich
economy   die Wirtschaft
edge   der Rand (-¨er)
edition   die Ausgabe (-n)
education   die Bildung
egg   das Ei (-er)
electricity   der Strom
to employ   beschäftigen
employed   berufstätig
employee   der/die Angestellte (-n) (adj. n.)
to encounter   begegnen (+ dat.)

end   der Schluss (-¨e); das Ende (-n)
energy   die Energie (-n)
to enter   eintreten~ (in + acc.)
entertainment   die Unterhaltung
entrance   der Eingang (-¨e); der Eintritt (-e)
environment   die Umwelt
environmental protection   der Umweltschutz
to estimate   schätzen
even   sogar
every   jeder/-e/-es
exact(ly)   genau
to exaggerate   übertreiben~
examination   die Prüfung (-en); das Examen (-)
example (of)   das Beispiel (-e) (für + acc.)
excellent   ausgezeichnet, hervorragend
except (for)   außer (+ dat.)
exception   die Ausnahme (-n)
exciting   aufregend
excursion   der Ausflug (-¨e)
exhibition   die Ausstellung (-en)
to exist   existieren
exit   der Ausgang (-¨e)
expensive   teuer; kostspielig
experience   die Erfahrung (-en)
experiment   der Versuch (-e)
to explain, to clarify   erklären
export (n)   der Export (-e)
to export   aus/führen, exportieren
to extend   verlängern
eye   das Auge (-n)

factory   der Betrieb (-e), die Fabrik (-en)
to fail (a test/exam)   durch/fallen
fairly   ziemlich
familiar   vertraut
famous   berühmt
fear   die Angst (-¨e)
feeling   das Gefühl (-e)
to fetch   ab/holen
finally   schließlich, zum Schluss
to finish   beenden
to finish (one's studies)   ab/schließen~
to finish work   Feierabend machen
flight   der Flug (-¨e)
fluent(ly)   fließend
to fly   fliegen~
focus, main area/subject   der Schwerpunkt (-e)
fog   der Nebel
to follow   folgen (+ dat.)
foot; on foot   der Fuß (-¨e); zu Fuß
to forbid   verbieten~
foreign language   die Fremdsprache (-n)
foreigner   der Ausländer/die -in
forest   der Wald (-¨er)

to forget   vergessen~
fork   die Gabel (-n)
to form   bilden
fortunately   glücklicherweise
to found   gründen
friendliness   die Umgänglichkeit (-en)
full   voll
full stop   der Punkt (-e)
fun   der Spaß (-̈e)
funny   komisch
further   weiter
future   die Zukunft

game   das Spiel (-e)
garbage   der Müll
garbage can   der Mülleimer (-)
garlic   der Knoblauch
gasoline   das Benzin
general(ly); in general   allgemein; im
　Allgemeinen
gentleman   der Herr (-en) (wk.n)
to get   bekommen~
to get along (with someone)   sich mit jemandem
　verstehen
to get up   auf/stehen~
gift   das Geschenk (-e)
girl   das Mädchen (-)
girlfriend   die Freundin (-nen)
to give   geben~
glad   froh
glance   der Blick (-e)
globalization   die Globalisierung
to go   gehen~
to go (in a vehicle)   fahren~
to go away   weg/gehen~; weg/fahren~
to go out   aus/gehen~
goal   das Ziel (-e); (in sport) das Tor (-e)
grade (at school or college)   die Note (-n)
green   grün
to grow   wachsen~
guest   der Gast (-̈e)
guesthouse   die Pension (-en)

hand   die Hand (-̈e)
to happen   geschehen~, passieren
hard-working   fleißig, arbeitsam
to have to   müssen
head teacher   der (Schul-) Direktor (-en) (wk. n.)/
　die -in
health   die Gesundheit
to hear   hören
heart   das Herz (-en) (wk. n.)
heating   die Heizung (-en)

help   die Hilfe (-n)
to help   helfen~ (+ dat.)
to hide   verstecken; verbergen~
history   die Geschichte (-n)
holiday   der Urlaub (-e)
honest(ly)   ehrlich
honey   der Honig
to hope   hoffen
hope   die Hoffnung (-en)
host(-ess)   der Gastgeber (-)/die -in
hot   heiß
hour   die Stunde (-n)
human being   der Mensch (-en) (wk. n.)

illness   die Krankheit (-en)
image   das Bild (-er)
to imagine   sich vor/stellen
immediately   sofort
importance   die Wichtigkeit, die Bedeutung
important   wichtig, bedeutend
impressive   beeindruckend
to improve   verbessern
income   das Einkommen (-)
independent   selbstständig; unabhängig
industrious   fleißig
information   die Auskunft (-̈e)
inhabitant   der Einwohner (-)
inn   die Gaststätte (-n)
instead of   anstatt (+ gen.)
insurance   die Versicherung (-en)
to intend   beabsichtigen
to introduce (a person)   vor/stellen
to introduce (a subject/object)   ein/führen
invitation   die Einladung (-en)
to invite   ein/laden~

jam   die Marmelade (-n); (traffic) der Stau (-s)
job   der Beruf (-e); der Arbeitsplatz (-̈e); die
　Stellung (-en)
joint   das Gelenk (-e)
joke   der Witz (-e)
journal   die Zeitschrift (-en)
journalist   der Journalist (-en) (wk. n.)/die -in
to judge   beurteilen
judge   der Richter (-)/die -in
juice   der Saft (-̈e)
to jump   springen~

kitchenette; lit. cooking niche   die Kochnische (-n)
knife   das Messer (-)
to know (a fact)   wissen~
to know (be acquainted with)   kennen~
knowledge   die Kenntnis (-se)

laboratory   das Labor (-s/-e)
lack   der Mangel (¨)
lady   die Dame (-n)
lake   der See (-n)
at last, finally   zuletzt
law   das Gesetz (-e)
Law   Jura; das Recht
to lay   legen
to lead   führen, leiten
leader   der Führer (-), der Leiter (-)
leaf   das Blatt (-¨er)
to leave   lassen~; verlassen~
lecture   die Vorlesung (-en)
left   links
legendary   sagenhaft
lesson   die Stunde (-n)
liberal (permissive)   freizügig
library   die Bibliothek (-en)
lid   der Deckel (-)
to lie   liegen~
to like   mögen, gern haben
limit   die Grenze (-n)
to listen to   zuhören (+ dat.)
litre   der/das Liter (-)
lively   lebendig
long   lang
to look at something   sich etwas an/schauen
to look for   suchen
to look forward to   sich freuen auf (+ acc.)
to lose   verlieren~
loud   laut
to love   lieben
low   niedrig
luck; to be lucky   das Glück; Glück haben
luggage   das Gepäck
to lunch   zu Mittag essen
lunch   das Mittagessen (-)

mad   verrückt
magazine   die Zeitschrift (-en)
majority   die Mehrheit (-en)
to manufacture   her/stellen
mark (final --), classification   die Gesamtnote (-n)
married   verheiratet
to match   passen
match   das Spiel (-e); der/das Match (-[e]s)
material   der Stoff (-e)
matter   die Sache (-n)
meal   die Mahlzeit (-en)
to mean   bedeuten
measure; take measures   die Maßnahme (-n); Maßnahmen treffen~
to meet   treffen~, begegnen (+ dat.)

member   das Mitglied (-er)
mental(ly)   geistig
meticulous   akkurat
metre   der/das Meter (-)
midday   der Mittag
middle   die Mitte (-n)
midnight   die Mitternacht
minority   die Minderheit (-en)
to miscount   verzählen
to moan (to whine)   jammern
month   der Monat (-e)
moon   der Mond (-e)
mostly   meistens
mother tongue   die Muttersprache (-n)
motorway   die Autobahn (-en)
mountain   der Berg (-e)
mouth   der Mund (-¨er)
to move (house)   um/ziehen~
movie – go to the movies   der Film (-e) – ins Kino gehen
music   die Musik
must (to have to)   müssen

name   der Name (-n) (wk. n.)
nation   das Volk(-¨er); die Nation (-en)
naturally   natürlich, selbstverständlich
near   In der Nähe (von + dat.)
nearly   nahezu
necessary   nötig, notwendig, erforderlich
needle   die Nadel (-n)
negotiation   die Verhandlung (-en)
neighbour   der Nachbar (-n) (wk. n.)/die -in
neither ... nor...   weder... noch ...
never   nie
nevertheless   immerhin, dennoch, trotzdem
news   die Nachrichten
news broadcast   die Nachrichtensendung (-en)
noisy   laut
nonsense   der Quatsch
normally   normalerweise
nose   die Nase (-n)
now and again   ab und zu
nuclear power   die Kernkraft, die Atomkraft
number   die Zahl (-en), die Anzahl (-en)
nurse (female)   die Krankenschwester(-n)
nurse (male)   der Krankenpfleger (-)
nutrition   die Ernährung

occasionally   gelegentlich
to occur   vor/kommen~
of course   natürlich
to offer   bieten~, an/bieten~
often   oft

only   nur
to open   öffnen, auf/machen
open   offen; geöffnet
open-minded   offen
opinion   die Meinung (-en)
opportunity   die Gelegenheit (-en)
to order   bestellen
other   ander -er/-e/-es
otherwise   sonst, ansonsten
ought to   sollen
overcoming   die Bewältigung (-en)
to own   besitzen~
own   eigen -er/-e/-es
owner   der Besitzer (-) /die Besitzerin (-nen)

page   die Seite (-n)
paint   die Farbe (-n)
to paint   malen
painting   die Malerei
parking place   der Parkplatz (-¨e)
part   der Teil (-e)
part (role)   die Rolle (-n)
part-time (lit. half days)   halbtags
to pass (an exam)   (eine Prüfung) bestehen
past   die Vergangenheit
payment   die Bezahlung (-en)
peculiar   merkwürdig; eigenartig
pension   die Rente (-n)
pensioner   der Rentner (-)/die -in
people   die Leute; das Volk (-¨er)
performance   die Leistung (-en)
to phone   an/rufen; telefonieren (mit + dat.)
photographer   der Fotograf (-en) (wk. n.)/die -in
physically   körperlich
picture   das Bild (-er)
place   der Ort (-e)
to place   setzen, stellen
to plan, to undertake   vor/nehmen~
plane   das Flugzeug (-e)
to play   spielen
to please, be pleasing   gefallen~ (+ dat.)
police officer   der Polizist (-en) (wk. n.)/die -in
population   die Bevölkerung (-en)
population density   die Bevölkerungsdichte (-n)
position   die Stellung (-en)
possibility   die Möglichkeit (-en)
power   die Kraft (-¨e); die Macht (-¨e)
precise(ly)   genau
to prefer   vor/ziehen~
prejudice   das Vorurteil (-e)
preparation   die Vorbereitung (-en)
to prepare   vor/bereiten
present   das Geschenk (-e)

present (time)   die Gegenwart
probably   wahrscheinlich
to produce   her/stellen, produzieren, erzeugen
profession   der Beruf (-e)
to prohibit   verbieten~
to promise   versprechen
proof   der Nachweis (-e)
protection   der Schutz
public   öffentlich
public   die Öffentlichkeit; das Publikum
to pull   ziehen~
pure   rein
to put   legen, stellen, setzen

quantity   die Menge (-n)
queen   die Königin (-nen)
quiet(ly)   ruhig; still

rail – by rail   die Bahn – mit der Bahn
railway   die Bahn (-en), die Eisenbahn (-en)
rain   der Regen
to ramble   wandern
rare(ly)   selten
to reach   erreichen
ready   fertig
reason   der Grund (-¨e)
to receive   erhalten~
recently   neulich
to recognize   an/erkennen~
to recommend   empfehlen~
red   rot
refrigerator   der Kühlschrank (-¨e)
to regret   bedauern
regular(ly)   regelmäßig
to regulate   regeln
relative   der/die Verwandte (-n) (adj. n.)
to relax   sich entspannen
reliability   die Zuverlässigkeit (-en)
reliable   zuverlässig
to remember   sich erinnern an (+ acc.)
to report   berichten
report   der Bericht (-e)
research   die Forschung (-en)
resistance   der Widerstand (-¨e)
to rest   sich ausruhen
restrained (reserved)   zurückhaltend
result   das Ergebnis (-se)
reunification   die Wiedervereinigung
to ride   reiten~
right   rechts
right (correct)   richtig
right (to)   das Recht (-e) (auf + acc.)
to rise   steigen~; (get up)   auf/stehen~

role   die Rolle (-n)
role model   das Vorbild (-er)
roof   das Dach (-¨er)
round (n)   die Runde (-n)
row   die Reihe (-n)
rubbish   der Müll
rubbish bin   der Mülleimer (-)
rule   die Regel (-n)
to run   laufen~

safe(ly)   sicher
satisfied   zufrieden
scenery   die Landschaft (-en)
scientist   der Wissenschaftler (-)/die -in
sea   die See (-n); das Meer (-e)
to search   suchen
secure(ly)   sicher
sense   der Sinn (-e)
to separate   trennen
series   die Reihe (-n)
to serve   dienen (+ dat.)
to set off   los/gehen~
to share   teilen
shift (work)   die Schicht (-en)
early shift   die Frühschicht (-en)
late shift   die Spätschicht (-en)
shop   der Laden (¨); das Geschäft (-e)
to show   zeigen
shower; take a shower   die Dusche (-n); sich
   duschen
to shrink   schwinden
to shut   schließen~
side   die Seite (-n)
similar(ly)   ähnlich
simple, simply   einfach
to sit   sitzen~
to sit an exam   eine Prüfung ab/legen
to skate   Schlittschuh laufen~
to ski   Ski fahren~, Ski laufen~
to sleep   schlafen~
slice – a slice of bread   die Scheibe (-n) – eine
   Scheibe Brot
slow(ly)   langsam
to smell (of)   riechen~ (nach + dat.)
snow   der Schnee
sociability   die Umgänglichkeit (-en)
sociable   gesellig
society   die Gesellschaft (-en)
solar energy   die Solarenergie (-n)
soldier   der Soldat (-en) (wk. n.)/die -in
sometimes   manchmal
soon   bald
speed   die Geschwindigkeit (-en)

to spend (money)   aus/geben~
to spend (time)   verbringen
splendid(ly)   großartig
spoon   der Löffel (-)
spring   der Frühling
to stand   stehen~
state   der Staat (-en)
state (condition)   der Zustand (-¨e)
station   der Bahnhof (-¨e)
to stay   bleiben~
step   der Schritt (-e)
to stop   auf/hören; halten~
story   die Geschichte (-n)
straight on   geradeaus
to stress   betonen
strict(ly)   streng
to stroll   bummeln
strong(ly)   stark
subject   das Thema (Themen)
subway   die U-Bahn (-en) (= Untergrundbahn)
succeed; We didn't succeed in ...   gelingen~; Es ist
   uns nicht gelungen, ...
to suffer   leiden~
to suffice (be enough)   reichen, genügen
to suggest   vor/schlagen~
summer   der Sommer
sun   die Sonne (-n)
sunshine   der Sonnenschein
supermarket   der Supermarkt (-¨e)
survey   die Umfrage (-n)
to swim   schwimmen~

to take   nehmen~
to take place   statt/finden~
to take up   beziehen~
to talk (about)   reden (über + acc.)
taste   der Geschmack (-¨e)
to teach   unterrichten
team   die Mannschaft (-en)
terrible   schrecklich
to thank   danken (+ dat.)
then   dann
thesis, dissertation   die Diplomarbeit (-en)
thing   das Ding (-e); die Sache (-n)
to think   denken~, glauben, meinen
thorough(ly)   gründlich
to throw   werfen~
tidy   ordentlich
time   die Zeit (-en)
tired   müde
topic   das Thema (Themen)
trade   der Handel
to trade   handeln

traffic   der Verkehr
traffic lights (set of)   die Ampel (-n)
train   der Zug (-¨e)
training   die Ausbildung (-en)
tram   die Straßenbahn (-en)
to translate   übersetzen
trend   die Entwicklung (-en); der Trend (-s)
to trust   vertrauen (+ dat)
truth   die Wahrheit (-en)
to try   versuchen
tube   die U-Bahn (-en) (= Untergrundbahn)
typical(ly)   typisch

umbrella   der Regenschirm (-e)
to understand   verstehen~
unemployment   die Arbeitslosigkeit
unity   die Einheit
upswing   der Aufschwung (-¨e)
use, usage   die Nutzung
to use   nutzen, benutzen, gebrauchen, verwenden
usually   gewöhnlich

vacation   der Urlaub (-e)
value   der Wert (-e)
various   verschieden
view   der Blick (-e)
village   das Dorf (-¨er)
to visit   besuchen
voice   die Stimme (-n)

wage   der Lohn (-¨e)
minimum wage   der Mindestlohn (-¨e)
waiter/waitress   der Kellner (-)/die -in
to want   wollen
war   der Krieg (-e)
to wash   waschen~
to watch TV   fern/sehen~
way out   der Ausgang (-¨e)
weak   schwach
to wear   tragen~
weather   das Wetter
wedding   die Hochzeit (-en)
week   die Woche (-n)
Welcome!   Willkommen!
well-known   bekannt
white   weiß
widow   die Witwe (-n)
widower   der Witwer (-)
winter   der Winter
world   die Welt (-en)
to worry   sich Sorgen machen
– Don't worry!   die Sorge (-n) – Mach dir keine Sorgen!
to write   schreiben~

yard   der Hof (-¨e)
to yawn   gähnen
year   das Jahr (-e)
yellow   gelb

zero   die Null (-en)

Grammar index